Real-World iOS Development

Best Practices from Startups, Teams, and Indies

Avi Tsadok

Apress®

Real-World iOS Development: Best Practices from Startups, Teams, and Indies

Avi Tsadok
Tel Mond, Israel

ISBN-13 (pbk): 979-8-8688-2814-0   ISBN-13 (electronic): 979-8-8688-2815-7
https://doi.org/10.1007/979-8-8688-2815-7

Managing Director, Apress Media LLC: Welmoed Spahr
Acquisitions Editor: Miriam Haidara
Editorial Project Manager: Marina Engler

Cover designed by eStudioCalamar

Distributed to the book trade worldwide by Springer Science+Business Media New York, 1 New York Plaza, New York, NY 10004. Phone 1-800-SPRINGER, fax (201) 348-4505, e-mail orders-ny@springer-sbm.com, or visit www.springeronline.com. Apress Media, LLC is a Delaware LLC and the sole member (owner) is Springer Science + Business Media Finance Inc (SSBM Finance Inc). SSBM Finance Inc is a **Delaware** corporation.

For information on translations, please e-mail booktranslations@springernature.com; for reprint, paperback, or audio rights, please e-mail bookpermissions@springernature.com.

Apress titles may be purchased in bulk for academic, corporate, or promotional use. eBook versions and licenses are also available for most titles. For more information, reference our Print and eBook Bulk Sales web page at http://www.apress.com/bulk-sales.

Any source code or other supplementary material referenced by the author in this book is available to readers on GitHub. For more detailed information, please visit https://www.apress.com/gp/services/source-code.

If disposing of this product, please recycle the paper

To Tammy, Maya (remember – 6!), and Harel, for supporting me through this book and the five before it, and to the quiet 5AM mornings in Tel Mond.

Table of Contents

About the Author

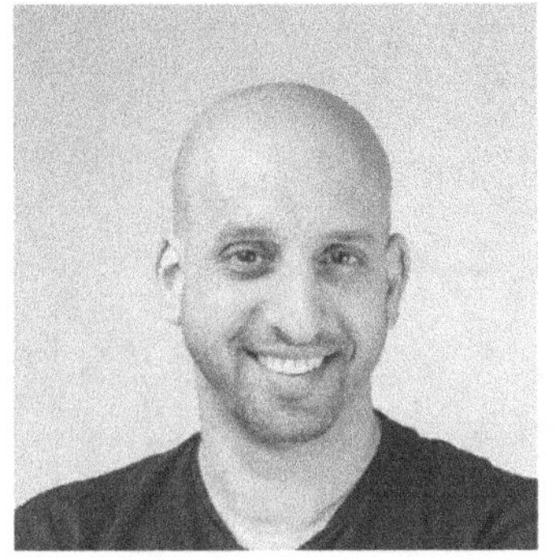 **Avi Tsadok** is an iOS developer and author of six books on Swift and iOS development. He has written best-selling titles such as *Mastering iOS Development* and *The Ultimate iOS Interview Playbook*. Avi has published dozens of technical articles and spoken at international conferences. He currently leads mobile development at Melio Payments, where he works on large-scale production systems used by thousands of businesses.

About the Technical Reviewer

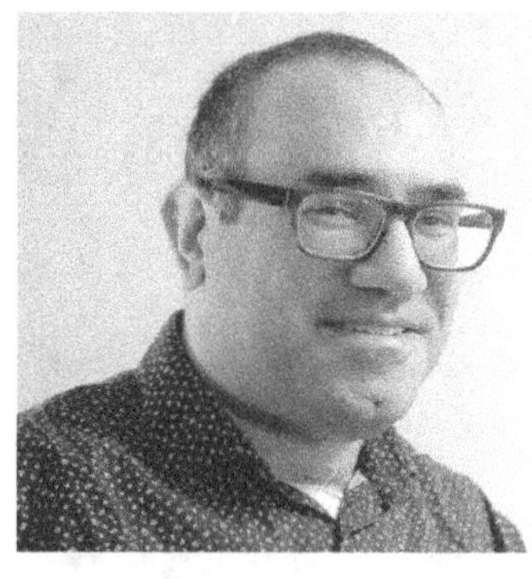 **Ahmed Bakir** is a mobile application development expert with over 20 years of experience in the software industry.

As an author, he has published three books on iOS and Internet of Things development, including *Program the Internet of Things with Swift*, which reached #3 on Amazon. As a professional, he has managed application engineering for global brands, including Chanel and Uniqlo. As an educator, he developed and taught the mobile programming certificate for the University of California San Diego's extension program. As an entrepreneur, he founded devAtelier in 2009, a Southern California–based app developer and consultancy that has shipped over 25 apps for their clients and the general public.

In his free time, you can find him on a never-ending quest to improve his coffee and watercolor painting skills.

You can find him online at `https://www.devatelier.com`.

Acknowledgments

I would like to thank the team at Apress for guiding this book from idea to reality. Your support and feedback made a big difference throughout the process.

This book would not exist without the developers who shared their work so openly. Thank you to Monika Mateska, Zlatko Kuvendjiski, Danijela Vrzan, Mikaela Caron, Oliver Binns, Vincent Pradeilles, Krzysztof Zabłocki, Stefan Blos, and Noam Efergan. You shared real decisions, real trade-offs, and real stories from production, and that is what shaped this book.

CHAPTER 1

Introduction

For every complex problem, there is an answer that is clear, simple, and wrong.

—H.L. Mencken

The Golden Age of Learning

Did you ever stop and think about how we learn and evolve as iOS developers? Some of us take courses. Others read blog posts. Some buy books, just like this one. Curious developers watch YouTube videos, attend conference talks, and constantly seek inspiration. These are all excellent sources of learning. They present clean architectures, clear patterns, and confident "best practices."

In recent years, something new has entered our lives – AI. With AI, we can learn faster than ever. We can get immediate explanations, real examples, and even working code. We can ask simple questions like "How do I build a login screen?" or broader ones like "What's the best architecture?" and receive fast, structured answers. It feels like everything is available to us at any moment.

At this point, we are surrounded by theory. And with that comes a strong feeling that there is a right way and a wrong way to build apps. If we just follow the principles we read about and apply the examples we see, things should work smoothly.

But once we start working in real teams on real projects, something feels off.

The Reality of iOS Teams

We have more knowledge than ever. In fact, we have access to almost everything. And yet, developers still struggle. We struggle to decide how to design screens, implement navigation, make code testable, build workflows, and set up CI/CD. We still see teams

1

© Avi Tsadok 2026
A. Tsadok, *Real-World iOS Development*, https://doi.org/10.1007/979-8-8688-2815-7_1

that disagree on fundamental decisions, from architecture to basic patterns. Even teams that use the same tools and consume the same content often work in completely different ways.

So, if knowledge is so accessible, why is there still so much confusion? Shouldn't things become simpler?

The answer is: not necessarily.

A Walk That Changed the Direction

A few years ago, I spoke at a conference in Paris. I have to admit that I didn't feel relaxed enough to go out for a walk with two other iOS developers until after my session. Up until that moment, I had been too focused on rehearsing my talk in the hotel room.

And you know what three iOS developers walking through the streets of Paris talk about. It's not soccer. We talked about how we build apps.

Each of us described our approach – our workflows, our decisions, and the way we think about development. We came from different companies, worked on different products, and operated under different constraints. Even our environments were different – different countries, different cultures, different teams. It quickly became clear that almost every factor that shapes development was different between us.

What surprised me the most was not that we disagreed. It was that we weren't arguing at all. The theory was clear to everyone. We all knew the patterns, the architectures, and the so-called best practices.

What we were actually doing was something else entirely. We were describing how we work in real life. And that was far more interesting. It was practical. It was honest. It was grounded in real decisions and real trade-offs. At that moment, a thought crossed my mind: I can write a book about this.

The Real Gap

That walk in Paris taught me something interesting, not only about development, but about iOS developers themselves. It made me realize that good developers want to understand what theory tells them to do, while great developers want to understand how things are actually done. And who are "they"? Other developers, of course.

We don't really need more definitions, abstract patterns, or blog posts trying to convince us that everything we've learned so far is outdated and that we should move on to the next big thing. What we are really looking for is something more grounded and more human.

At the end of the day, we are humans, and humans are drawn to stories, especially stories about other people. We want to understand how others think, make decisions, and deal with real constraints. That kind of knowledge is practical, relatable, and much easier to connect with.

Theory explains what should work, but reality shows what actually works. And the gap between those two is exactly what this book is about.

Why Theory Falls Short

Theory is not our enemy, and as professional developers we should seek of learning theory as much as we can. So why do I say that theory is not everything? Let's try to break this down.

Theory Is Too Generic

Theory assumes ideal conditions. We create three folders in Xcode – UI, Business Logic, and Data – and call it architecture. We add a coordinator and believe navigation is solved.

In a way, it reminds me of Apple's first SwiftUI presentation, where a few lines of code were enough to build a list, something that used to take us 150 lines in UIKit. It looked incredible, almost too good to be true.

But we all know what happens next. Reality is much more complex.

Most presentations ignore what it actually means to be an iOS developer. Maintaining an existing codebase, working as part of a team, coordinating with QA and a product manager, and dealing with deadlines. These demos assume a clean environment, where everything is under control and nothing stands in the way.

In reality, there is always legacy code, sometimes even Objective-C. Even if we can refactor, we don't always have the time. This is a business, and deadlines are real.

We might design a great user experience, but product managers and designers have their own plans. What we end up building is not exactly what we imagined, and often not what the demo promised. In fact, it can be different enough to make the demo almost irrelevant.

That leads me to the next point – static.

Theory Is Static, Development Is Dynamic

Theory presents a snapshot in time. It describes how we should build things as if the problem is stable. Think about it. At some point in the past, someone faced a problem and built a solution. And you know what? That solution might have been a great fit for that developer, and it might even fit our app today.

But if you are a real developer, you probably recognize a different reality. Real apps behave more like living systems. They evolve, scale, change direction, and constantly introduce new problems. They are not perfect creations. They have strengths and weaknesses, and those shift with almost every commit.

The solution we consider "correct" today can easily become tomorrow's limitation. What once helped us move fast can later slow us down. What felt like a clean abstraction can turn into unnecessary complexity as the product grows.

At the end, the theory is not wrong. It is simply incomplete over time.

Real Teams Are Contextual

This is perhaps the most meaningful point in the book, and it explains why theory alone is not enough. What works for an indie developer is not necessarily relevant for an R&D department with multiple mobile teams. What makes sense for a health app may not apply to a fintech product with strict regulations. Even the pace and rhythm of work can differ dramatically, and that directly influences how teams test and build their CI/CD pipelines, and even how they use Git.

In real development, every decision comes with a trade-off. This is something theory rarely emphasizes, yet these trade-offs shape our day-to-day work. Culture, regulations, scale, and people all play a role. They influence dozens of decisions we make every day, often under pressure and with limited options.

These decisions are rarely about choosing what is "best." More often, they are about choosing what fits the current reality – what aligns with the product, the team, and everything that already exists.

And if that's not enough, here comes what I call the "AI illusion."

The AI Illusion

At this point, I want to take a step back. Blog posts, conference sessions, and YouTube videos are not completely disconnected from reality. They do talk, at least to some extent, about context and constraints. It's far from perfect, but it's there.

However, in recent years, a new player has entered the field: AI. If theory was already easy to access online before tools like ChatGPT, large language models have made it even more accessible. We can ask a question and get an instant answer. We can generate architectures, structures, design patterns, and, in many cases, what appears to be a complete solution.

But AI doesn't just make theory accessible. It makes it feel personal. The answer is tailored to our exact situation. And that is the illusion.

What these systems actually give us is what is most commonly correct. As we'll explore in Chapter 10, these models are not reasoning about our specific team or product. They are predicting the next word based on patterns they have seen before. There's nothing wrong with that, but it creates a sense that the solution fits our needs better than it really does.

What AI cannot show us is how real teams work. It cannot explain why one team chose a certain architecture while another rejected it. It cannot reveal the trade-offs behind those decisions, or the constraints that shaped them.

In many ways, the rise of AI is exactly why I chose to focus this book on real teams rather than theory.

And now, let me make this a bit more personal.

My Personal Journey

This is my sixth book, which is a nice achievement. Over the years, I've written about testing, Core Data, Swift Package Manager, and general iOS development. I always believed that theory is essential for becoming a great iOS developer, and I still do.

But my journey didn't start there. I began without a formal computer science background and without real development experience. Back in the days of iOS 2, that didn't matter much. If you knew how to build a `UITableView` and write a bit of Objective-C, you were already "an iOS developer."

At that point, I was living inside what we call the Dunning–Kruger effect. In simple terms, beginners tend to overestimate their abilities, while more experienced developers become aware of how much they still need to learn. I lacked experience and theoretical knowledge. What I did have was confidence.

Over time, that confidence shifted. I started to understand the value of patterns, architecture, and deep technical thinking. That realization stayed with me and became the main driver behind writing more and more books about how to build good iOS apps.

However, none of my previous books answered this question: how do real iOS teams actually work? This is also why this book is different. For the first time, I'm not focusing on what I know, but on what others know. In many ways, this book represents the other side of that same journey – the moment you realize that even after so many years, you still don't know enough. One of the interviewees told me, "I wish I had this book when I started to develop for iOS" (will let you guess who it was). Or, in other words, the other side of the Dunning–Kruger effect.

Who This Book Is For

The easiest answer I can give is this: every iOS developer. But the reality is a bit more nuanced.

Let's start with who this book is not for. If you are completely new to iOS development or Swift, some parts of this book may not resonate with you. This is not a guide on how to build your first UI, learn design patterns, or navigate between screens. The book assumes you already have some experience, whether as an indie developer or on a team.

It also requires a certain mindset. This book is built around real-world practices, and those often challenge what we think we know. If you are looking for clear rules or a single "correct" way to build apps, this might not be the right place. The goal here is to explore different approaches, question assumptions, and sometimes let go of ideas that once felt obvious.

This book is for iOS developers who have already built an app or two, for indie developers who are balancing everything on their own, and for team leads who make trade-off decisions every day. It is for developers who want to understand not just what works, but why different teams choose different paths.

How to Read This Book

Unlike many books that follow a step-by-step approach, this book takes a different path. Each chapter focuses on a specific area of iOS development. Some explore testing, others architecture or design, and later chapters move into workflows and team practices. There is a natural flow from one topic to the next, so reading the chapters in order is recommended but not required.

Each chapter begins with a brief introduction to the topic, then moves into real-world perspectives from developers and teams. In many cases, these perspectives do not fully align. You may encounter conflicting opinions, different approaches, and even opposite conclusions. This is intentional. The goal is not to present a single correct answer, but to expose you to the range of decisions teams make in practice.

As you read, you may find yourself agreeing with some approaches and questioning others. That's exactly the point. This book is designed to challenge assumptions and encourage you to think about what fits your own context.

At the end of most chapters, you will find a section that highlights the tools used by the interviewees. This is a practical way to connect the ideas in the chapter with your own work and explore how they might apply to your day-to-day development.

What You'll Gain

By the end of this book, you will start to see iOS development differently. Instead of looking for the "right" way to build an app, you will begin to understand why different teams make different decisions. You will recognize that architecture, testing strategies, workflows, and data management are not fixed rules, but choices shaped by context.

You will develop a stronger intuition for trade-offs. When you read about a pattern or a best practice, you will be able to ask the right questions. What problem does this solve? What does it cost? And more importantly, does it fit my current situation?

This book will also expose you to real-world approaches from different teams. You will see how developers operate under constraints, adapt to scale, and balance speed, quality, and complexity. These examples are not meant to be copied directly, but to expand your thinking and help you make better decisions in your own projects.

Finally, you will gain confidence. Not the confidence that comes from following rules, but the confidence that comes from understanding them. The confidence to choose your own path, justify your decisions, and evolve your approach as your app and your team grow.

Let's start our unique journey with the first topic – architecture and design patterns.

CHAPTER 2

Architecture and Design Patterns

Architecture needs to serve the company goals.

—Vincent Pradeilles, iOS developer

Introduction

In software books, it's often tempting to start with the small details and slowly work our way outward. But when it comes to iOS development, it's usually smarter to begin with the **big picture**. Architecture and design patterns form the skeleton of our apps – shaping how we organize our code, how teams collaborate, and ultimately how well the product serves its goals. They are not just a theory but a practical link between the app in your hand and the company's larger vision.

In this chapter, we will

- Explore Vivino's real-world app architecture

- Clarify the meaning of "architecture" versus "design patterns"

- Take a tour through the "architectural zoo"

- See how design patterns solve everyday problems

Based on the interviews, one thing is clear: everyone has strong opinions on architecture. Yet rather than starting with the definitions, it's best to explore an actual use case first. That's why we begin with **Vivino**. Their story highlights not only the choices they made but also the trade-offs and pressures that shaped those decisions.

A. Tsadok, *Real-World iOS Development*, https://doi.org/10.1007/979-8-8688-2815-7_2

Starting with the Story of Vivino

Imagine you're at a dinner party. Someone pours you a glass of wine, and you love it. However, at this point, you don't really know how to proceed – should you take a photo of the label and upload it to Google images? Should we search for the wine's name and hope for an online shop to buy it? Save it in notes? But, as Steve said, there's an app for that.

Meet **Vivino** – one of the world's most popular wine apps (they call it – *19,366,500 wines in your iPhone*). The Vivino app is basically a wine scanner and discovery platform: a user can point their camera at a wine label, and the app recognizes the wine and pulls up information such as reviews and pricing, and even helps them purchase it.

I'll admit – I'm more of a beer man, but I also know that wine is an extremely popular drink, and that makes the Vivino app a very popular one with more than 50 million users worldwide. This kind of scale requires an architecture that can handle complex data, a UI that supports social features, stable networking, and crucial search capabilities.

Designing Vivino's app architecture is, without any doubt, an ongoing challenge. Building these kinds of apps seems complex, but what about maintaining them over time? Adding more features, fixing issues, or onboarding new developers are also essential requirements.

After speaking with **Monika Mateska**, one of Vivino's iOS developers, I understood that one of the things that is important to the team is to keep things simple and pragmatic while supporting future product iterations.

So how does Vivino keep this all running so smoothly while still shipping new features at scale? Let's dive in!

Examine Vivino's Architecture

One of the most popular architecture concepts is the "Three-layer architecture," which consists of the UI, Business Logic, and Data layers. However, the Vivino team decided to base their app on **four layers**:

- **Features Layer**: The Features layer contains the different end-user features – wine scanning, search, profile page, and more. If you imagine patterns like MVVM – yeah, that's part of it.

- **Components Layer**: The Components layer contains reusable building blocks that serve the different features. For example, UI components such as buttons and text fields, as well as text formatters and validators. The code inside the Components layer is feature agnostic – if it serves a specific feature, it should be part of the Features layer.

- **Foundation layer**: This layer contains business rules, user cases, and the app's business logic – these are often called "Domain logic." If the Components layer shares UI code across different features, the Foundation has nothing to do with UI and focuses only on shared logic.

- **Data Layer**: As its name states, the Data layer is all about data: managing persistent stores, API clients, and caching.

The fourth-layered architecture Vivino uses helps them establish a robust app that they can maintain over time. It focuses on sharing UI building blocks and business logic across different features. The structure Vivino chose is considered relatively deep and aims to serve multiple squads working on a single app.

Vivino's model is just one approach. Across iOS development, we know that different teams pick different styles. So, the question is – is that the perfect architecture for a mobile app? Before we answer that question, let's try to define the different definitions.

Understanding the Definitions

Architecture is a slippery term. For years, "experts" tried to convince us of the perfect architecture for our projects (not just mobile apps), but in a way that was an overblown task. Not because of their skills and knowledge, but because of the way we work on our code. Unlike a `class` or a `struct`, architecture isn't something we can point to in Xcode and define when it begins and ends. It's more of an abstract approach to organizing code, setting boundaries, planning data flows, and reflecting on the decisions we make and the trade-offs we accept. In other words, architecture is **less about syntax and more about strategy**.

But why listen to me? Let's hear what other developers have to say about this topic!

Listening to Developers

You know what they say – *"ask 10 developers about architecture, and you'll quickly run out of whiteboard markers"* (I'm kidding, no one really says that, but you have to admit it is true!). And what do you know? That's precisely what I did!

So, what do they say? Some look at it as a philosophy, some – just a tool.

Vincent Pradeilles, who worked on **Photoroom** and apps for the biggest banks in France, is clear about that:

> *Architecture is the way we organize code to meet the organization's goals. That is why **there's no absolute truth,** and there isn't this one architecture that fits one organization and not another.*

For Vincent, architecture sets the boundaries of what is possible, and that's an interesting phrase. For example, in the banking apps he worked on, the architecture wasn't built around business logic because the business logic operations were mainly handled on the backend. That isn't the case with the **Photoroom app,** where the business logic runs on the device; therefore, its architecture is different.

Zlatko Kuvendjiski, who works at public safety technology company Axon in London, reinforces Vincent's words but from another angle. For him, architecture is also about testability and long-term evolution. In his **personal app**, he uses **TCA (The Composable Architecture)** together with **a Swift Package per feature**. This structure enforces clear boundaries and improves testability, even if it introduces some complexity.

At **Axon**, however, his team uses a more traditional **MVVM** approach – but the underlying principle is the same: the goal isn't architectural purity, but the ability to maintain and evolve the app over time under real-world pressure.

Defining the Terms

Model–View–ViewModel (**MVVM**) is an architectural pattern used in iOS development that separates the user interface from the business logic. The **Model** represents the app's data, the **View** displays the UI and handles user interaction, and the **ViewModel** prepares data for the view and coordinates the presentation logic. By placing this logic in the ViewModel, MVVM keeps views lightweight and improves testability.

At this point, we discussed what Monika, Vincent, and Zlatko had to say about architecture, but there's one thing we haven't mentioned, and that's MVVM. And it's a good chance to clear things up about the different terminologies.

Architecture is about organizing our code to meet our (or our company's) goals. On the other hand, design patterns are just reusable solutions that help us solve recurring problems.

Think of building a house. Deciding how many floors you'll have and what each floor is for – **that's architecture.** Choosing spiral stairs versus a straight staircase, or an open-plan living room versus closed rooms – **that's design patterns.** Architecture defines the big picture, while patterns solve recurring, more minor problems.

And that brings us back to the question: is Vivino's architecture the perfect one or the common one? Or maybe the question is broader – what types of architectures do we have? I think it's a good idea for us to make a small visit to the *"architectural zoo."*

Visiting the Architectural Zoo

Now that we understand what an architecture and a design pattern are, we want to examine our options, and that's, well, a little tricky. There's a reason I called it the *"architectural zoo"* rather than the "architectural market." We don't have a shelf where we can simply pick one architecture and be done with it. Instead, architectures are like animals in a zoo – each has its own nature. Some look the same, but they behave differently. Some thrive only in the desert, and some are built for the cold.

However, we can still discuss some basic principles and draw examples of common architectures and their goals.

Let's begin with the first and perhaps the most obvious one – *context-driven architecture.*

Context-Driven Architecture

We've already talked about building an architecture for a specific goal, but we never named that idea. And here it is. Vincent's line that *"architecture must meet the company's goals"* felt obvious, yet it stuck with me. Why? Because most of us, when starting a new codebase or reshaping an old one, are attracted to what we already know. If we spent 3-4 years in a small team using a classic three-layer setup, there's a good chance we'll reach for the same architecture as an indie – even when our new constraints are totally different.

The idea is to pause and ask: **what does this product and team actually need?** The answers should shape the structure – not the other way around.

Here are some of the questions we can ask:

- How many user-facing features do we expect our app to have?

- How much heavier will the on-device logic be versus the backend?

- How many teams will work on our app in parallel?

- What is the navigation strategy in our app?

- How much do we care about testing?

- What do we think about the offline-first policy or caching policy?

The above checklist isn't complete, but it highlights where to focus. Suppose our app keeps **most logic server-side** and does **little local caching**, while prioritizing **polish and speed in the UI**. For this example, the right fit would usually be a **lean, UI-first architecture** backed by a **robust networking layer** (Figure 2-1).

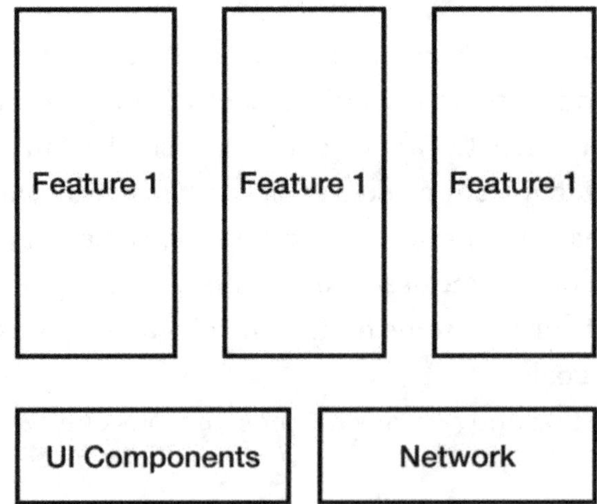

Figure 2-1. *An architecture for a light UI-based features app*

Figure 2-1 shows an architecture that is quite different from the classic three-layer structure we usually see. A classic three-layer structure often consists of a UI layer, a business layer that holds most of the app's logic, and a data layer. However, in this case, we see some changes. First, notice what's missing: we don't have a dedicated business layer, since we're not planning to perform any significant logic or computation on-device. We also don't include a persistent store, which makes avoiding the business layer even more logical.

On the other hand, we do have a solid networking component that we can share across the different features we're going to build, and a UI components library that allows us to reuse elements and keep our interface consistent.

Finally, we expect our features to remain independent and distinct from one another. This kind of architecture serves well what Vincent reminded us: architecture should always serve the company's goal.

Now that we have a basic skeleton of our app architecture, we can discuss modularization.

Separating Wisely

Planning a context-driven architecture is about matching the way we work to the product's actual requirements. But as Krzysztof Zabłocki warned me in our interview: *"Don't try to predict the future."* At first, that sounds like the opposite of planning ahead.

Krzysztof, who has led iOS development at *The New York Times* and *Headspace* and authored frameworks used by tens of thousands of developers, has learned this lesson through years of experience: projects rarely grow into what we initially imagine. Patterns shift, requirements evolve, and even product goals can change completely. Counting on stability is the fundamental mistake.

Instead of trying to lock in the "perfect" architecture, we should **design for change**. That means making our projects as flexible as possible – splitting them into modules and libraries so that one piece can be replaced, updated, or re-implemented without disrupting the rest. In other words, plan for the present, but build for the unknown.

But what does this look like in practice? Is modularization just about organizing folders in Xcode, or is it something deeper? From my interviews, this question was at the heart of many discussions.

Let's go back to Vivino. While their architecture has historically evolved inside a single Xcode project, from Objective-C to Swift, and through several structural shifts, they **do use Swift Package Manager for all external dependencies today**. Their internal modules, however, are still implemented as in-project frameworks, and the team is **now exploring a gradual migration of those internal frameworks into Swift packages.**

Other teams, however, have already taken the next step – using Swift Package Manager not only for external libraries but also to structure their internal modules. This gives them more precise boundaries, easier reuse, and more flexible testing strategies. Let's look at what they had to say.

Understanding the Idea Behind Modules

For many developers, simplicity is the name of the game. Take **Danijela Vrzan**, an indie developer from Canada, who favors a straightforward, single-module setup in her personal projects. But in her previous team, the requirements were different. *"When the company grew, we started to modularize our code with Swift Packages. That move reduced build times and made it easier to work at scale."*

Danijela's experience wasn't unique. **Noam**, from Yazio, uses Swift Packages for a similar reason: to keep the team productive as the user base grew. At Yazio, the entire app is organized into Swift Packages, enabling parallel development and maintainability across a large codebase.

At this point, we can see the tension: on one hand, keeping things simple; on the other, organizing code for growth and clear separation. But developers also use the Swift Package Manager in their **personal projects**. Oliver Binns, a manager at Deloitte Digital, heavily uses packages in his side apps. For Oliver, this isn't about scale or team size – it's about boundaries. By enforcing clear interfaces between code components, packages make their projects more stable and easier to maintain, no matter how small they are. As Krzysztof put it, it's a way of *building for the unknown.*

What Oliver and other developers emphasize is that having **clear boundaries** between different parts of a project makes it far less prone to issues when changes occur simultaneously. It's like in a zoo: each animal has its own enclosure, so they don't get in each other's way. In the same way, when code is encapsulated correctly, a fix in one place is less likely to "bite" into another part of the app.

So how do we achieve this separation in practice? Let's look at some approaches to **encapsulating code** – the way Oliver, Krzysztof, and Danijela have done in their projects.

Encapsulating Code Using Swift Packages

In a perfect world, we could sit in a room and plan all the packages our app will ever need, complete with their interfaces and boundaries. But reality is different. Not only can we not predict the future, but most of us face the challenge of **modularizing an existing app** rather than starting fresh. And even when it *is* a new app, it's almost impossible to anticipate every service or library from day one.

Modularization, then, isn't a one-time exercise. It's an **ongoing process** that must keep pace with the dynamic, ever-changing nature of maintaining a project.

So, where do we start? With the bottom of the stack obviously.

Starting with the Bottom of the Stack

We know – it's tempting to start encapsulating the exciting, user-facing parts: flows, features, and views.

But a module is **isolated by design** (that's the whole point). If we start with a feature first, it won't have clean access to the **underlying services** it depends on – business logic, data/persistence, networking, logging, feature flags, and so on.

So, we should actually start from the **bottom of the stack** – the parts on which most of the project depends – and move upward. Once those foundations are modular, feature modules can rely on them without leaking details. See Figure 2-2.

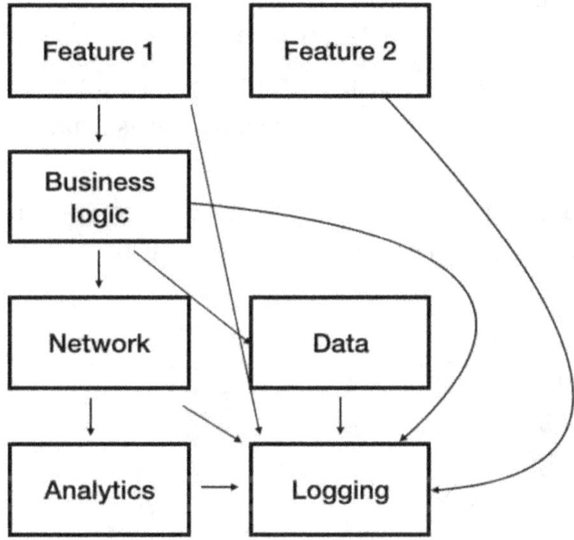

Figure 2-2. *The app components stack*

Figure 2-2 shows a typical app structure with several layers and components. If we try to sketch our own app in the same way, we quickly discover where to begin. Notice how the **Logging** component in Figure 2-2 doesn't depend on anything else, yet everything else depends on it. That makes it a natural candidate to modularize first.

This principle applies to other bottom-level services too – Networking, Analytics, or even a Design System. These are relatively independent, widely reusable, and stable over time, making them ideal starting points before moving up to business logic or features.

The next step after selecting the component we want to encapsulate is to create a new Swift Package and declare its interface.

Declaring the Interface

From the interviews I've done, it seems that defining the **interface** is the number one reason developers are so passionate about modularizing their apps.

But what does it really mean to have *clear boundaries*? Why can't we just settle for `internal` and `private` methods? Aren't those already boundaries?

The difference with a Swift Package is that it **splits a component into two parts**: the **public API** and the hidden implementation. That creates a contract between the package and the rest of the app. In other words, a package is like another product, and the package manifest makes that official.

When we start thinking in terms of APIs and contracts, good things happen.

Take the Logging library we just mentioned. Inside the package, we can hide any implementation details we want, such as custom logic, third-party dependencies, and tools. None of that leaks out. The only thing the app sees is what we decide to mark as `public`.

By encapsulating the Logging library in a Swift Package, we can define a clear contract where the rest of the app only sees the public API:

```swift
import Foundation

public enum LogLevel: String {
    case debug = "DEBUG"
    case info = "INFO"
    case warning = "WARNING"
    case error = "ERROR"
    case critical = "CRITICAL"
}

public final class Logger {

    public static let shared = Logger()

    public func log(_ level: LogLevel, _ message: String, context: [String: Any]? = nil) {
        let formattedMessage = formatMessage(level: level, message: message, context: context)
        output(formattedMessage)
    }
```

```swift
// MARK: - Internal Implementation

private func formatMessage(level: LogLevel, message: String, context:
[String: Any]?) -> String {
    let timestamp = ISO8601DateFormatter().string(from: Date())

    if let context = context, !context.isEmpty {
        let contextString = context
            .map { "\($0.key)=\($0.value)" }
            .joined(separator: ", ")
        return "[\(timestamp)] [\(level.rawValue)] \(message) | \
        (contextString)"
    } else {
        return "[\(timestamp)] [\(level.rawValue)] \(message)"
    }
}

private func output(_ message: String) {
    print(message)
}
}
```

And from the rest of the app:

```swift
import Logger

Logger.shared.log(.info, "App started")
Logger.shared.log(.debug, "Fetched items", context: ["count": 12])
Logger.shared.log(.error, "Network request failed", context: ["endpoint":
"/feed"])
```

Notice how the app can only access what we've marked as `public`. The internal details stay hidden inside the package, forcing us to think in terms of interfaces and responsibilities. That's the real power of modularization.

Now that we have a Swift Package, one of the questions I had was – can we reuse it across projects and apps? I must say that the answers I got surprised me.

Reusing the Swift Package

We already know we can reuse a Swift Package within the same app; that's part of the idea of encapsulating code. But here's the thing – if we invested the efforts of creating a "product" with a clear contract and advanced and valuable implementation, wouldn't it be natural to reuse them across our apps?

We just talked about the Logging library – imagine we do the same for networking, analytics, common tools, and more. Creating a new app and importing these libraries to start on an advanced stage sounds extremely productive.

Yeah, in theory.

In reality, things are different.

Reusing Swift Packages across projects was one of the follow-up questions I asked during the interviews. I was expecting at least one developer to say, "Sure, that increases the speed of my development and improves the maintenance." However, no developer said this is what they do.

Digging deeper, I started to understand why. The idea of reusing code across projects may sound like heaven, but as Krzysztof reminded me, *don't try to predict the future.*

In practice, developers almost always tailor their packages to the needs of the current project. That's the top priority. A package may start out looking generic, but it quickly evolves into something shaped by the product it lives in – and that makes it unsuitable for sharing.

Vincent put it clearly: *"In reality, it doesn't work. It takes too much time and effort to maintain it."* Once you share a library between projects, you suddenly inherit a new issue: cross-project bugs, backward compatibility, versioning, and the need to retest existing apps after every change.

The message from the field is clear: **Swift Packages are for modularizing apps, not for creating universal libraries.**

So, if that's the case, is splitting our app into modules the common approach? Well, not exactly. Let's see a different opinion about this topic.

Keeping It Simple (But Not Stupid)

At this point in my interviews, I was under the impression that working with Swift Packages was the standard among iOS developers. Developers like Zlatko and Oliver even told me they modularize their personal projects, because they find it so compelling.

And then I met **Mikaela Caron**, an indie developer from the United States who favors speed and simplicity over complex architectures. She has a good reason for it. *"I just want to ship new apps and get things done!"* she told me. It sounds obvious, but it perfectly captures the trade-off between flexible architecture and delivery speed.

Sure, a carefully modularized architecture makes it easier to maintain an app, add new features, and fix bugs – but not everyone needs that. Mikaela has already published about four indie apps, and for her, the overhead of Swift Packages would just slow her down. Her focus is on shipping quickly, learning fast, and enjoying the process.

In her apps, Mikaela primarily works with the **MVVM design pattern**, especially when building with SwiftUI. Her ViewModels don't just manage view state – they also handle business logic and networking. It's a leaner approach than what you'd find in larger teams, but it's on purpose.

And that's the point: in Mikaela's case, the architecture certainly serves her goals of shipping fast. What might look "too simple" in a corporate environment is exactly what gives her the speed and freedom she needs as an indie developer.

We've already seen a spectrum of opinions and approaches – and that's just the beginning. Throughout this book, you'll encounter even more ways of looking at the same problems. But for now, we need to make things practical. Let's refine what we've learned so far into more precise guidance, so we can move from theory into something you can apply in your own projects.

Picking the Right Architecture

In the previous paragraph, we already understood there's a large spectrum to pick from, so let's try to be a bit more practical and group it into several types (Figure 2-3).

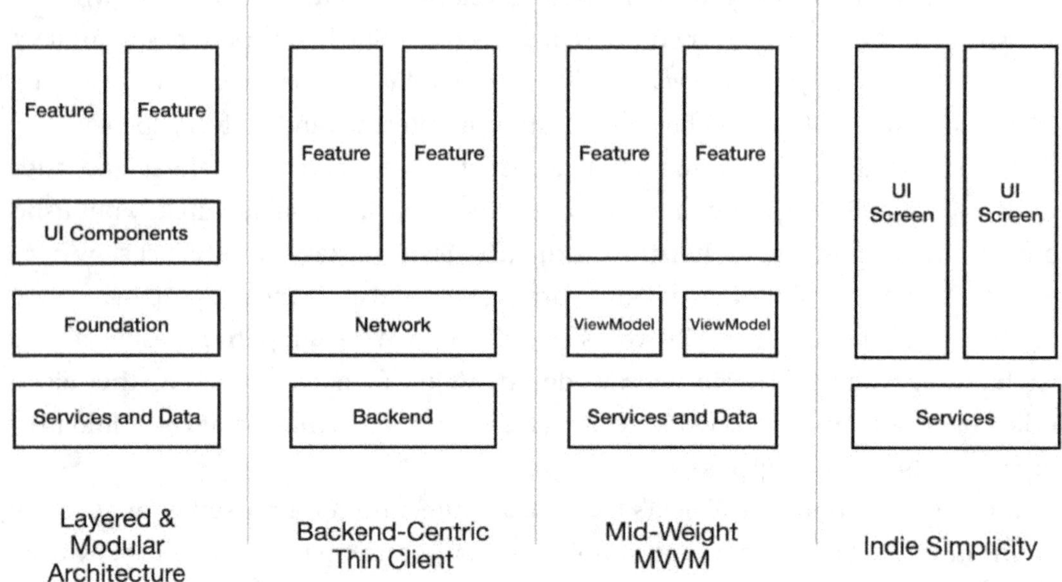

Figure 2-3. *The different types of architecture*

Figure 2-3 shows the main architectural types I encountered during my interviews. Remember, each serves a specific goal, so we should always reflect on how they compare in real-world requirements.

- **Layered and Modular Architecture:** Code is organized into layers or packages. Business logic, UI components, and services are shared across features. This approach enables clear testability and parallel development. Monika's Vivino app, Zlatko's Axon, Oliver's Deloitte, and Vincent's Photoroom are strong examples. It's well-suited for larger apps with multiple squads and significant on-device logic.

- **Backend-Centric Thin Client:** Most business logic lives in the backend. The client focuses on UI and network calls, with minimal on-device logic. This architecture is well-suited to environments where server-side control is crucial, such as banking, fintech, and regulated industries. Vincent's banking projects are a good example.

- **Mid-Weight MVVM:** The ViewModel (defined earlier in the chapter) acts as the glue between the UI and the data services. In this style, most of the business logic sits in the ViewModel, with no dedicated business/Foundation layer. It works well for small teams and apps that favor simplicity and speed, and that don't require modularization.

- **Indie-Simplicity:** Here, the ViewModel and UI together handle everything: state, business rules, and networking. There's no persistence layer or package structure. This approach is ideal for solo developers, small apps, or cases where delivery speed matters more than long-term maintenance. Mikaela's indie apps are a clear example.

These four templates show how different teams approach architecture depending on their goals and constraints. But architecture only gives us the big picture – the skeleton of the app. To make it move, we also need the muscles and joints. That's where **design patterns** come in.

Solving Problems with Design Patterns

By now, we've seen that architecture is about the "big moves": layers, modules, backend versus client decisions. But once we're inside that structure, our everyday work takes place on a smaller scale. How should a view talk to its data? Where does the state live? How do we keep controllers from growing into monsters? These are the questions design patterns are meant to answer.

We're zooming in now to talk about how each module or layer is actually implemented. The good news is: we don't have to reinvent the wheel. The iOS community is mature, and for almost every recurring problem, there's already a solution. How do I always say? – There's a pattern for that.

There's a Pattern for That

Think about it: building a list of items fetched from storage? There's a pattern for that. Syncing data from the backend and caching it locally? There's a pattern for that, too. Most of the code we write day to day falls into well-trodden patterns we've seen in tutorials, blog posts, or past projects.

That's why I asked developers in my interviews which patterns really mattered to them. The first and most important topic that came up was **UI patterns** – MVC and MVVM. And honestly? Their answers didn't surprise me... let's see.

Architectural Design Patterns

Building UI Using MVC and MVVM

Many years ago, before SwiftUI and Combine, almost every iOS screen was built with
UIKit, Apple's UI framework. And in those early days, one design pattern ruled them all:
MVC – Model-View-Controller.

Why MVC? Simply because that's what Apple showed in WWDC sessions and code
samples. Most iOS developers were new to the platform, and MVC felt like the official
way to separate screen responsibilities.

Over time, apps grew more complex. It wasn't enough to just show data – we needed
to manage state, keep files small, and write code we could test. MVC often collapsed
under that weight. Controllers grew enormous, juggling networking, state, and UI logic
simultaneously. Developers renamed it **"Massive View Controller."**

The obvious evolution was to split out the controller's responsibilities into a
ViewModel. The ViewModel manages state, talks to the model, and leaves the view
"dumb" and declarative. That approach – **MVVM** – quickly became one of the most
common patterns in iOS.

With the arrival of **SwiftUI**, MVVM felt almost unavoidable. SwiftUI's declarative
style and state-driven updates fit perfectly with the ViewModel idea. But MVVM wasn't
the only option. Developers also explored the **MVP** (Model-View-Presenter) and more
structured approaches like **VIPER** (View-Interactor-Presenter-Entity-Router).

So, MVC gave us structure, MVVM slimmed down our controllers, and SwiftUI
pushed us even further in that direction. But what happens in the wild? Do teams stick to
these patterns? Do they mix them? Or do they bend them until they barely look like the
diagrams in blog posts? Let's look at what developers told me.

Understanding Vivino's Relationship with VIPER

Vivino's story is fascinating here because their architecture is relatively unique (four
layers) and they had to scale quickly – both in developers (three squads) and in users
(millions worldwide).

This scale pushed their iOS team to invest heavily in architecture and design
patterns, perhaps more than most. They wanted their screens to be testable (don't worry,
we'll get to testing in the coming chapters) and to enforce a strict separation of concerns
throughout the app.

For Vivino, **MVC** wasn't a good fit. In the **UIKit** era, many teams faced the same issue: controllers that grew too large and became hard to manage. **VIPER**, already in use before Monika joined, turned out to be the more scalable choice for their complexity. Its **Interactor** layer provided a clean place for complex business logic, such as wine match percentages, user preferences, and data pulled from multiple endpoints. And the **Router** helped tame Vivino's intricate navigation flows – from scanning a label, to preview, to details, to purchase – in a predictable way.

In short, MVC would have led to overly large controllers, and **MVVM** may not have provided sufficient separation at the time. **VIPER** promised a structured approach, smaller units, and better testability, which made sense for Vivino's scale.

So, let's say a few words about what **VIPER** actually is.

Diving into VIPER

VIPER is one of those patterns that sounds intimidating at first glance. The name stands for **View, Interactor, Presenter, Entity, and Router** – five separate components that together replace the "Massive View Controller" problem.

The idea is simple: instead of dumping everything into one giant controller file, we break it into smaller roles, each with a clear responsibility.

Let's see what VIPER looks like (Figure 2-4).

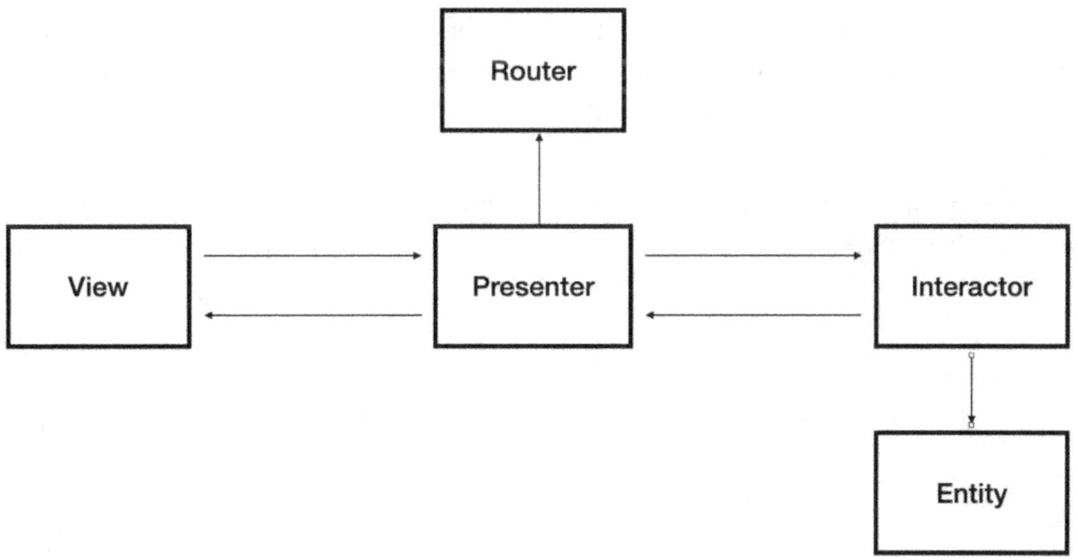

Figure 2-4. *The VIPER design pattern*

Figure 2-4 shows the different VIPER components and how they communicate with each other. Let's list them and explain their role:

- **View**: Displays information and forwards user input.

- **Interactor**: Contains the business logic and decides "what happens" when an action is triggered.

- **Presenter**: Coordinates between the View and the Interactor, preparing data for display. This component is also relevant in the MVP (Model-View-Presenter) design pattern.

- **Entity**: The data models that move through the system.

- **Router**: Handles navigation.

If MVC felt like three actors crowding onto one stage, VIPER makes it into five actors with clearer lines. The **promise** was better separation of concerns and, more importantly for Vivino, easier **testability**. You can test an Interactor in isolation, or check that a Presenter formats data correctly without pulling in the whole UI.

Of course, this separation comes at a price: boilerplate. Writing five files to build a single feature can feel heavy, especially for small apps or indie projects. But for Vivino, with three squads working in parallel and millions of users, the overhead was worth it. VIPER gave them the structure they needed to keep UIKit under control.

And yet, Vivino isn't sticking with VIPER forever. Like many teams, they're evolving toward MVVM as SwiftUI becomes the dominant framework. Patterns come and go, but the need they're trying to solve – making complex apps maintainable – remains the same.

Let's look at Figure 2-5, now with our new information about the different design patterns Vivino uses.

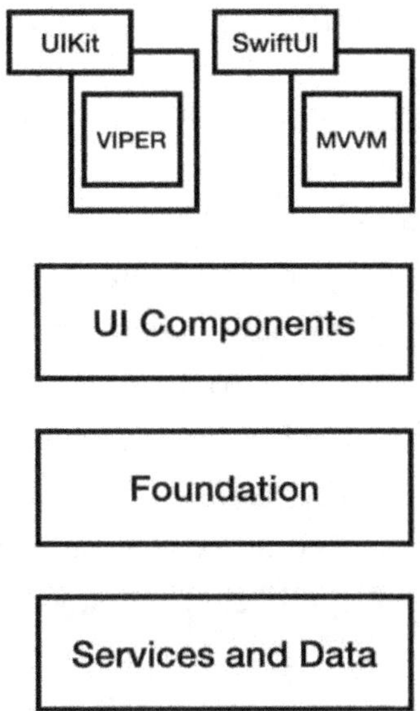

Figure 2-5. *Vivino UI design patterns*

Figure 2-5 shows how different UI design patterns can coexist in the same app. So asking *"Do you build your app with MVVM or VIPER?"* isn't really the right question. These patterns aren't app-wide choices; they're tools suited to specific screens or contexts.

As Vivino's case shows, teams often make different decisions over time – UIKit screens structured with VIPER, SwiftUI screens built with MVVM. The point isn't to be consistent at all costs, but to pick the pattern that fits the framework, the team, and the problem at hand.

So far, we've talked about the **big picture** (architecture) and the **local picture** (UI design patterns like MVC, MVVM, and VIPER). But something is still missing. Architecture and patterns define the *shapes* of our code, yet they don't explain how the pieces talk to one another. Every feature needs data, every screen needs services, and every layer needs to know which other layer it can communicate with.

In other words, we need to talk about the **glue**: the mechanism that connects these parts without coupling them together. That's where **Dependency Injection** comes in.

Gluing the Pieces Together with Dependency Injection

Let's talk about an important part of building software: **dependencies**. For junior developers, this topic may feel like a non-issue – it's easy just to call a class directly, use static methods, or rely on a singleton.

But for more experienced developers, **Dependency Injection** becomes essential. Coupling code, interfaces, and logic together creates major issues over time and makes testing far more complicated than it needs to be.

Think of Dependency Injection as glue. You can use **superglue** (singletons or static calls) to connect parts quickly. It works fast, but it's messy and nearly impossible to undo later. Or you can use **bolts and screws** (e.g., constructor injection), which takes more effort up front but gives you flexibility and clean removal.

So, the question is: what kind of glue do developers actually use in practice? To answer that, let's start by looking at **protocols, testing, and Singletons.**

A Little Bit About Protocols, Singletons, and Testing

The title of this section might seem a little off at first glance, and it may look like I've mixed terms. But when I spoke with developers about how they implement dependency injection, I noticed a strong correlation between DI, protocols, and testing.

Now, to be clear: **you can implement dependency injection without protocols.** Here's a simple example:

```
class NetworkService {
    func fetchData() -> String {
        return "Fetched data from the network"
    }
}

class UserViewModel {
    private let networkService: NetworkService

    init(networkService: NetworkService) {
        self.networkService = networkService
    }
```

```
func loadUser() {
    print(networkService.fetchData())
}
}
```

In this code, `UserViewModel` depends on `NetworkService`, and we inject it via the constructor. This example is a perfectly valid DI example. But in practice, many of the developers I spoke with don't stop there. They add **protocols** on top – not because DI requires it, but because protocols make testing easier, enforce boundaries, and scale better as projects grow. The overhead of adding a new dependency to the constructor isn't worth it if we don't fully decouple it using protocols.

Adding a protocol also adds more work, but the value it adds overcomes that. Look at the following diagram (Figure 2-6).

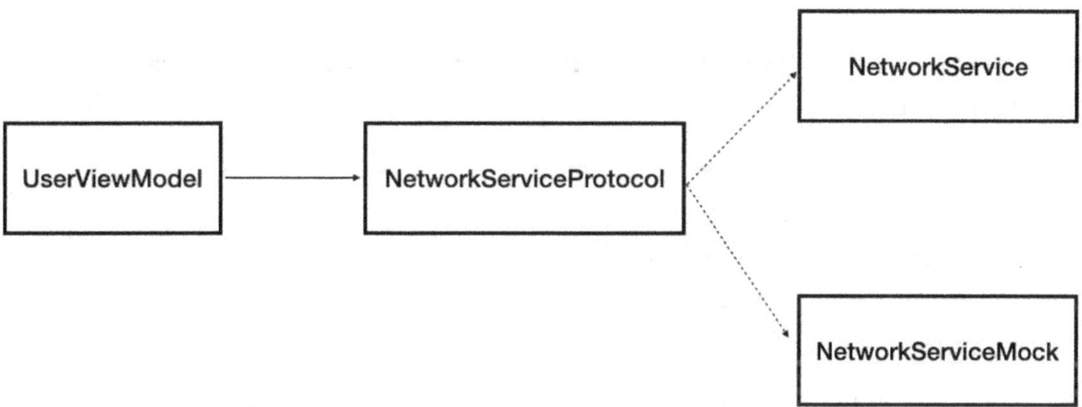

Figure 2-6. *Protocol-based dependency injection*

Figure 2-6 shows the opportunities protocol-based dependency injection provides. The ability to swap `NetworkService` with a `NetworkServiceMock` is powerful: it helps when backend APIs aren't ready, makes unit testing easier, and even improves SwiftUI previews. That's part of why developers often tie DI so closely to testing.

But there's another side to the dependency story – the shortcut many of us have used: the **Singleton**. A Singleton restricts a class to a single, shared instance and makes it globally accessible. It's convenient for services like logging or analytics, but the tradeoffs are hidden dependencies and tighter coupling.

In my interviews, the same developers who leaned heavily on protocol-based DI (like Noam Efergan and Zlatko Kuvendjiski) also warned against overusing Singletons.

Oliver Binns put it well: *"Even the few Singletons we use, we still inject them. That way, we keep the benefits of testing and avoid spreading global state."*

Here's a code snippet of how to inject a Singleton:

```
class UserViewModel {
    private let networkService: NetworkService

    init(networkService: NetworkService) {
        self.networkService = networkService
    }

    func loadUser() {
        print(networkService.fetchData())
    }
}

let viewModel = UserViewModel(networkService: NetworkService.shared)
viewModel.loadUser()

class FakeNetworkService: NetworkService {
    override func fetchData() -> String {
        return "Fake data for testing"
    }
}

let testViewModel = UserViewModel(networkService: FakeNetworkService())
testViewModel.loadUser()
```

In this code, we can see how we initialize the UserViewModel and inject the Singleton NetworkService.shared. We can also see how to create a FakeNetworkService and inject it when we need to test the UserViewModel or just avoid the actual implementation with our custom one.

Exploring an Interesting Tool: Swift-Dependencies by Point-Free

So far, we've seen how most developers manage dependency injection manually – through constructors, setters, protocols, and sometimes singletons. But some teams go further and use tools to make DI easier and more consistent.

One of the great things about interviewing developers is that I always learn new tricks and frameworks I hadn't tried before. **Zlatko Kuvendjiski** told me about a library called `swift-dependencies`, created by Point-Free – the same team behind the well-known Composable Architecture (TCA).

The goal of `swift-dependencies` is to bring structure to dependency management. It gives developers an alternative to singletons, makes dependencies explicit, and provides built-in solutions for testing and SwiftUI previews.

Once we add the `swift-dependencies` package as a dependency (oh, the irony) to our project, we can start using it with macros and enums.

Let's take a common use case: an `AuthClient`. Many developers would normally implement this as a singleton. Instead, we'll define it as a struct:

```
struct AuthClient {
    var signIn: @Sendable (_ email: String, _ password: String) async
    throws -> UserSession
}

struct UserSession: Equatable, Codable {
    var token: String
    var userEmail: String
}
```

Unlike the protocol-based dependencies we saw from other developers, Point-Free takes a slightly different approach. Here, the dependency is expressed as a stored property that holds a function:

```
var signIn: @Sendable (_ email: String, _ password: String) async throws ->
UserSession
```

It may not look like a protocol, but it effectively **acts like one**. For example:

```
let live = AuthClient(
    login: { username, password in
      try await API.login(username, password)
    },
    logout: { try await API.logout() }
  )
```

Here, we initialize a new `AuthClient` and pass in the actual implementation of the `signIn` function. Even without the `swift-dependencies` library, this is already a neat way to avoid protocols and make swapping, stubbing, or overriding implementations much simpler.

Now that we've defined the `AuthClient`, we can add real, test, and preview implementations by creating an enum that conforms to the DependencyKey protocol:

```swift
private enum AuthClientKey: DependencyKey {
    // Real production implementation
    static let liveValue: AuthClient = .init { email, password in
        try await API.login(email, password)
    }

    // Default for tests (safe, deterministic)
    static let testValue: AuthClient = .init { _, _ in
        .init(token: "TEST_TOKEN", userEmail: "test@example.com")
    }

    // Nice for SwiftUI previews (fake latency)
    static let previewValue: AuthClient = .init { email, _ in
        try await Task.sleep(nanoseconds: 500_000_000)
        return .init(token: "PREVIEW_TOKEN", userEmail: email)
    }
}
```

The DependencyKey protocol is at the heart of how `swift-dependencies` works. Using it, we identify each dependency and define its implementations for production, testing, and previews.

Next, we register it by extending DependencyValues:

```swift
extension DependencyValues {
    var auth: AuthClient {
        get { self[AuthClientKey.self] }
        set { self[AuthClientKey.self] = newValue }
    }
}
```

DependencyValues holds the list of all dependencies available in the project. From here, using the dependency in a ViewModel is straightforward:

```swift
final class SignInViewModel: ObservableObject {
    @Dependency(\.auth) var auth

    func signIn() async {
        do {
            let session = try await auth.signIn(email, password)
            self.session = session
        } catch {
            self.errorMessage = (error as? LocalizedError)?.
            errorDescription ?? "Something went wrong."
        }
    }
}
```

The @Dependency property wrapper handles everything for us, returning the correct implementation based on whether we're in production, running tests, or building SwiftUI previews.

In short, the `swift-dependencies` library offers an elegant way to replace singletons and inject custom implementations, while making testing and previews first-class citizens.

Summary and Takeaways

Architecture and design patterns are never one-size-fits-all. From Vivino's layered system to Mikaela's indie pragmatism, the lesson is simple: architecture must serve the product and the team, not the other way around.

What we've learned:

- **Architecture Is Strategy:** It sets boundaries and shapes how code evolves with company goals.

- **Design Patterns Solve Recurring Problems:** MVC, MVVM, VIPER, and others are just tools – they are not our goal.

- **Context Matters:** A banking app, a photo editor, and an indie project each lead to different approaches, and that's perfectly fine.

- **Plan for Change, Not Perfection:** As Krzysztof reminded us, predicting the future leads to brittle designs – flexibility wins.

- **Dependency Injection and Clear Boundaries Pay Off:** They make testing, previews, and maintenance far easier in the long run. However, we should consider the trade-offs they bring.

In the end, there's no perfect architecture. What matters is aligning code structure with your team's goals, your product's scale, and your ability to adapt.

And architecture is just one side of building apps that work in the real world. The other side? Deciding **what to build, how to validate it, and how to know if changes actually improve the product.** That's where experimentation comes in.

In the next chapter, we'll dive into **A/B testing and feature experimentation** – what makes our app move in the right direction.

CHAPTER 3

A/B Testing and Experimentation

Optimizing the paywall with experiments is crucial, even on a small scale.

—Krzysztof Zabłocki

Introduction

In the previous chapter, we explored app architecture and design patterns – the skeleton that supports our features and business logic. But architecture is only the starting point. Once we set the foundation, an app must continue to evolve, guided by data and user behavior. That's where experiments come in.

In this chapter, we will

- **Look at Yazio,** a team running dozens of experiments in parallel

- **Learn the foundations of A/B testing,** including the mindset shift, common challenges, and the math behind significance

- **See how different teams approach experimentation,** each with its own culture and constraints

- **Explore phased rollouts and feature flags,** and why they belong in the same conversation

A. Tsadok, *Real-World iOS Development*, https://doi.org/10.1007/979-8-8688-2815-7_3

By the end, you'll see how experimentation connects architecture with growth – and why the ability to control who sees what, and when, is as important for developers as it is for product managers.

Now, let's start strong – with 40 experiments running at once!

Having 40 Experiments at Once

When Noam joined Yazio, one thing became immediately clear: almost nothing shipped without an experiment. On any given day, the app might be running 30 or 40 A/B tests simultaneously – new paywall variations, onboarding tweaks, different notification timings – all quietly competing in the background.

For developers, this meant every feature was provisional. You didn't just "build the thing" and release it; you built two or three versions and let the data decide. It was an ongoing cycle of hypotheses, implementations, and measurements.

At first, Noam found it exhilarating. The culture was relentlessly data-driven: intuition and gut feelings were interesting, but they didn't settle arguments. Numbers did. But it also demanded discipline. Running dozens of tests in parallel required careful instrumentation, feature flagging, and constant vigilance to prevent tests from interfering with one another.

What Yazio illustrates is the full embrace of A/B testing: not a one-off tool, but a way of life. And it raises the question – why don't all teams work this way?

Starting with the Basics of A/B Testing

Before we dive in, let's start with the fundamental question: **what is an A/B test?**

An A/B test – also known as **split testing** – is when you create two or more variations of the same feature, layout, or text and compare their performance to see which one works best.

At first glance, A/B testing might sound like a product manager's responsibility. But in reality, it has a significant impact on iOS developers. Many developers – especially seniors – are deeply involved in product decisions, and indie developers often **are** the product managers. On top of that, experimentation introduces new challenges for engineers, including privacy constraints, maintenance, and increased testing complexity.

To truly understand A/B testing, teams first need to shift their mindset – stop seeing decisions as final and start seeing them as experiments.

Shifting Our Mindset

Why is shifting our mindset toward A/B testing so hard?

At first, we might assume the difficulty is technical. In reality, the most significant barrier isn't code or tools – it's psychological. The root challenge lies in how we, as humans, make decisions and cling to our beliefs.

Several forces make this shift difficult:

- **Ego and Ownership**: We don't just create ideas; we identify with them. When an experiment fails, it can feel like *we* have failed.

- **Desire for Certainty**: A/B testing forces us to live in uncertainty, waiting for data instead of trusting our instincts.

- **Sunk Cost Bias**: Rolling back a feature after investing weeks or months is painful. Even when the data says it performs worse, we resist removing it.

- **Illusion of Expertise**: Senior developers and product managers often believe their instincts are enough. A/B testing challenges that sense of authority.

In short, we need to accept that our best ideas may be wrong, and that users – not us – have the final say.

To see the difference between instinct and data, let's look at Figure 3-1.

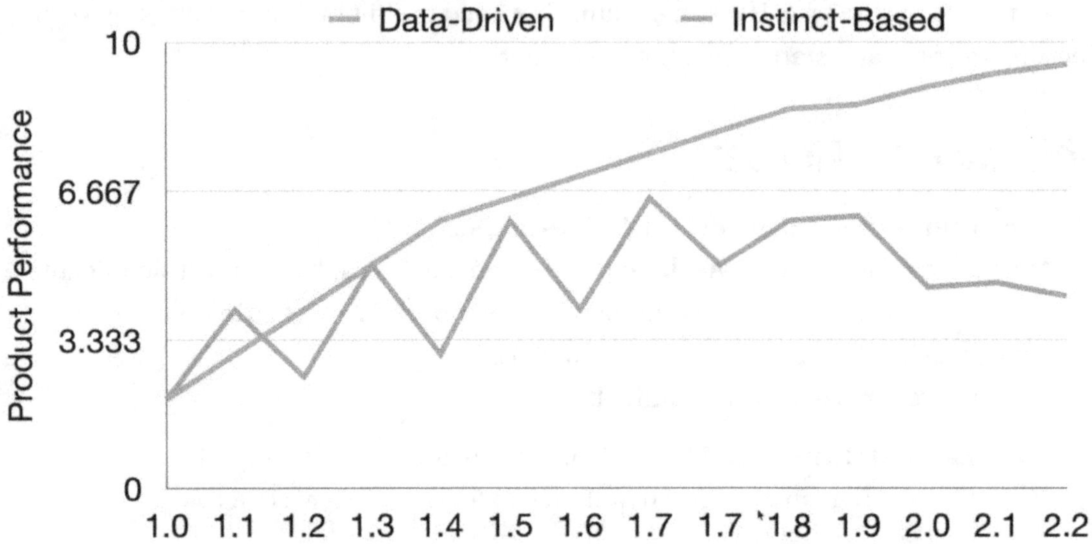

Figure 3-1. *A data-driven process versus an Instinct-based one*

Figure 3-1 shows a hypothetical app by its versions, and how each approach shapes product performance over time – whether measured by conversions, engagement, or another key metric.

- **Instinct-Based Approach:** Can sometimes lead to good results, but just as often falls back. The jumps up and down reflect the risks of relying on gut feeling.

- **Data-Driven Process:** Produces steadier, incremental improvements as experiments validate or reject changes. It may feel slower, but it is more reliable.

Over time, the data-driven path outperforms instinct. But even once we overcome these mental hurdles, mobile A/B testing brings its own technical challenges. Let's explore those next.

Listing the Challenges of A/B Testing on Mobile

iOS development brings unique challenges in privacy, deployment, performance, cross-platform consistency, and more. These challenges apply not only to "regular" iOS development but also to managing A/B tests.

Think about it: running experiments means analyzing user behavior and delivering changes in real time. Those requirements run directly against Apple's design philosophy, which emphasizes stability and predictability for users.

Here are some of the main obstacles:

- **App Store Release Cycle**: Unlike the web, we can't push experiments instantly. Each new variant requires an App Store submission, which takes time, effort, and manual review. Even after approval, users don't update immediately, leaving multiple versions in the wild. This makes experiment analysis more complex.

- **UI Instability**: Apps should launch as fast as possible, often before A/B configurations load. As a result, the interface can suddenly change while a user is in the middle of a session. Features may appear or disappear in front of them, creating confusion and invalidating results.

- **Privacy Regulations**: Experiments rely on tracking user behavior. But compliance with frameworks like GDPR, CCPA, and Apple's App Tracking Transparency requires careful anonymization and limits on what can be measured. These regulations make analyzing results harder.

- **Code Cleanup**: Setting up an experiment is hard enough, but removing it afterward is just as challenging. Developers must delete code paths, retest affected areas, and remove backend configurations to prevent technical debt.

These issues make A/B testing on mobile anything but trivial. And yet, the biggest challenge for many iOS developers isn't technical at all – it's knowing how to design and run experiments correctly. So, before we explore how teams in the field approach it, let's go over the foundations of A/B testing.

Going Over the A/B Testing Foundations

Managing A/B tests requires expertise beyond what many iOS developers usually practice. It touches on product management and data analysis – topics far removed from our usual conversations about design patterns, architecture, or Swift code.

And yet, A/B testing and product thinking are part of our reality as iOS developers. That's why it's important to understand the basic terms.

The basics start with **control groups and variants**. If we look back at Figure 3-1, we can see that data-driven apps tend to improve steadily over time. This happens because experiments always run against a baseline – or, in other words, the current version of the app. That baseline is the **control group**, while the new feature or change that we test is the **variant**. We can have multiple variants, but there is always one control. The idea is simple: every test should prove an improvement against what already exists.

But what does "improvement" mean? An A/B test is only helpful if it's tied to a **metric**. This could be conversion rate, feature engagement, or retention. Too often, teams try variants without agreeing on precisely *what* they want to improve. Without a clear metric, we can't judge whether a variant is truly successful.

We discuss A/B testing in the context of product management because iOS developers often live close to the UI, the experience, and feature ownership. But there's one more critical concept, borrowed from statistics, that we need to understand: **statistical significance**. It ensures that the differences we see in results are real – not just random chance.

Let's talk about it, because that's a topic that is crucial to understand, especially for those who usually work on a small scale, like indie developers.

Understanding What Statistical Significance Is

From the interviews I conducted, it's clear that teams usually perform A/B testing in large-scale apps like Vivino, Yazio, and Photoroom. Part of the reason is the challenges we discussed earlier – managing experiments is complex. For indie developers who already carry the full weight of design and development, it can feel overwhelming.

But there's another reason: **scale.** To trust experimental results, we need to reach a level of statistical significance, and we'll understand this using a coin experiment.

Why Sample Size Matters

The best way to understand this is with a coin flip.

- If we flip a coin five times, we might get four heads and one tail. That looks biased, but the sample is far too small to draw any conclusion.

- If we flip it 100 times, the results get closer to 50 heads and 50 tails.

- By 10,000 flips, we can be confident the ratio will be very close to 50–50.

This simple example shows why **sample size matters** when making decisions from experiments.

Now, let's return to A/B testing. In small-scale apps, usually built by indie developers, it's risky to approve a new variant if the sample size is too small. Imagine we run an onboarding experiment and find that seven out of ten people finish onboarding in Variant B, versus five out of ten in Variant A.

It's tempting to say Variant B "wins," but with such a tiny group, that difference could easily be luck – just like flipping four heads out of five tries.

So how can we tell if an experiment is statistically significant? How do we know if a difference is real, or just noise combined with sample size?

Well, the answer is from the space of math, and I'll explain it even though we can use online tools to calculate it. We will explain it through a real use case – onboarding.

Measuring Significance

Let's look at a real example. Suppose we run an onboarding experiment:

- **Variant A:** 1,000 users, 40 conversions (4%)

- **Variant B:** 1,100 users, 33 conversions (3%)

Step 1: Calculate the pooled conversion rate:

$$p = \frac{40 + 33}{1000 + 1100} = \frac{73}{2100} = 0.348$$

This value represents the average conversion rate across both groups.

Step 2: Calculate the standard error (SE):

$$SE = \sqrt{0.0348 * 0.9652 * \left(\frac{1}{1000} + \frac{1}{1100} \right)} \approx 0.0080$$

The SE tells us how much the results might vary if we ran the same test repeatedly with the same sample size. In other words, it measures **reliability**.

Don't worry if the equation looks a little frightening – there are great online tools that do the dirty work for us. What I want to do here is to explain how it works under the hood.

Step 3: Calculate the z-score:

$$z = \frac{0.04 - 0.030}{0.0080} \approx 1.25$$

The z-score compares the observed difference to the SE.

Now comes the critical step: plotting this on the **normal distribution curve** (Figure 3-2).

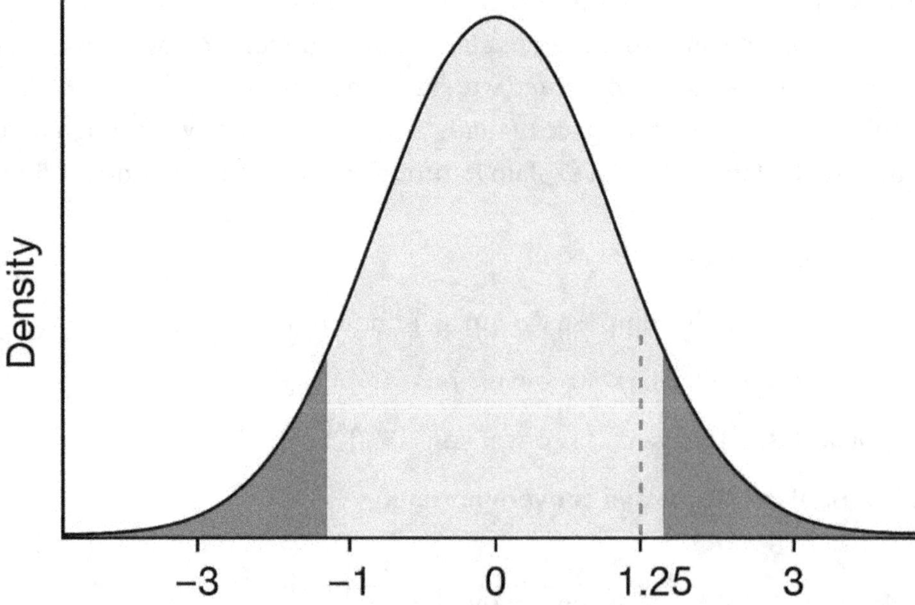

Figure 3-2. *The z-score in the normal distribution curve*

Looking at Figure 3-2, we see that a z-score of 1.25 falls in the gray region of the curve. For 95% confidence, we need a z-score greater than 1.96. Since our result doesn't cross that threshold, it's **not statistically significant**. In practice, this means we would need to either run the test longer (collect more users) or see a larger difference between variants to reach a trustworthy conclusion.

This example shows why even with 1,000 users per group, an experiment can still fall short. Combine that with the overhead of maintaining experiments, and many indie developers choose to skip A/B testing altogether. But scale isn't the only factor – the size of the difference also matters. Which leads us to the following question: even if 1,000 users per group aren't enough, how do large-scale teams like Vivino or Yazio manage to run dozens of experiments at once?

Let's see how A/B testing looks in the wild.

We don't have to do the math by hand! Several online tools can do it for us: Evan **Miller's A/B Test Calculator** – (https://www.evanmiller.org/ab-testing/) or **Optimizely Sample Size Calculator** (https://www.optimizely.com/sample-size-calculator/#/?conversion=3&effect=20&significance=95) are just two tools out of hundreds that can help us with planning and analyzing our tests.

See How Teams Run A/B Tests in the Wild

We saw that indie developers often skip A/B tests due to scale and overhead. Large-scale apps are different – experimentation is part of the culture. Why? Because the very challenges that overwhelm indies are manageable at scale.

For a start, a large user base means results come in faster. Fast results enable teams to decide quickly whether to iterate on an experiment or roll out a winning variant. Faster decisions prevent experiments from piling up, which would otherwise create too many active combinations and make testing nearly impossible.

There's another factor: **analysis.** Running and analyzing several experiments at once is hard for small teams, but larger organizations have dedicated analysts, data pipelines, and tools to handle it.

Let's look at Figure 3-3.

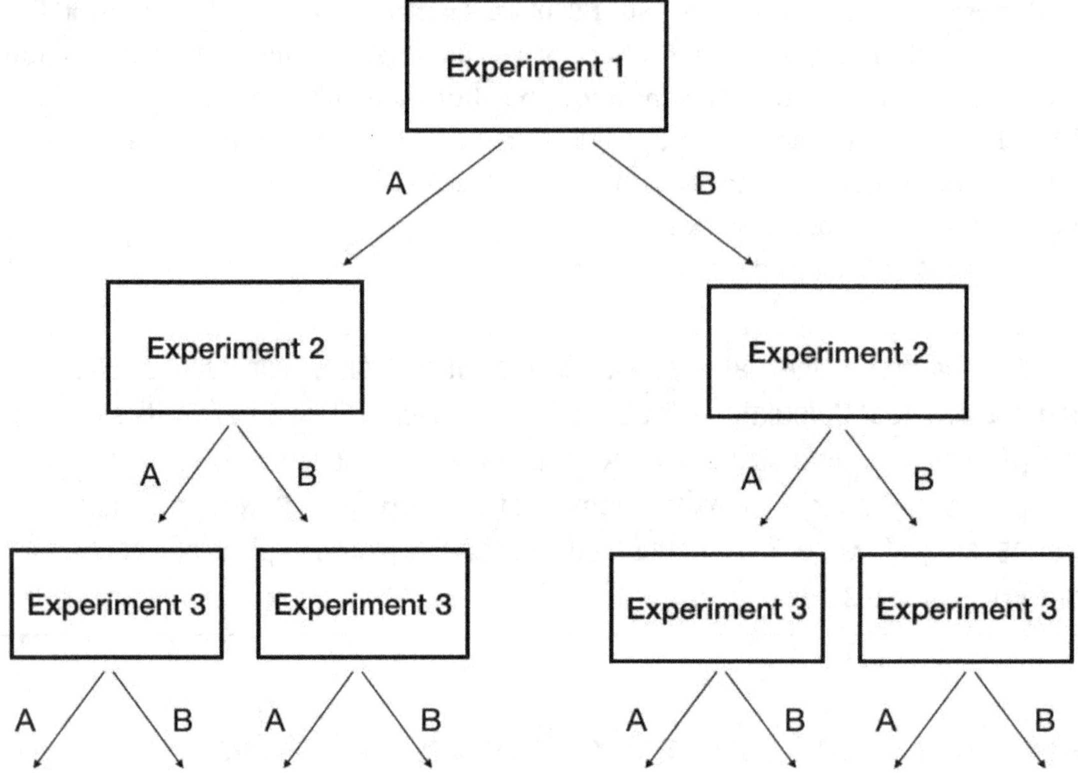

Figure 3-3. *Three experiments running at the same time*

As shown in Figure 3-3, three experiments with two variants each already yield eight distinct combinations. And that's with only two variants – add more, and the number of possible user experiences skyrockets.

At this point, you might wonder: doesn't this mean teams should run only one experiment at a time?

The answer is no – and here's why.

Consider Jeff Bezos' perspective at Amazon:

> *Our success at Amazon is a function of how many experiments we do per year, per month, per week, per day.*

> —Jeff Bezos, Amazon CEO and Founder

Bezos' strategy was simple: every experiment is an opportunity, almost like money lying on the floor. Every screen or feature that we don't test is considered unoptimized – meaning lost potential revenue or missed improvements.

From this perspective, experiments aren't extra work on top of product development – they're the **core engine** of improvement.

And still, we see that managing too many experiments is a real challenge. The combinations multiply quickly, and analysis becomes harder with every new test. Is it even possible to keep this under control?

For Noam and his team at **Yazio**, the answer is yes. Let's hear about Yazio's story.

Running Almost 50 Experiments at Once

Yazio, a health app from the UK, serves over **100 million users** – definitely not our standard app. At this scale, the ability to run many experiments at once isn't just helpful, it's crucial for growth.

Think about it: with such a massive user base, every small decision about the user experience – whether it's onboarding content, a new paywall design, or even the color of a button – can immediately influence critical metrics like conversion, engagement, and retention. Managing multiple experiments simultaneously, and doing so effectively, becomes a requirement, not a luxury.

To handle this, the Yazio team relies on **GrowthBook**, an open source platform for A/B testing and feature flags. GrowthBook lets them roll out variants, segment users, and measure impact with confidence. Without this kind of infrastructure, running dozens of parallel tests would quickly spiral into chaos.

A Few Words About GrowthBook

There are many A/B testing platforms available, each with its own focus. To make sense of what really matters when choosing one, let's use **GrowthBook** as a case study. This section isn't about recommending GrowthBook as the best tool – it's about using it to highlight the criteria any team should consider.

GrowthBook is an open source platform for feature flags and A/B testing. Compared to enterprise tools like **Split.io** (used by Vivino), it's lightweight and flexible. Its open source nature makes it especially attractive in industries where privacy and regulation are critical, such as fintech or healthcare, because teams can host and control their own data pipelines.

Looking at GrowthBook's core capabilities gives us a checklist for evaluating tools:

- **Feature Flags:** The ability to hide, show, or gradually roll out features, plus kill switches for risky flows

- **Experimentation:** Built-in statistical analysis, so teams don't have to calculate significance on their own

- **Integrations:** Connectors to data warehouses like Snowflake, BigQuery, or Postgres, which make experimentation work within existing pipelines

These might sound like basics, but not all platforms provide them. For example, gradual rollouts and proper statistical handling are sometimes missing in lighter-weight tools.

Teams choose GrowthBook because it's open source, cost-effective, and scalable – Yazio runs 40 experiments in parallel with it. On the flip side, its dashboards are less polished than those of enterprise platforms, and it works best if you already have strong analytics practices in place.

Here's what GrowthBook's dashboard looks like (Figure 3-4).

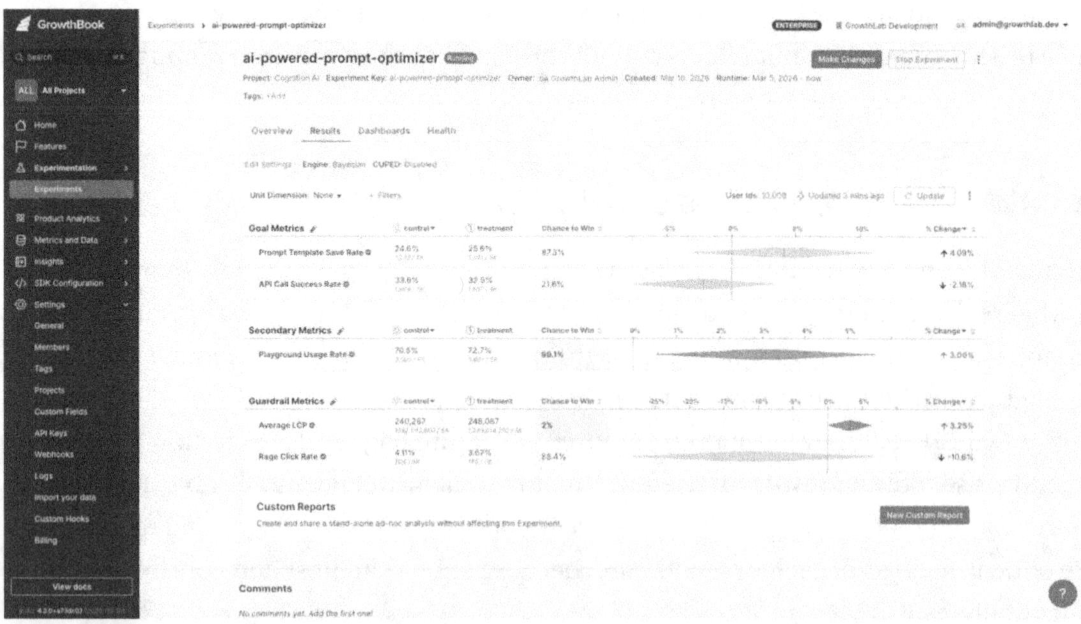

Figure 3-4. *GrowthBook Dashboard (provided by GrowthBook)*

So, the point here isn't "use GrowthBook." The fact is that evaluating GrowthBook helps us see what matters: **flags, experimentation support, data integration, and the right balance between cost, flexibility, and usability.** Whatever tool you choose, these are the criteria to check.

Figuring the Experimental Velocity Formula

The fact that Yazio runs so many experiments at once, combined with Jeff Bezos' view of experiments as "money on the floor," brings us to an important idea: **experimenting velocity**.

Experimenting velocity is not an official scientific term, but when we talk about A/B tests, it can serve as a compass, helping us understand how quickly our app can learn and grow.

The formula looks like this:

$$\text{Velocity} \propto \text{Number of Users} \times \text{Number of Experiments}$$

What this means is simple:

The more experiments we run, the more likely we are to discover improvements.

The larger our user base, the faster each experiment reaches statistical significance.

In practice, an indie app with 10,000 monthly active users might only manage a few A/B tests at a time, each taking weeks to collect enough data. In contrast, an app at Yazio's scale can run dozens of experiments in parallel, each reaching significance within days.

Every development team wants its app to grow at the maximum possible velocity. If the user base size is fixed, the variable we can control is the **number of experiments.** But how do we know how many experiments we can realistically handle before complexity overwhelms us?

This is where Zlatko's experience offers another perspective.

Segmenting Our Users

We saw how Yazio handles dozens of experiments running simultaneously. Noam even admitted, "It causes headaches to run experiments derived from other experiments sometimes, but it almost always pays off." For Yazio, this kind of experimentation is essential for growth.

However, not all teams take this approach. The balance between velocity and complexity depends on scale, culture, and priorities. Zlatko, working on a smaller-scale app in his previous company, told me his team ran no more than four experiments simultaneously. But even with just four experiments, each with two variants, the math quickly explodes: **four experiments produce 16 different combinations**.

What made this trickier is that Zlatko's team in his previous company, cared about only one metric: ARPU (average revenue per user). If ARPU moved, and multiple experiments were live, which experiment caused the shift?

His team developed several strategies to handle this problem:

1. If we want to measure one experiment in isolation, we can segment the user in the **control group for the other experiments**. In that way, the only change we see is from the one experiment we are testing. The main problem is that this approach reduces the sample size available for each variant.

2. Another option to solve that is to **split experiments by geography**. For example, run a paywall in Germany and subscription flow in France. This way, we avoided interference because the different user groups don't overlap. However, there's a distinct downside here – we are assuming users in different geolocations behave similarly, and obviously, that's not the case.

3. The last option is to segment the user across all experiments and **create a results matrix**. For example, if we have two experiments (A/B and C/D), we will have the following segments: Segment 1 (A+C), Segment 2 (A+D), Segment 3 (B+C), and Segment 4 (B+D). In this case, we have four segments because that's the number of combinations from two groups. However, for four groups, this number jumps to 16 segments, meaning the number of users per segment shrinks dramatically.

In short, Zlatko's team traded velocity for reliability. While Zlatko's team carefully limited the number of simultaneous experiments, Vivino pushed experimentation further – often juggling three in parallel and concluding them quickly.

Conclude Experiments Quickly

At Vivino, one of the world's largest wine apps, experimentation is still an essential part of the culture but handled with more structure. As Monika explained:

We have, for example, three running experiments in parallel that could, of course, affect the end result users see. We are actually trying to conclude as many experiments as we can. In the last period – I believe we are at 30ish right now – but that does not mean that each experiment affects the other. There are mostly three experiments affecting a certain user experience at a time.

In practice, Vivino typically runs **about three experiments at once**, and over the years, they've conducted more than 30 in total. Their emphasis is not just on starting experiments, but on **concluding them quickly**, which keeps the codebase clean and the bold results.

To make this possible, Vivino combines **Split.io** and **Mixpanel**:

- **Split.io** manages feature flags and experiment rollouts.

- **Mixpanel** handles analytics, capturing which variant a user sees and how it affects behavior.

This toolchain allows product managers to define success metrics and developers to focus on building and instrumenting variants.

The lives of Noam, Zlatko, and Monika show how challenging A/B testing can be, each wrestling with their own issues. Most of what we've seen so far has focused on managing the sheer number of combinations, which makes experimentation complex to run at scale. But not every industry struggles with combinations. Some face an entirely different kind of challenge – one where even running an experiment at all can be risky. Let's see what Vincent has to say about that.

The Trust Problem in A/B Testing

Earlier in this chapter, when we listed the challenges of running experiments on mobile apps, privacy came up as one of the most significant issues. It's easy to see why: the whole purpose of experiments is to analyze user behavior and adapt the experience accordingly.

Often, that also means segmenting users by location, age, gender, or other properties, to understand which direction to take the app or its features. In practice, being "data-driven" can feel like a call to collect as much user data as possible. But while Apple is already cautious about this approach, in some industries it can become a significant roadblock.

In Chapter 2, we saw how Vincent handled business logic in banking apps. Based on his experience, banking apps are especially challenging to experiment with. Collecting user data is far from straightforward: in most cases, explicit consent is required, and sensitive information such as transaction history, income, and even demographics cannot be used casually for analysis.

But the issues don't stop there. At its core, A/B testing is about showing variants. In a wine app, it's acceptable if two users see slightly different designs. In a banking or fintech app, however, that very same practice can raise suspicion. For many users, an inconsistent interface feels unsafe. In fact, offering different variants is uncomfortably close to how phishing and scams work – tricking users with slightly altered screens. Being in an experimental group could, in itself, damage trust, thereby undermining the experiment's results.

The lesson is clear: A/B testing isn't equally viable across all industries. Whether it makes sense depends not just on technical feasibility, but also on the industry's risk profile and the company's culture around privacy and trust.

Even though Vincent struggled to run experiments in the banking industry, that doesn't mean he has nothing to say about experimentation. In fact, his later work at Photoroom shows a very different side of the story – one where A/B testing became a practical tool for growth. Let's take a closer look at his experience there.

Finding the Right Places to Experiment?

Up until now, we've discussed the importance of A/B testing and the challenges of running experiments – from controlling them over time to dealing with privacy. But we haven't yet answered a simple question: **what exactly are we testing?**

By now, we can already see that implementing A/B testing comes at a cost. Showing a user one feature or another is actually the easy part. The more complex parts are choosing the right testing service, integrating analytics, analyzing results, and cleaning up code once an experiment is concluded. With this overhead in mind, it's critical to focus on the areas that matter most.

Based on Vincent's experience at Photoroom, we can identify the "usual suspects" when it comes to high-impact screens and features:

- **Monetization (Paywalls and Subscriptions)**: According to Vincent, this is the most important place to run experiments. If an app has a paywall, small design or copy tweaks can directly influence revenue. Localization is another factor: when supporting multiple locales, experiments should segment users by culture and habits, since responses to pricing and messaging can vary widely.

- **Onboarding Flows**: Onboarding is another key area for testing. This is the user's first impression of the app and often the moment where they provide initial information or set up their account. Optimizing onboarding flows can dramatically affect retention. For example, you might test shorter versus longer onboarding, static walkthroughs versus interactive tutorials, or even the navigation patterns that support different flows (such as the Coordinator pattern).

- **Feature Discoverability**: Photoroom also ran experiments around feature placement. Moving tools to different areas of the UI helped them measure which setup encouraged users to discover and adopt features more often. Improving discoverability drives engagement and increases the product's perceived value.

In practice, we can test almost anything in an app. But the highest-impact areas are those directly tied to **revenue** and **onboarding**. These are the places where small changes can have outsized effects on the product's success.

Defining what to test is just the beginning. Running reliable experiments requires robust infrastructure: internal tools, debugging methods, and analytics pipelines. This is where Krzysztof's experience sheds light on how teams keep experimentation under control.

Keeping Experiments Under Control

The primary strength of experiments – providing different experiences for different users – is also their biggest weakness. As we saw with Zlatko and Monika, running just four experiments in parallel can already create up to 16 different combinations. The result is unpredictability: our app may behave in ways that are hard to debug, test, or keep stable. One key takeaway is to conclude open experiments as quickly as possible. But what else can we do?

According to Krzysztof, experiments are not just feature flags. They require **tools, analytics, and debugging pipelines** to stay under control.

To begin with, teams need **internal dashboards and monitoring**. Visibility is essential not only for product managers but also for developers. We must be able to see which variant a user was exposed to and track exactly what happened during their session.

In addition to visibility, developers and QA engineers need the ability to **force the app into a specific experiment state**. Without this, debugging becomes guesswork. The solution is to provide mechanisms – overriding feature flags on the backend, setting environment variables, or using internal debug screens – that allow engineers and support staff to reproduce any variant combination. This also supports automated testing, since unit tests need to run against predictable states.

Finally, there is the **cleanup problem**. Leaving concluded experiments and "dead" feature flags in the code creates technical debt and confusion. Code that feels obvious today may become unrecognizable a few months later. Proper finalization of experiments must therefore include code cleanup and removal of unused flags.

Look at the following code example:

```swift
struct HomeView: View {
    @State private var tasks: [Task] = []

    var body: some View {
        VStack {
            if FeatureFlags.newOnboardingEnabled {
                if ExperimentManager.shared.variant(for: "onboarding_flow")
                == "A" {
                    NewOnboardingView()
                } else if ExperimentManager.shared.variant(for:
                "onboarding_flow") == "B" {
                    SimplifiedOnboardingView()
                } else {
                    LegacyOnboardingView()
                }
```

```
    } else {
        LegacyOnboardingView()
    }

    TaskListView(tasks: tasks)

    if FeatureFlags.showConfettiOnCompletion {
        ConfettiView()
    }
            }
        }
}
```

At first glance, this code looks reasonable, but a closer look reveals the problem: the onboarding_flow experiment has already concluded, Variant B won, and the team chose to keep SimplifiedOnboardingView. Yet all branches remain in the code – Variant A is dead, the fallback is irrelevant, and the feature flag is no longer needed. What remains is a decision that was already made, but still lives in the code.

The broader lesson is clear: experimentation at scale is not just about deciding between "A" or "B." It's about building the infrastructure to design, run, monitor, debug, and conclude experiments reliably. Without strong tools, experiments quickly turn from an engine of growth into a source of chaos.

What's interesting is that controlling what the user sees, or experiences, is relevant not only to A/B testing. There's more to come in this area.

Why A/B Testing Is Only Part of the Story

Up until now, we've discussed everything related to running experiments on iOS – from basic terms to challenges and tooling. But in almost every interview, two related practices kept coming up alongside A/B testing: **feature flags** and **phased rollouts**.

So, let's look at these practices for a moment.

A **feature flag** is a technique that allows us to remotely hide or show (turn on or off) a feature without redeploying. In simple terms, it's a conditional code path that can be turned on or off at runtime. That's its biggest strength: we don't need to ship a new build to change user behavior.

Here's a code example:

```swift
struct HomeView: View {

    var body: some View {
        VStack {
            if FeatureFlags.isNewTaskInputEnabled {
                NewTaskInputView()
            } else {
                LegacyTaskInputView()
            }

            TaskListView()
        }
    }
}
```

This example shows a feature flag controlling which UI the user sees. By updating the value remotely, the team can switch between implementations instantly – without releasing a new version of the app.

Controlling it remotely makes feature flags powerful across all platforms, not just mobile. On iOS, submitting a new version to the App Store is just the tip of the iceberg. Before submission comes scoping, development, QA, and the review process – all of which take time. With feature flags, we can bypass much of this pipeline when making incremental or controlled changes.

A **phased rollout**, on the other hand, is a way to deploy a feature gradually under supervision. Typically, we start by exposing the feature to a small subset of users (say, 1–5%). We then monitor stability, crash reports, errors, and behavior before expanding the rollout. If everything looks good, we increase exposure gradually until it's available to everyone.

It's worth noting that Apple provides a phased rollout option for App Store releases. Look at Figure 3-5.

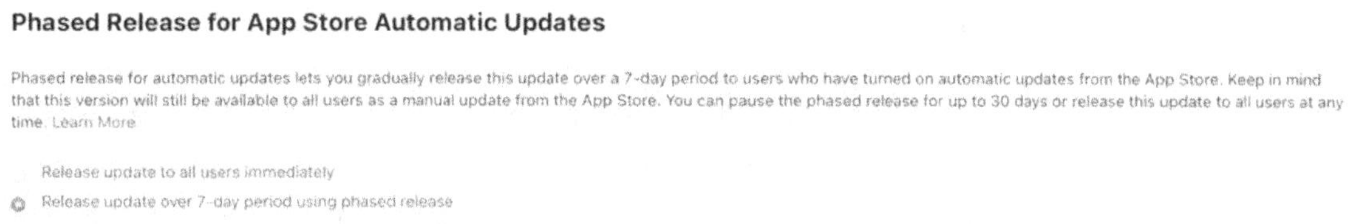

Phased Release for App Store Automatic Updates

Phased release for automatic updates lets you gradually release this update over a 7-day period to users who have turned on automatic updates from the App Store. Keep in mind that this version will still be available to all users as a manual update from the App Store. You can pause the phased release for up to 30 days or release this update to all users at any time. Learn More

   Release update to all users immediately

○ Release update over 7-day period using phased release

Figure 3-5. *Phased Release from App Store Connect*

Figure 3-5 shows how the Phased Release Rollout is a built-in feature in App Store Connect. While App Store Connect allows us to roll out an entire version, some tools let us apply the same principle at the feature level using feature flags.

While these practices have different immediate goals than A/B testing, in the end, they all serve the same purpose: **controlling who sees what, and when.**

And that's part of the reason why they also have the same challenges.

Same Challenges, Different Names

Controlling what the user sees is a powerful capability – it provides flexibility and creates growth opportunities. However, the same challenges we discussed with A/B testing – cleanup, debugging, unpredictability, privacy concerns – also apply to feature flags and phased rollouts.

For example, too many active flags cause the same combinatorial explosion as too many experiments. Remember the math: just four feature flags create 16 possible combinations. Add a fifth, and you're already at 32. On top of that, we don't remove old flags; they pile up as technical debt and clutter the codebase.

Because we can apply feature flags to almost anything, they serve more than product needs. Their primary value is **code flexibility**. This is why feature flags aren't just a product manager's tool – they're just as important for us, the developers.

But what does this mean for iOS developers if we're not even running A/B tests? The answer, as several indie developers pointed out in interviews, is that **feature flags are still valid on their own.** Even without experiments, flags let us hide unfinished features, safely roll them out when ready, or turn them off instantly if something goes wrong. In other words, feature flags are a lightweight way for developers to gain control and reduce risk, even without a formal experimentation framework.

Feature Flags in the Wild

Based on the interviews, we can see a strong correlation between A/B testing and feature flags. And honestly, that's not surprising. Once a team invests in experiments, it's only natural to add feature flags as well. The infrastructure for toggling features and removing dead code already exists, so the additional cost is relatively low.

But what about indie developers and feature flags?

Before these interviews, I assumed indie developers avoided A/B testing because of scale, but I thought that feature flags would be a different story. After all, flags don't require a huge user base or weeks of statistical analysis. They simply provide flexibility and safety – two things indie developers also need.

Yet the reality turned out to be different. For indie developers, the overhead of maintaining feature flags often outweighs the benefits. The reasons came up again and again in the interviews:

- **Infrastructure:** No matter how we look at it, feature flags require supporting infrastructure. It's not just about adding a library to the app; it also means building the proper tooling. For example, the ability to force the app into a specific state for debugging isn't something most indie developers invest in.

- **Testing Burden:** Larger teams can rely on QA to cover the different flag combinations of an app (and even then, it's a challenge). For indie developers, the entire testing burden falls on one person. At that scale, it's often not worth it.

- **Risk Tolerance:** As Mikaela pointed out, one of the privileges indie developers have is the ability to take risks that larger companies cannot. And here, "taking risks" doesn't mean "being brave" – it means moving faster, accepting that small issues may slip through, and prioritizing speed of delivery over absolute safety.

In short, while feature flags and A/B testing go hand in hand for larger teams, many indie developers choose a different path: they embrace simplicity and risk-taking over the overhead of maintaining flags.

Summary

Experiments and feature flags are not just technical practices – they are cultural ones. Running experiments provides a safe way to guide our app toward steady growth and goals. Even small teams can experiment, as long as they recognize the constraints and the costs involved.

In this chapter, we revisited the basics of A/B testing and the challenges that come with it. We saw how different teams approach experimentation, the tools they use, and why A/B testing is only part of the story. Feature flags and phased rollouts complete the picture, giving developers and product teams the flexibility to control who sees what, and when.

This chapter blended iOS development, product thinking, and even a bit of math. And speaking of culture, the next chapter turns to another place where engineering and culture meet: **testing**.

CHAPTER 4

Testing Our Apps

Hundreds of unit tests. Only a handful of UI tests – and they'd better be good.

—Oliver Binns

Introduction

Every iOS developer has a love–hate relationship with testing.

We know it saves us, but it also slows us down.

We praise it on blogs and conference stages, yet curse it when our build breaks.

Still, across every developer I spoke with, one truth remains:

Testing isn't just about code - it's about confidence.

In this chapter, we will

- Explore unit tests, testable code, and their ripple effects

- Draw the line on what's worth testing (and what isn't)

- Uncover the different testing layers and introduce a new model

- Dive into the tools developers use today - from XCTest to Maestro

I promise - this is going to be an exciting chapter.

Together, we'll explore that blurred line between **quality and efficiency**, and discover how real iOS teams find their balance.

Let's start with **Oliver Binns**.

© Avi Tsadok 2026
A. Tsadok, *Real-World iOS Development*, https://doi.org/10.1007/979-8-8688-2815-7_4

When Tests Break (or Save) the Day

Oliver Binns takes testing seriously. For him, testing isn't just a checklist item - it's part of the team's culture. At Deloitte Digital, his team aims for 80–95% coverage with **hundreds of unit tests**, layers on snapshot testing, and even guards the most critical flows with a handful of carefully chosen UI tests. Some developers on the team even practice TDD, which says a lot about their testing-first mindset.

Oliver never framed it this way directly, but the message is clear: in his world, testing is woven into the daily rhythm of building apps.

On the other side, Danijela also mentioned using snapshot tests, but in her view, they added too much noise to day-to-day work.

That raised a question I carried through many of my interviews: ***when do tests stop saving our day and start breaking it? Where's the line between tests that accelerate us and tests that turn into overhead?***

Here's a small confession. My very first book was *Pro iOS Testing* (Apress). Back then, I believed testing was a pillar of developer culture - and I wasn't wrong. But these interviews gave me the missing half of the picture: authentic voices from the field, showing how different teams actually test, what they invest in, and where they cut corners.

Let's start at the bedrock of it all: unit tests.

Unit Testing (But Not the Whole House)

If architecture is the skeleton of our app, unit tests are its daily **health check**. Their goal is simple: verify that the smallest pieces of code behave exactly as expected. But what counts as the "smallest piece"? It could be a formatter, a ViewModel method, or just a simple function.

Unlike integration tests, unit tests run fast and local - no backend, no UI, no network. What's interesting about unit tests is that writing them doesn't just test our code - it shapes it. To write good tests, we need testable code. Over time, that discipline pushes our entire codebase toward cleaner design, and that's a big use. Let's understand why.

Writing Testable Code

Here's a simple example:

```swift
class UserManager {
    func fetchUserName() -> String {
        let url = URL(string: "https://api.example.com/user")!
        let data = try! Data(contentsOf: url)
        let json = try! JSONSerialization.jsonObject(with: data) as!
        [String: Any]
        return json["name"] as? String ?? "Unknown"
    }
}
```

The `UserManager` example above includes a function called `fetchUserName` that makes a network request and returns the user's name.

At first glance, this looks fine. But if we try to test it, we hit a wall:

- The function depends **directly on the network** (`Data(contentsOf:)`).

- We **can't run it without internet access** and a real server.

- We **ignore errors**.

- There's no way to **inject a mock** response.

Unit tests have to be consistent, fast, and reliable - and this function gives us none of that.

Now let's adjust it to be testable:

```swift
protocol NetworkService {
    func fetchData(from url: URL) throws -> Data
}

class RealNetworkService: NetworkService {
    func fetchData(from url: URL) throws -> Data {
        try Data(contentsOf: url)
    }
}
```

```
class UserManager {
    private let networkService: NetworkService
    private let url = URL(string: "https://api.example.com/user")!

    init(networkService: NetworkService) {
        self.networkService = networkService
    }

    func fetchUserName() throws -> String {
        let data = try networkService.fetchData(from: url)
        let json = try JSONSerialization.jsonObject(with: data) as!
        [String: Any]
        return json["name"] as? String ?? "Unknown"
    }
}
```

Two changes made a huge difference:

- The function now **throws errors**, making failures easier to test.

- We inject a **protocol-based network service** to replace the real network with a mock in tests.

Let's see another example of how to make our functions more "pure," and by doing so, more testable.

Here's a simple function that returns a greeting message based on the current time:

```
func getGreeting() -> String {
    let hour = Calendar.current.component(.hour, from: Date())
    if hour < 12 {
        return "Good morning"
    } else {
        return "Hello"
    }
}
```

The logic is clear - if the hour is before 12, return *"Good morning."* Otherwise, return *"Hello."*

But there's a problem: we can't control or predict the result in a test. Run this in the morning, and it passes. Run it in the afternoon, and it fails.

Now, let's make it pure by passing the current hour as a parameter:

```swift
func getGreeting(for hour: Int) -> String {
    if hour < 12 {
        return "Good morning"
    } else {
        return "Hello"
    }
}
```

Now the function is independent of system time. This is what we call a pure function - its output depends only on its input. Pure functions are deterministic, predictable, and therefore manageable to test.

The lesson is clear: to make code testable, **separate logic from infrastructure**. Logic is ***what we do*** ("Take some JSON, parse it, return the user's name"). Infrastructure is ***how we get*** the raw material ("Fetch data from the network").

When we couple logic and infrastructure, tests become fragile and slow. When they're separated, tests become fast, reliable, and easy to write. That's the foundation of unit testing.

The Side Effects of Testable Code

Here's the funny thing about testable code: once we make code testable, we've already improved it. And not just the code - the team too.

So how does testability reach beyond the codebase? The answer lies in what I call the **ripple effect**. The moment we aim to write unit tests, we naturally start reshaping our design. We split logic from infrastructure, create purer functions, lean more on dependency injection, and push our projects toward modular boundaries.

But the ripple doesn't stop at code. Testability also changes how teams work together. It affects how developers collaborate with QA engineers, how product managers think about release confidence, and even how comfortable teams feel with refactoring. In short, testable code isn't just a technical improvement - it's a cultural one.

Everything I wrote here is not part of my imagination - based on the interviews, there's a strong correlation between how much developers invest in testing and how their apps are built.

- Teams that invest heavily in unit tests almost always rely on protocols, dependency injection, and modularization to make that possible.

- Teams that skip testing (such as indie developers) often also skip dependency injection or modularization, since these practices add overhead without an obvious benefit.

Always keep in mind - there's no single *"right"* or *"wrong"* approach here. Every team weighs effort, requirements, and cost, then decides which testing approach brings their app closer to its goals.

With that in mind, let's move forward and see what developers actually choose to test - and how they do it.

Drawing the Line: What's Worth Testing

We can talk about the importance of testing, culture, habits, and tools all day long. But the million-dollar question remains: **what's actually worth testing?**

From the interviews, one thing is clear: there isn't a single answer. Different teams draw the line in various places. What we do see, though, are three distinct approaches that keep showing up - each shaped by company scale, culture, and priorities.

Let's start with the first one: **test everything.**

Test Everything

At first glance, *testing everything* might sound naive or exaggerated. How can anyone practically test everything? Isn't that just a waste of time?

But the interviews told a different story. For some teams, aiming for very high coverage isn't just possible - it's logical. This **Coverage-Driven** approach is most common in larger teams, where quality gates are strict, and developer turnover is high. In those environments, dozens of hands touch the codebase. High coverage acts as insurance against regressions and helps new developers build confidence quickly.

Take Oliver's team at Deloitte Digital. Structured into several smaller squads, they push for **80–95% coverage**, with hundreds of unit tests guarding their business logic and feature packages. But what really stands out isn't the numbers - it's the mindset. As Oliver put it, *"high quality is a whole team responsibility, and we shouldn't kick things over the fence to a separate QA team."* His team tries to automate as much testing as possible.

Danijela's previous team followed a similar path. Coverage there reached **90%+** across unit, snapshot, UI, and integration tests. She admitted it added stability, but also a lot of *noise*. Still, for a large team with many developers contributing in parallel, testing served as a safety net to ensure scale.

And it looks like the simplest way to enforce "testing" everything is just to integrate that as part of the pull request.

A **pull request (PR)** is a (not only) GitHub feature for proposing code changes before merging. It's the review stage where teammates check quality, run tests, and give feedback. A PR can be anything from a one-line bug fix to an entirely new feature – either way, it's where testing becomes part of the workflow.

We saw that *"test everything"* is a valid approach to testing. It works well for large teams, where any developer can accidentally break the codebase, and it serves as a strong gatekeeper before we merge or deploy changes.

But this approach comes with a cost. It's not just about writing more tests - it's also about running them, keeping them fast, and maintaining them over time. Code evolves, and every change risks breaking existing tests.

That's why *"test everything"* isn't suitable for every team. With that in mind, let's move on to the next approach: **selective testing**.

Selective Testing

With **Selective Testing**, teams don't try to cover every line of code or chase high coverage numbers. If *"test everything"* is about blanket coverage, *"selective testing"* is about being pragmatic. The focus is on tests that are stable, valuable, and fast to run.

Developers in this camp often start with the **happy path**, while edge cases come later - if at all.

For Zlatko, this meant focusing on **ViewModels and utilities**, while Monika described a clear separation at Vivino: developers concentrate on unit tests for the logic, and QA engineers automate broader workflows.

Selective testing follows the **80–20 rule**: cover the parts that matter most, and stop before the return on effort drops too low. Figure 4-1 illustrates this point.

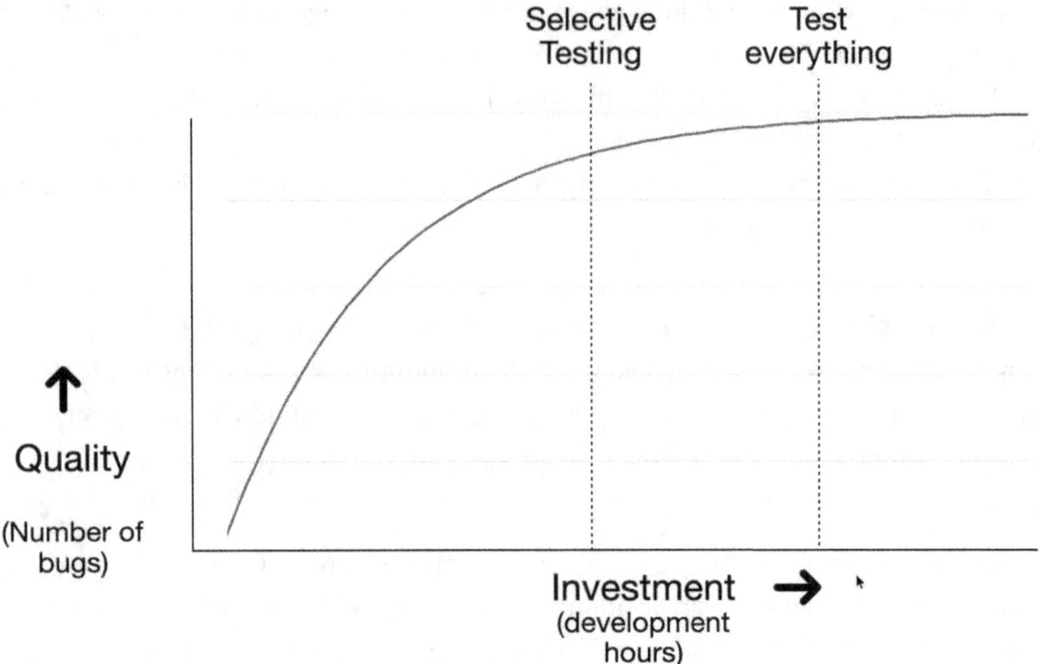

Figure 4-1. *ROI (Return on Investment) of testing*

Figure 4-1 shows how the two approaches we've discussed - *Selective Testing* and *Test Everything* - stand next to each other on the ROI curve. The figure isn't exact science, but it's easy to see the inflection point at which adding more tests doesn't yield much additional quality. *Selective testing* teams stop there, while *test-everything* teams push further.

We've seen how **test-everything** teams aim to cover as much as possible, often driven by scale and strict quality gates. And we've seen how **selective testing** teams take a more pragmatic approach, adapting their testing efforts to what makes sense for them. Both methods are valid.

And that inflection point in Figure 4-1? It doesn't exist as an exact spot in real life, but it's a valuable way to imagine the trade-off - the moment a team decides, *"It's not worth the extra effort."* That point is subjective, and each team defines it for itself.

But there's still another way to look at testing - not from scale or coverage, but from the **business point of view**.

Business Context-Driven

When we think about it, **every testing approach should keep the business context in mind.** Remember - the goal of an app isn't just to be technically perfect; it's to serve the business behind it.

The difference here is focus.

Up to this point, we've looked at testing as a technical question - about quality, coverage, and how much a team can handle with its given size and resources. But in some industries, testing isn't about coverage at all. It's about **protecting trust, compliance, and actual money.**

Consider this: we're building a peer-to-peer payments app. Many things could go wrong, but the team is small - too small to test even half the codebase. Does that mean they shouldn't test? Of course not. They'll focus their limited efforts on what matters most - the **payment flows**. Because if those fail, the company loses money and users lose trust.

Vincent Pradeilles, who worked on banking apps, put it best:

The goal is to prevent bad situations that could harm the company. Not all bad situations are bad for the company, so we test in ways that make sense for the organization.

What Vincent highlights is that testing should follow **business value**, not lines of code. For an e-commerce app, that means focusing on checkout, payment processing, and discounts - not on whether the wish list sorts alphabetically. That extra edge case in the shipping flow might not boost your coverage metrics, but it will help you sleep better at night.

Each industry - and each team - must find out **what could hurt the company if it breaks.**

In fintech, losing trust or failing to comply can be catastrophic. In consumer apps, a crash in onboarding translates directly to churn - and churn is money lost. And for indie developers, where there's no QA team to rely on, the rule is simple: test what could kill user trust.

Ultimately, **the most valuable tests are those that protect the business.**

So Where Do We Draw the Line?

The insights I gathered from the developers I spoke with were fascinating. Each of them contributed a small piece to a much bigger picture – how we, as developers, should think when we approach testing.

If we want to compare testing to something in the real world, it's a lot like **insurance**.

What's most important to protect - the critical business elements, or the codebase as a whole?

Do we need full coverage, or do we already have other "insurance policies" in place - like QA, support, or monitoring?

Every insurance policy has its price, and every team decides what they're willing to pay. There's no right or wrong here, only what fits the team's context and the business behind it.

In the end, deciding **what to test** is like choosing **what to insure** - it all comes down to understanding what truly matters, and how much it's worth protecting.

But there's one question left - what about indies?

What About Indies?

Sometimes, when I work on my side projects, I catch myself wondering whether I should add tests or not. Not because tests aren't necessary - we already know they are - but because when you're a **solo developer**, writing tests isn't always that obvious.

For starters, indie apps are usually simpler. We're not talking about complex fintech platforms or social navigation giants - most indie apps are small enough to test manually in minutes. And while an indie project might technically include *a developer, a team lead, a product manager,* and *a designer*, in reality, they're all the same person. One person juggling all those roles. That's a lot to carry.

And let's not forget: an indie developer's time is **costly**. There's no salary behind those hours - only the hope that the next feature or release moves the app forward. Every decision comes with a trade-off between writing a new test, promoting the app, or building a new feature. Sometimes, writing a test just isn't the most effective use of time.

So, it's not surprising that many indie developers invest little, if any, effort in testing.

Danijela keeps just a few unit tests in her personal projects - a sharp contrast to the 90%+ coverage she had when working on a large team. **Mikaela** doesn't use unit tests at all, choosing instead to spend her limited time on building and marketing her apps.

One thing is worth noting, though: indie developers don't have a QA process. There's no safety net. Sometimes, a simple unit test can be that net - a small investment that saves hours of debugging later.

In the end, testing for indies isn't about discipline or dogma - it's about **trade-offs**. And sometimes, the most intelligent decision is to test less and ship faster.

Even though we've already discussed how different teams decide **what** and **how much** to test, we've mainly focused on **unit tests** - the foundation of any testing strategy. But testing doesn't stop there. There are more layers to explore, each adding its own kind of confidence and value.

Let's take a closer look at these different layers of testing - and see how developers across teams approach them in their own unique ways.

The Layers of Testing

Most iOS testing tutorials stop at unit tests - and for good reason. They're fast to write, easy to maintain, and are the foundation of almost every test plan. **Unit tests check the smallest units of behavior in our code in isolation, such as a function, a method, or a ViewModel action. Their goal is to verify that a single piece of logic gives the expected result without depending on the UI, the network, or external systems.** But they're also just the beginning.

Beyond unit tests, there's a whole ecosystem of testing layers that bring our apps closer to real life:

- **Integration tests** verify how different parts of the system work together - for example, how a ViewModel interacts with the data store, or how the business logic layer handles real backend responses.

- **UI tests** simulate how users actually experience the app: tapping buttons, signing in, navigating screens.

- **Snapshot tests** freeze a moment in time - storing a visual reference (like a screenshot or JSON output) and comparing future results against it to catch unexpected changes.

- **Performance tests** go even deeper, measuring how fast or efficiently our code runs after every update.

Each of these layers gives us confidence from a different angle. Together, they form a complete safety net - one that ensures not just that the app works, but that it keeps working as it evolves.

But every safety net has a cost.

When I asked Krzysztof Zabłocki about testing, he said:

"Unit tests are the most important. Even if you have a thousand of them, they're still fast – as long as you mock time, network, and control the environment. That's what keeps your codebase safe without slowing you down."

And he's right. Running thousands of unit tests might take just a few seconds - a small price to pay for a stable foundation.

But that balance quickly changes as we move up the testing ladder. A single integration test that hits the backend can take longer than all your unit tests combined. And one end-to-end UI test - logging in, performing an action, waiting for animations - can take as long as several integration tests together.

The real cost, though, isn't just time. It's consistency.

Tests that depend on external services aren't isolated. They break for reasons beyond our control - a flaky network, a slow server, or a new API version. And every broken test adds up to **maintenance debt.**

That's why testing is a balancing act: the closer we get to real-world behavior, the higher the value - and the higher the cost.

That balance is the foundation of the **testing pyramid.**

The (Non-existent) Testing Pyramid

In one of my earlier books, *Pro iOS Testing* (Apress), I wrote about the **Testing Pyramid** - an elegant model suggesting a balance of **50% unit tests, 30% integration tests, and 20% UI tests**.

Look at Figure 4-2.

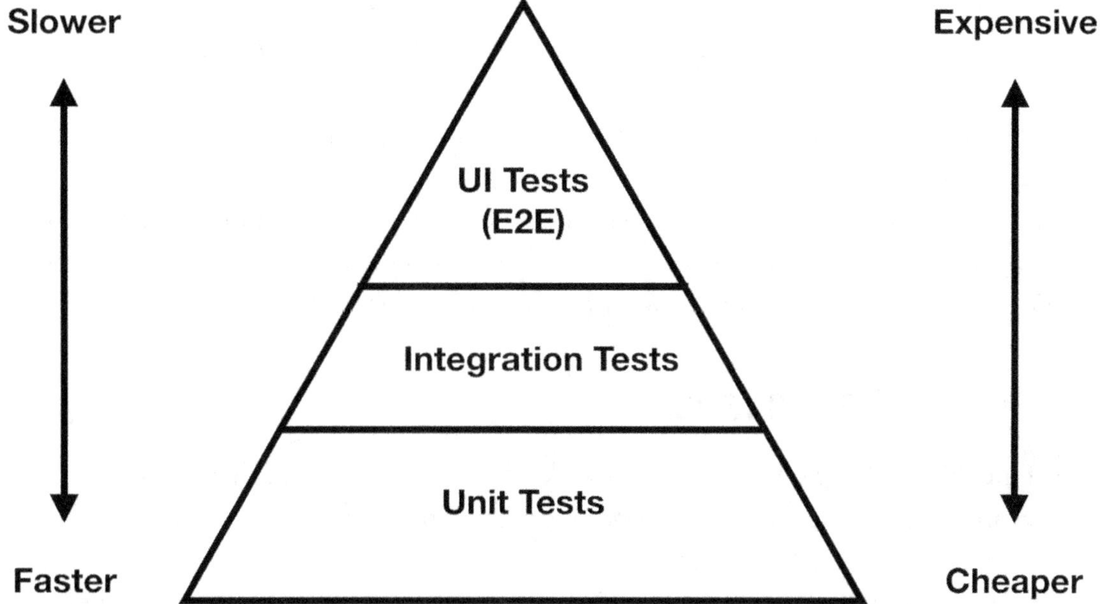

Figure 4-2. *The Testing Pyramid (from "Pro iOS Testing" by Apress)*

Figure 4-2 visualizes the testing pyramid idea - the more complex the test, the fewer we should have.

And that idea makes perfect sense.

On paper.

Why *on paper*? Because after talking with different iOS teams, I realized that this neat pyramid rarely exists in real life - at least not in the world of iOS development.

Teams like **Oliver's** or **Danijela's** lean heavily on **unit tests** because their scale demands speed and reliability.

Integration tests? Barely.

Let's linger on integration tests for a moment. Their goal is to verify how two or more units work *together,* once we have already covered them with unit tests.

For example, imagine a ViewModel responding to a button tap that updates a local store. Writing an integration test for that flow takes time - it runs slower, often requires special setup, and still depends on code that's already been tested in isolation.

And that's the easy case.

Now, picture an integration test that touches a backend.

Double the effort. Triple the runtime. And reliability? Downhill. Most developers simply don't see the return on that investment.

UI tests, however, get a different kind of respect. Developers who care about key user journeys often think, *"If I'm going to invest in a slow, unreliable test, it might as well test what the user actually sees."*

And that logic holds up - we often see teams maintaining just a few UI tests for their most critical flows.

In the end, the real-world testing pyramid looks far less like a pyramid and more like a **testing landscape** - a vast plain of unit tests, dotted with a few integration peaks and a handful of UI tests standing guard over the main paths users take through the app.

The Testing Landscape

One of the things I keep repeating in my books is that there's always a gap between **theory and reality** - and we should remember that gap whenever we read books, watch tutorials, or follow "how-to" guides.

Testing is one of those topics that looks *amazing* in theory. It promises structure, confidence, and quality. It even touches culture and mindset. And trust me - I've been there. When I wrote my first book, *Pro iOS Testing*, I dove deep into these models, including the well-known **Testing Pyramid**.

The problem is that the pyramid describes testing as layers - clean, proportional, and geometric. But in the real world, testing isn't geometry. It's geography.

The **Testing Landscape** model takes the idea of the pyramid and fits it to reality - a reality shaped by the teams I interviewed for this book.

So, let's do a quick case study.

Picture a vast landscape stretching endlessly toward the horizon. Those open fields are our **unit tests** - fast, reliable, and everywhere they can be. They form the broad foundation that supports everything else. Not just 50% of the surface like the pyramid suggests - they're scattered across every testable class and function, filling the ground beneath our feet.

Now, look closer. Across the fields, we'll find **small hills and rivers** connecting different zones - these are your **integration tests**. They flow between systems, linking ViewModels, stores, and services together.

And in the distance, you'll see a few **tall mountains** rising above everything else. Those are your **UI tests** - rare, high-effort, but essential for the most critical user journeys. **Snapshot tests** live in that same terrain - high points you visit when visuals or state changes matter most.

Do you see it? The real testing model isn't a perfect pyramid - it's a **living landscape**. It's something we **map, navigate, and evolve** over time. The goal isn't to stack layers neatly on top of each other - it's to understand our terrain and place our mountains, hills, and rivers exactly where they make sense.

And just like every continent has its own geography, each **team, company, and developer** has its own **testing landscape** - shaped by priorities, constraints, and culture.

Let's visualize what that landscape might look like (Figure 4-3).

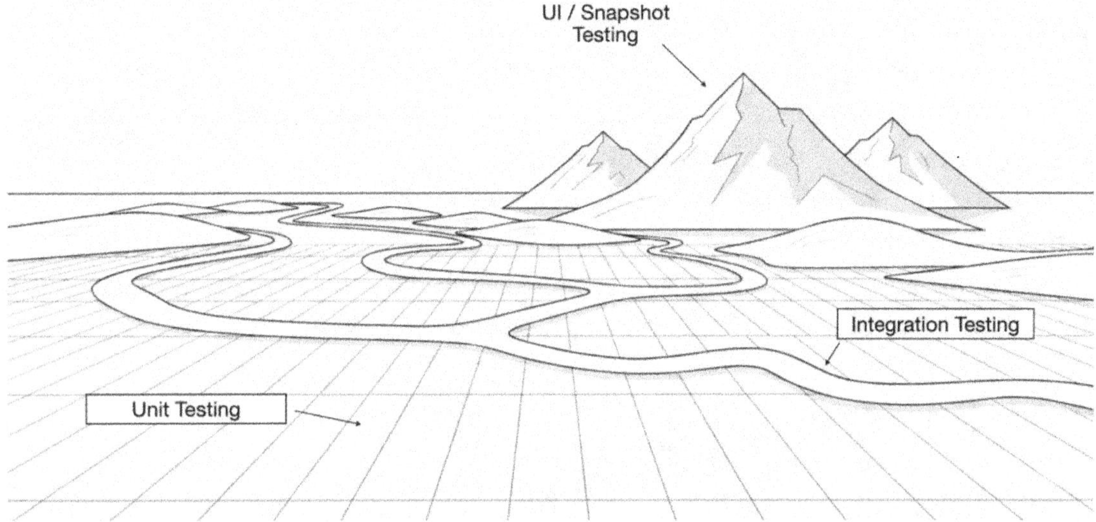

Figure 4-3. *The testing landscape*

Figure 4-3 looks a little different from most figures in this book - and that's intentional. Geometry can't capture how testing really behaves. In reality, **unit tests** are spread across the entire foundation, covering most of the surface. **Integration tests** appear like rivers and hills, connecting systems. And **UI and snapshot tests** rise like tall mountains - rare, high-effort, but vital for the most critical flows.

Take a moment to imagine your own app, your own team.

What does your testing landscape look like?

We've talked about philosophies, strategies, and the different shapes testing can take across teams. But ideas alone don't build tests - tools do. The frameworks and utilities teams choose are what turn theory into everyday practice. So, let's see what iOS developers actually use in the wild to bring their testing culture to life.

Tools of the Trade

Apple gives iOS developers a solid set of testing tools out of the box – **unit**, **performance**, and **UI** testing frameworks that are reliable and well-integrated with Xcode.

Still, many teams choose to go further, adopting additional frameworks to sharpen their testing experience - tools that make tests more expressive, faster, or easier to maintain.

These tools aren't mandatory. They don't replace Apple's frameworks - they refine them. They improve **readability**, **capabilities**, and **reliability**.

But before we look at the tools themselves, it's worth taking a short step back.

All of these frameworks - whether XCTest, Quick & Nimble, or SnapshotTesting - build on the same basic **testing methodology**.

As I often say, *tools are just tools*. They don't define the way we test - the **methodology defines them**.

So before diving into the toolbox, let's quickly revisit the **core structure of a test** – the three simple steps every test shares: **Given, When, and Then.**

The Testing Methodology

"Given–When–Then."

You've probably seen those three words before. They're part of a standard structure for writing tests - a way to describe behavior, not just check results. It's also known as **BDD (Behavior-Driven Development)**.

Other variations exist, like **Arrange–Act–Assert** or **Setup–Exercise–Verify**, but here's the thing: the **names change, the logic stays the same.**

And that logic is essential.

One of the biggest reasons some developers avoid testing isn't that they dislike tools - it's that they focus *too much* on the tools. They get stuck on syntax or frameworks instead of understanding the simple, repeatable structure that makes any test work.

The idea is built on three stages:

1. **Arrange/Given**: Prepare the data and the test state. Initialize
   classes, inject dependencies, or stub network calls - whatever it
   takes to make the test deterministic. This step might be tedious,
   but it's the most important one. It often takes the longest time, too.

2. **Act/When**: Perform the actual action: call the function, trigger the event, or, in a UI test, simulate the user interaction.

3. **Assert/Then**: Verify the result. This is where you confirm that you meet your expectations - that your code behaved exactly as it should.

I know - these steps may sound obvious. But many developers who struggle to start testing fail because they skip or blur them. They mix setup and verification, or they forget to isolate the action they're testing.

Here's a short XCTest example that shows these steps in practice:

```
// Arrange
let calculator = Calculator()

// Act
let result = calculator.add(2, 3)

// Assert
XCTAssertEqual(result, 5)
```

In this test, we're checking how our `Calculator` class handles the `add()` function.
We start with the **Arrange** step and set up the `Calculator`.
Then we **Act** by calling the function.
And finally, we **Assert** the expected outcome - that 2 + 3 equals 5.
That's it. Three steps. Every test, from the simplest unit test to the most complex UI flow, follows this rhythm. Once you internalize it, the rest - the tools, the frameworks, the naming conventions - all fall into place.
Before we go over the tools developers use in practice, let's talk about how testing tools work under the hood.

How Testing Tools Really Work

What happens when we press ⌘U in Xcode?
If you haven't asked yourself that yet, now's the time to wonder.
Because if we want to delve into the tools developers use every day, we should first understand how testing tools actually work.

When we start running tests in Xcode, it feels like magic - green checks appear, and we get that satisfying "All tests passed" message. But behind the scenes, something much simpler is happening.

At the end of the day, the tools we use don't do anything particularly smart or complex. After all, their job is to run the code we wrote - *we're* the ones who worked hard on it.

To make this possible, the testing tool creates something called a **test bundle** - a small program responsible for running our tests.

The Test Bundle

When we run our tests, Xcode compiles our app and also builds a separate product: a **.xctest bundle**.

This bundle is essentially a **dynamic library (.dylib)** that contains

- Our test classes (subclasses of XCTestCase or annotated @Test types)

- Metadata about those tests (names, methods, and attributes)

- The test runner entry point - usually xctest

The first step is for Xcode to run this test bundle using the `xctest` executable, passing it the compiled code.

If you've ever noticed the "Executable" setting under your scheme configuration in Xcode, that's part of this mechanism.

We can think of every "Test" run as Xcode saying:

"Build the app as usual, but instead of launching it directly, launch the test runner executable and tell it to load my tests."

Look at Figure 4-4.

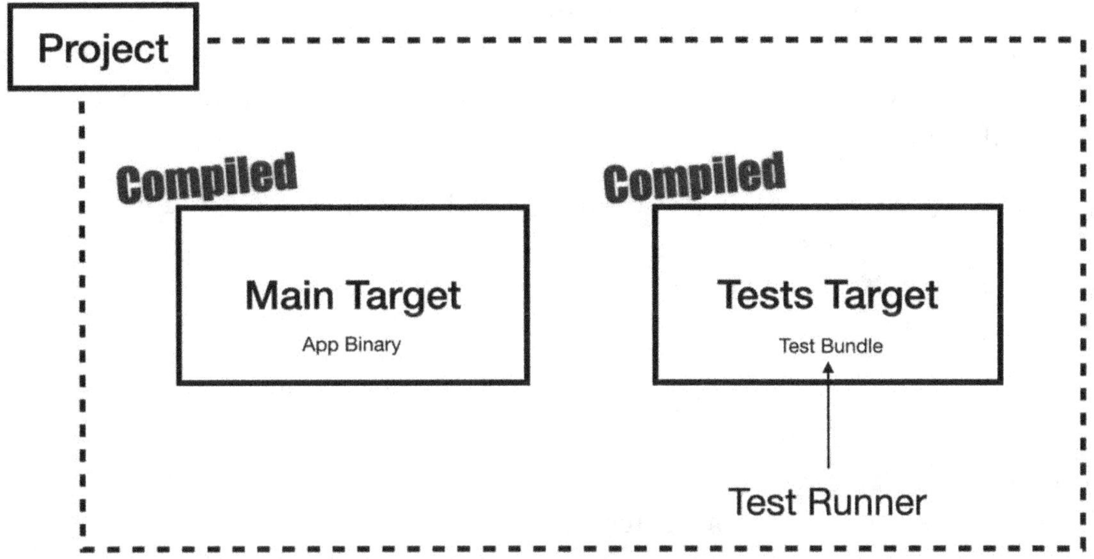

Figure 4-4. *What Xcode runs when we press ⌘U*

Figure 4-4 shows exactly what we've discussed - injecting another product (a dynamic library, for that matter) together with the test runner that executes the test functions.

It's an elegant and straightforward way to test our app without modifying our production code.

And speaking of test functions - let's try to build a small test runner ourselves.

The test runner will help us better understand how testing tools really work.

Building a Test Runner Ourselves

If we want to create a test function and run it, we don't actually need any special framework.

Remember what I said earlier - a test is simply code that runs inside our app, initializes a class, and calls one of its functions.

Consider the following code in our app:

```
class Calculator {
    func add(_ a: Int, _ b: Int) -> Int {
        return a + b
    }
}
```

This snippet shows the same `Calculator` class we saw earlier under *The Testing Methodology* section.

To test it, we can simply create a function called `testAddition` (no Xcode needed!) along with a small `assert` helper:

```swift
func assert(_ condition: @autoclosure () -> Bool, _ message: String) {
    if !condition() {
        print("✗ Test failed:", message)
        exit(1)
    }
}

func testAddition() {
    print("▶ Running testAddition...")

    // Arrange (Prepare)
    let calculator = Calculator()

    // Act (Action)
    let result = calculator.add(2, 3)

    // Assert (Verify)
    assert(result == 5, "Expected 2 + 3 to equal 5, but got \(result)")

    print("✓ testAddition passed!")
}
```

This simple snippet already behaves like a miniature testing framework.

It prepares the data, performs the action, verifies the result, and prints the outcome.

At its core, that's precisely what **XCTest** and **Swift Testing** do - only with more automation: test discovery, structured reporting, setup and teardown, and code coverage.

Understanding What Frameworks Add to the Table

By now, we realize that frameworks don't do the heavy lifting - we do.

Developers write code, write tests, and maintain them.

So why do we even need a testing framework?

After all, frameworks don't test our app for us. They simply run the test functions we've written.

But frameworks are *built for scale.* Running a single test function is easy - we don't need a framework for that.

Once we have dozens or hundreds of tests, though, we need more - much more.

For a start, we need a way to discover all the test functions we've written automatically.

Frameworks do that by scanning our code and identifying test functions using conventions such as the test prefix in XCTest or the @Test annotation in Swift Testing.

This discovery process saves us from manually maintaining a test list and lets us run everything in one go.

Next, we need to **prepare and clean up** before and after each test.

Frameworks handle that for us with setup and teardown steps, giving each test its own clean environment.

This keeps tests isolated, deterministic, and reliable - if one test fails, it won't break the others.

After the tests finish running, we need **structured reporting** that tells us what passed, what failed, and why.

Some frameworks display this with a nice UI inside Xcode - green checkmarks for success, red crosses for failure - while others output detailed reports for CI systems to consume and track over time.

Clear reporting turns a wall of logs into actionable feedback.

Finally, there's **code coverage** - another valuable feature frameworks add to the table.

Coverage tools show us how much of our code is being tested and highlight the areas that aren't.

As we saw earlier in this chapter, some teams treat coverage as a measurable goal, while others use it simply as a guideline for quality and confidence.

All these features - discovery, lifecycle management, reporting, and coverage - are what turn a few test functions into a **real testing ecosystem**.

They don't change what a test *is*, but they make it possible to run hundreds or even thousands of them reliably, repeatedly, and at scale.

Now, let's see what tools developers use today to bring all of this to life.

Testing Tools in Practice

At this point, we understand the correlation between testing, company culture,
and goals.

We also know that the hard work lies in writing testable code and crafting the tests
themselves, while running them is actually quite simple.

Now it's time to explore the tools developers use in their day-to-day work - starting
with the most fundamental ones: **XCTest** and **Swift Testing**.

Three Generations, Same DNA

For more than a decade, XCTest has been part of every iOS developer's toolkit.

It's reliable, robust, and yet simple to use.

Apple introduced XCTest in 2013, but iOS developers didn't start testing their apps
in 2013.

So how did they do it before XCTest existed?

If we go a bit further back, we find that the design and philosophy of XCTest were
built upon an older framework called **OCUnit** - the standard for iOS testing before 2013.

OCUnit (Objective-C Unit) was part of a larger family of frameworks known as **XUnit**,
which shaped the foundation of unit testing across programming languages.

A test in OCUnit would look something like:

```
- (void)setUp {
    [super setUp];
    mathObject = [[MyMath alloc] init];
}

- (void)tearDown {
    [mathObject release];
    mathObject = nil;
    [super tearDown];
}

- (void)testAddPositiveNumbers {
    NSInteger result = [mathObject addNumber:5 withNumber:7];
    STAssertEquals(result, 12, @"Expected 5 + 7 to equal 12");
}
```

```
- (void)testAddNegativeNumbers {
    NSInteger result = [mathObject addNumber:-5 withNumber:-7];
    STAssertEquals(result, -12, @"Expected -5 + -7 to equal -12");
}
```

Notice the familiar structure: `setUp` and `tearDown` methods for preparing and cleaning up before and after each test, test functions with the `test` prefix, and assertion functions to validate results.

If you've ever worked with XCTest, this should look familiar - and that's no coincidence.

When Apple introduced XCTest, it was built from the ground up with OCUnit's design and philosophy in mind.

Here's the same test rewritten in XCTest:

```
(void)setUp {
    [super setUp];
    self.mathObject = [[MyMath alloc] init];
}

- (void)tearDown {
    self.mathObject = nil;
    [super tearDown];
}

- (void)testAddPositiveNumbers {
    NSInteger result = [self.mathObject addNumber:5 withNumber:7];
    XCTAssertEqual(result, 12, @"Expected 5 + 7 to equal 12");
}

- (void)testAddNegativeNumbers {
    NSInteger result = [self.mathObject addNumber:-5 withNumber:-7];
    XCTAssertEqual(result, -12, @"Expected -5 + -7 to equal -12");
}
```

As we can see, the structure barely changed.

Keeping the same naming conventions for `setUp` and `tearDown`, as well as the `test` prefix, helped developers transition smoothly from OCUnit to XCTest.

What changed was the modern integration with Xcode, better tooling, and more substantial support for Apple's evolving ecosystem.

Over the years, XCTest has evolved - and so have iOS developers and the Swift language itself.

Developers began demanding more: better test hierarchies, a more natural Swift syntax, and improved support for asynchronous and cross-platform testing.

XCTest, while stable and proven, still carried the weight of its Objective-C roots.

Its reliance on inheritance, its verbose async testing, and its limited structure made it feel dated in the Swift era.

To overcome these limitations, Apple introduced **Swift Testing** - a modern, Swift-native, and open source framework designed to make testing feel at home in the language itself.

Here's what the same test looks like with Swift Testing:

```swift
@Suite("MyMath Tests") struct MyMathTests {
    let mathObject = MyMath()

    @Test func addPositiveNumbers() {
        let result = mathObject.addNumber(5, withNumber: 7)
        #expect(result == 12)
    }

    @Test func addNegativeNumbers() {
        let result = mathObject.addNumber(-5, withNumber: -7)
        #expect(result == -12)
    }
}
```

This example highlights several essential improvements.

It's shorter and cleaner - no need for `setUp` and `tearDown` since we can use standard Swift initialization.

There's no inheritance, no subclassing, and no prefixes - just pure Swift.

The syntax feels natural, expressive, and modern, with the `@Suite`, `@Test`, and `#expect` constructs making the intent clear.

Swift Testing represents the same philosophy that started with OCUnit and matured through XCTest - but written for the next generation of developers.

Three generations, one shared DNA.

The XCTest Domination

Sometimes it's best to start with the bottom line - every developer I interviewed still uses **XCTest** in one way or another.

There are a few good reasons for that.

First, **Swift Testing is still new**, and adoption, especially in testing, takes time.

Think about it: there's little reason to rewrite hundreds of existing tests just to migrate them to a new framework if everything already works.

Second, many projects still contain Objective-C code.

And when we need to test Objective-C components, we still need XCTest.

The continued dominance of XCTest isn't driven by excitement - it's driven by **stability**.

With testing frameworks, change comes slowly.

XCTest may not be glamorous, but it's reliable, integrated, and predictable.

Oliver, Danijela, Zlatko, Monika, Krzysztof, and Stefan all rely on XCTest for the majority of their tests.

Now that we've established that, let's explore how the transition toward **Swift Testing** is actually unfolding.

When XCTest Learns Swift

Many new iOS capabilities and APIs experience slow adoption, often because of **backward compatibility**.

However, what's interesting about **Swift Testing** is that it doesn't require a minimum iOS version.

We don't ship it with the app - we run it exclusively on the developer's machine.

And yet, its adoption has been slower than expected - for good reasons.

As mentioned earlier, migrating existing test suites to Swift Testing is expensive and delivers almost no business value.

But that's not the only factor.

In large teams, all developers are already familiar with **XCTest**, and it's far easier to keep using what everyone knows.

Many teams have also built their own small utilities, helpers, and conventions around XCTest - making it even more convenient to stay where they are.

In practice, Swift Testing adoption usually starts **at the edges**.

Remember Chapter 2, "Architecture and Design Patterns"?

Some teams organize their code using Swift packages, and those boundaries often become the testing frontier.

For example, **Oliver** mentioned using Swift Testing in new packages – a perfect way to experiment without disrupting legacy code.

So yes, we often see Swift Testing **extend** XCTest, but not replace it.

XCTest remains the main testing framework - the stable core that teams still build around. Another tool that extends XCTest is Quick and Nimble, which Monika uses. Let's uncover it.

Quick and Nimble for Expressive Testing

Unit tests have two traits that make them special.

First, they're **structured** - every test follows the *Given–When–Then* pattern we discussed earlier in *The Testing Methodology* section.

Second, each test describes a specific use case, with clear context and expectations.

Quick and Nimble (`https://github.com/quick/nimble`) take both of these ideas a few steps further.

Together, they form one of the most popular frameworks for **Behavior-Driven Development (BDD)** in Swift.

Monika Mateska and her team use Quick and Nimble to make their tests more expressive and uniform - every test follows the same structure and reads almost like a sentence.

Let's look at an example:

```swift
class LoginManagerSpec: QuickSpec {
    override func spec() {
        describe("LoginManager") {
            var manager: LoginManager!

            beforeEach {
                manager = LoginManager()
            }

            context("when given valid credentials") {
                it("should complete successfully") {
                    waitUntil(timeout: .seconds(1)) { done in
```

```
manager.login(username: "test", password: "1234") {
result in
    expect(result).to(equal(.success(true)))
    done()
}
}
}
}

}
```

Even though Quick and Nimble are built on top of **XCTest**, they look and feel entirely different.

The `context` block represents the **GIVEN** part, describing the current state.

The `it` block is the **WHEN**, defining the action.

And the assertion inside - `expect(...).to(equal(...))` - expresses the **THEN**, validating the outcome.

You might notice how the `expect` function resembles Swift Testing's syntax.

That's not a coincidence - both share the same goal: to make expectations human-readable.

But Nimble goes further, offering a rich library of **matchers** (`to(beNil())`, `to(contain())`, `to(throwError())`, and more) that make writing tests easier and clearer.

This style of testing enforces a consistent pattern across the team, improving readability not only for developers, but also for **QA engineers** and even **product managers** who review test behavior.

It's not always obvious why a team should adopt frameworks like Quick and Nimble, but for teams like **Vivino**, where many developers collaborate on the same codebase, tools like these can make testing more expressive, structured, and enjoyable - once everyone gets used to them.

Mocking Our Tests

Creating mocks is one of the most critical parts of writing tests.

Remember - we want our tests to be **consistent, deterministic, fast,** and **easy to run.**

And by "mocking," we mean **mocking our dependencies** - replacing real implementations with lightweight versions that simulate behavior in a controlled way.

When we discussed testable code earlier in *Writing Testable Code*, we replaced a network service with a mock that adhered to the same protocol.

This is the most common and most straightforward approach to dependency mocking - and it works well.

But protocol-based mocks aren't the only way to go.

In Chapter 2, we mentioned the `swift-dependencies` (`https://github.com/pointfreeco/swift-dependencies`) library, which Zlatko's team uses extensively.

One of its most powerful features is the ability to provide **different dependency values for different environments** - production, tests, or even SwiftUI previews.

Here's the same snippet from Chapter 2, showing how we can use `swift-dependencies` to mock our tests:

```swift
private enum AuthClientKey: DependencyKey {
    // Real production implementation
    static let liveValue: AuthClient = .init { email, password in
        try await API.login(email, password)
    }

    // Default for tests (safe, deterministic)
    static let testValue: AuthClient = .init { _, _ in
        .init(token: "TEST_TOKEN", userEmail: "test@example.com")
    }

    // Nice for SwiftUI previews (fake latency)
    static let previewValue: AuthClient = .init { email, _ in
        try await Task.sleep(nanoseconds: 500_000_000)
        return .init(token: "PREVIEW_TOKEN", userEmail: email)
    }
}
```

By defining multiple environments, Zlatko's team can **switch behaviors automatically** - live for production, deterministic for tests, and simulated for previews.

It's an elegant way to build testability into the architecture itself.

Another interesting approach is not mocking the dependency, but **mocking the server itself.**

Oliver Binns and his team use a tool called **Imposter**, which launches a local HTTP server that simulates real responses.

Imposter allows them to test their network layer directly while keeping tests deterministic and fast.

Here's an example of a simple Imposter configuration file:

```
{
  "imposters": [
    {
      "port": 8080,
      "protocol": "http",
      "stubs": [
        {
          "predicates": [{ "equals": { "path": "/user/1" } }],
          "responses": [
            {
              "is": {
                "statusCode": 200,
                "headers": { "Content-Type": "application/json" },
                "body": { "id": "1", "name": "Avi", "email": "avi@ios.com" }
              }
            }
          ]
        }
      ]
    }
  ]
}
```

This JSON defines a mock server, its endpoints, and the responses it should return. Now, we can call it directly from our Swift code:

```swift
final class UserService {
    func fetchUser() async throws -> User {
        let url = URL(string: "http://localhost:8080/user/1")!
        let (data, _) = try await URLSession.shared.data(from: url)
        return try JSONDecoder().decode(User.self, from: data)
    }
}
```

Here, instead of injecting a mock dependency, we inject a **mock environment**.

Our code doesn't even need to know it's talking to a fake server - it just works.

Working with a fake server makes the tests cleaner, more realistic, and easier to maintain.

Another interesting approach about mocking data I found with Stefan Blos - mocking data is not only for testing, but it's also for SwiftUI previews. So, Stefan invested in sharing mock data between SwiftUI previews and tests - mock once, enjoy twice!

Mocking - whether through **protocols**, **swift-dependencies**, or **mock servers like Imposter** - is a cornerstone of stable, robust testing.

It's what transforms fragile, unpredictable tests into reliable safety nets that teams can trust.

Next, let's talk about a different kind of test - snapshot testing.

Catching Changes Using swift-snapshot-testing

Up until now, we've focused on logic tests, mostly unit tests.

Snapshot tests, however, are less about **logic** and more about **appearance**.

Instead of asking *"Did it work?"*, snapshot tests ask, *"Does it look the same?"* - and that's an entirely different perspective.

Visual changes in a view can come from many sources: logic updates, rendering changes, modified presentation code, or even SDK updates that subtly alter how a screen looks.

It's almost impossible to catch these issues with unit tests alone.

Snapshot testing captures a view, stores it as a reference, and compares future versions against it.

Sometimes, even a single pixel difference can trigger a failure - and that's its power.

Of course, we can define thresholds to avoid making snapshot testing painful.

And because of that potential friction, most iOS developers avoid snapshot testing altogether.

Like code coverage, it's usually **big teams** that invest in it - those who need a stronger "insurance policy" to guard against visual regressions.

Two of those developers are **Oliver Binns** and **Noam Efergan**, who both use `swift-snapshot-testing` by **Point-Free** (`https://github.com/pointfreeco/swift-snapshot-testing`).

Here's an example of how `swift-snapshot-testing` works in practice:

```
struct ProfileCardViewTests {
    @Test func profileCardView() {
        // Arrange
        let view = ProfileCardView(
            name: "Avi Tsadok",
            role: "iOS Developer",
        )

        // Act & Assert
        assertSnapshot(of: view, as: .image)
    }
}
```

In this example, we create a view with fixed parameters to ensure determinism, then call `assertSnapshot` to compare the rendered result with previous iterations.

At first run, the framework renders our SwiftUI view into an image and saves it to disk as a reference snapshot. That .png file is the source of truth. On future runs, the framework renders the view again and compares it pixel-by-pixel with the source of truth it saved earlier. If everything matches, the test passes; if something changes, the test fails, and we get a diff.

Snapshot testing isn't limited to images - it can also capture JSON responses, `Data` objects, or any other serializable value. It even supports testing across multiple trait collections, like different devices or color schemes.

For large teams, where visual consistency can easily break, snapshot testing provides valuable safety nets.

But as **Danijela** wisely noted, when not done carefully, it can just as easily add noise instead of confidence.

And to finish our toolset, let's turn to a completely different type of test – UI tests.

End-to-End Testing with Maestro

End-to-end testing, or in the iOS world, **UI testing**, isn't a straightforward type of test.

The idea sounds simple: simulate user behavior by running the app and interacting with it like a real user would - tapping, scrolling, and navigating through the interface - all while treating the app as a **black box**, without touching its internal logic.

However, as **Krzysztof Zabłocki** reminded me, he prefers unit tests, and lots of them.

The reason is simple: **unit tests are deterministic, fast, and require almost no maintenance.**

UI tests, on the other hand, are the opposite - they're slower, more fragile, and demand ongoing maintenance.

Despite that high cost, what surprised me most was that **almost every developer I spoke with implements some form of UI testing.**

None of them rely on it heavily, but all agreed it's valuable for verifying their **most critical user journeys**.

Oliver Binns uses UI tests for key flows such as onboarding and payments.

Zlatko includes them as part of his suite but replaces them with unit tests whenever possible.

And as we already know, **Vincent** focuses on flows that are critical to the company's business goals.

Taken together, this pattern reflects the same **testing landscape** we explored earlier in this chapter:

Most developers do write UI tests, but only for the **mountaintops** of their apps, the high-value flows where a bug could cost the company money or trust.

One team that takes a slightly different approach is **Noam Efergan's** team at **Yazio**.

While most teams still use **XCTest** for UI testing, Noam's team relies on a modern, declarative tool called **Maestro** (`https://github.com/mobile-dev-inc/Maestro`).

The idea behind Maestro is to make UI testing **cross-platform, simple, and readable.**

Instead of writing code, tests are defined in **YAML scripts** that describe user interactions in plain language.

Here's a real-world Maestro example of a "happy path" sign-in flow:

```
appId: com.company.app
name: Login happy path
steps:
  - launchApp
  - tapOn: "Sign in"
  - inputText:
      text: "avi@example.com"
  - tapOn: "Next"
  - inputText:
      text: "correct-horse-battery-staple"
```

```
- tapOn: "Continue"
- assertVisible: "Welcome, Avi"
```

We don't need any prior testing experience to understand what this script does.

It launches the app, taps on **Sign in**, enters credentials, and verifies that the expected welcome message appears.

As **Noam** explained, Maestro is *"a convenient tool to work with"* - it supports subflows, selectors, state setup, and integrates seamlessly with CI pipelines.

But even with tools like Maestro, **methodology still matters**.

A good framework doesn't replace a good foundation.

To make tests deterministic, we still need strong **state setup** and **test infrastructure**, just as Krzysztof emphasized.

And we still need to follow established best practices, like the **Page Object Model,** which structures screens as modular objects that encapsulate their locators and actions (you can read more about it in my book "Pro iOS Testing").

Maestro can simplify UI automation, but it's not magic.

The principles of reliable testing remain the same - clear structure, controlled state, and focus on what truly matters.

Summary

This chapter was a long one - but testing is a big topic, and developers have a lot to say about it!

We explored what makes code testable, the different philosophies teams follow, the **Testing Landscape** model, and the tools that power real-world testing today.

I finished this chapter feeling genuinely optimistic.

The culture and maturity of iOS development have evolved dramatically over the past decade, and testing is now an essential part of every developer's toolkit.

That's good news - not only because tests improve quality, but because of the **ripple effect** they create across architecture, collaboration, and culture.

Now that we understand *how* developers test, it's time to *see how they automate it.*

Let's move forward and explore how teams bring all of this into their **CI/CD pipelines** - because our journey through iOS development is far from over.

CHAPTER 5

CI/CD and Release Pipelines

We submit every Friday and release every Monday. Jenkins runs everything for us - when it behaves.

—Monika Mateska, Vivino

Introduction

In the previous chapter, we talked about **testing** - a huge topic that tells the story of teams through the lens of their culture.

But that story isn't complete without linking it directly to the **CI/CD pipelines** that carry those tests into production.

Most iOS developers don't consider CI/CD an exciting topic.

It's often seen as a world of scripts, servers, and automation.

Yet, just like testing, it reveals so much about how teams actually work - their habits, their priorities, and their rhythm.

In this chapter, we will

- Explore the **human side of automation**

- Describe **the method behind the machines** and the steps that bring code to life

- Review **the tools developers use** to build and release confidently

- And finally, uncover **the best practices from the field**

Let's jump right in - with **Danijela Vrzan** and her story.

A. Tsadok, *Real-World iOS Development*, https://doi.org/10.1007/979-8-8688-2815-7_5

The Human Side of Automation

In her previous team, **Danijela Vrzan** used to push her code to CI/CD and wait for the process to finish.

The pipeline ran unit and snapshot tests, handled signing, and uploaded the build - a routine that still took about **40 minutes** to complete on GitHub Actions.

Even though the company had a dedicated platform team maintaining the CI/CD setup, they deliberately chose the slower GitHub Actions over more complex solutions - for one simple reason: **simplicity.**

So why wait forty minutes for a build to finish?

Because unlike many other aspects of iOS development, this time it's **not about speed** - it's about **trust and consistency.**

But what do those words really mean?

Many iOS developers aren't fully aware of what happens when they press *Build* in Xcode.

Think about it for a second: building locally means taking *your* current codebase, linking *your* local versions of dependencies, and producing a binary - often skipping tests or other safety checks. When your teammate hits the build button, the process looks identical but might not be - slightly different code, different dependency versions, a missing environment variable, or maybe they run tests while you don't.

That inconsistency isn't always bad. Local builds are fast and flexible - they don't take 40 minutes like Danijela's and can speed up the development process.

But when a build becomes the foundation for testing, distribution, or release, **speed must give way to consistency**.

Trust in the build means trusting that everyone - every machine, every branch, every commit - goes through the same process, every single time.

And that shift, from speed to trust, is what CI/CD is really about.

Now, let's dive in a find out about the method behind the machines.

The Method Behind the Machines

At this point, we already understand that CI/CD is more about **consistency and trust** than speed.

But what exactly does "CI/CD" mean?

The two terms are often bundled together, and for many developers, "CI/CD" is just a buzzword for a process they don't fully understand.

Let's break it down and see what's actually behind it.

As the name implies, CI/CD consists of two parts:

- **CI (Continuous Integration)**: Every code change is automatically built, tested, and merged.

- **CD (Continuous Delivery/Deployment)**: Every commit can safely reach users, at any time.

The real goal of CI/CD is **reliability through repetition** (which, ironically, is what I'm doing now - repeating that CI/CD is all about trust).

Setting up a CI/CD process creates a **pipeline** that our code flows through - starting with a defined event and ending in a safely delivered app.

Figure 5-1 illustrates this concept.

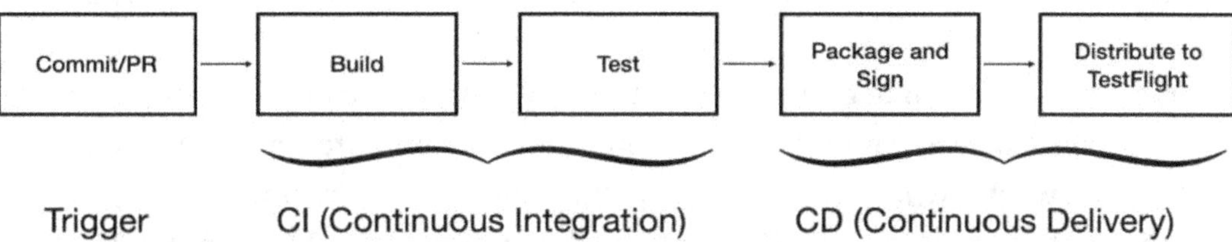

Figure 5-1. *The anatomy of a CI/CD pipeline - from code commit to TestFlight distribution*

Figure 5-1 shows the classic skeleton of a CI/CD pipeline for most iOS teams.

A pipeline begins with a **trigger** - typically a commit or pull request.

While it's possible to start the process manually, it's far more logical to tie it directly to a code change.

After pushing our code, the **build** and **test** stages ensure that the version is stable and high-quality - that's the **CI** part.

Then come **packaging, signing, and uploading** - the **CD** part.

The vision behind this pipeline is simple but powerful: we don't want to manually organize our work into "versions."

Instead, every code change enters one side of the pipeline, and a new TestFlight build - ready for users - comes out the other.

This idea has long been common in backend engineering, but as you'll see throughout this chapter, **iOS developers are catching up fast.**

Looking back at Figure 5-1, we can see a common CI/CD pipeline we probably find in most teams and developer. As I mentioned in the previous section, the process begins with a trigger. So, let's say a few words about it.

Triggering the CI/CD

Every pipeline begins with an event - **the trigger.**

Most teams tie it to a **commit or pull request**, though it can also be a **scheduled job** (like nightly builds) or even a **manual trigger** for special release cases.

From the interviews, it's clear that nearly all teams with an established CI/CD process trigger on **pull requests** and **merges**.

And it's easy to understand why - after all, the "CI" in CI/CD stands for **Continuous Integration**.

It means that whenever we add a new feature or fix a bug, we integrate it back into the codebase - and we want that integration to automatically verify the stability of the app.

Some teams even **block merging** until the CI/CD process completes successfully.

In that sense, the trigger reflects much more than a configuration setting - it mirrors **how the team works**, what runs in their pipeline, and even their **culture**.

For example, Monika from Vivino explained that they trigger builds not only on pull requests but also on every merge to `main` and `develop`.

The choice of trigger and what runs afterward reveals how the team approaches integration and delivery.

If your goal is **continuous delivery**, you'll want a pipeline that's always ready to ship.

That means running the *full* process - build, unit tests, UI tests, and snapshot tests - on every change. Yes, the same process we see in Figure 5-1.

It's part of the reason **Danijela's builds** took 40 minutes in her previous team.

On the other side, some developers prefer a lighter approach.

Krzysztof, for instance, runs UI tests only on **scheduled nightly builds**.

During regular development, his CI focuses on fast-running unit tests: "They're practically free," he says, "so let's make a lot of them."

From the interviews, two main patterns emerge:

1. **Production-Ready**: Every commit to `main` or `develop`, and every pull request, triggers a full pipeline that builds a version ready to deploy.

   This approach is most common among larger teams with frequent releases.

   These teams want immediate feedback on breaking changes and the confidence that every build could go to production.

2. **Feedback-First**: The pipeline runs primarily on pull requests, focusing on unit tests for speed.

   Full CI/CD runs, including UI and snapshot tests, are scheduled (often nightly).

   This method prioritizes quick feedback and is especially suited to **smaller teams or indie developers**.

These two patterns reflect the main purpose of CI/CD:

either getting quick feedback about your app's stability or making sure there's always a build ready to ship.

Speaking of builds - let's talk about them.

Building Our App

We saw that the previous step of "triggering" is critical as it defines when and what will happen - and that's a lot for a step! However, triggering the process doesn't do any practical work. So, the first step that does something is the build step.

Before we dive into the build step, let's try to frame its scope. The build is where everything becomes real - our code turns into an actual product. It's the foundation of everything that follows.

And every iOS developer knows - building a project not only takes time, but it's also an extremely complex task. We'll have to resolve dependencies, install libraries, link everything together, compile hundreds of classes, and thousands of files! Our machines work very hard to perform this sensitive step, and so do the CI/CD machines. The build step is really the heartbeat of every pipeline and probably the longest and most important part.

We'll start the dive by setting up the environment.

Step 1: Setting the Environment

The build step is not just the compile process we usually run on the local machine - it's much more than that.

To start the process, we need to set up the environment: the Xcode version and the macOS version. An important thing to bear in mind is how closely the CI/CD environment aligns with the environment developers have on their local machines.

Sometimes, developers install a newer Xcode version while the version on the CI machine remains old. This situation can cause the local codebase to build successfully but fail in the CI process. In addition, different developers can have different environment versions - what does that mean for building? For testing?

As Zlatko and Monika both told me, keeping these versions aligned is not negotiable.

"Yep, we do," they said almost identically, "mostly because of consistency and to make sure there are no unintended bugs that were missed during local testing."

Danijela described a more structured approach. At *her previous company*, the infrastructure team handled Xcode upgrades centrally. "Once our infra team made sure everything was ready for a new Xcode version," she explained, "that's when we were allowed - and required - to update on our work computers."

In practice, this synchronization prevents surprises: if a build passes locally, it will probably pass on the CI machine.

The CI's fixed environment becomes the anchor - a single, verified state that ensures consistency across developers and machines, keeping one of the most fragile parts of the pipeline stable.

Now that we have the environment set up, let's set the project by resolving dependencies first.

Step 2: Resolving Dependencies

Another aspect where consistency is important is **resolving dependencies**. In Chapter 2, we've talked about swift packages in the context of our app architecture. We saw that in most teams, packages are part of the project repository (a.k.a. local packages). However, when we deal with third-party swift packages/pods or remote packages, the package version can be different from one machine to another. So, in the CI machine, we need to make sure we are consistent with the project dependencies.

Now that we have everything set up for the actual build process, some of the developers take advantage of the CI to keep their code to a high standard by linting their code.

Step 3: Perform Linting on the Code

We've talked about the consistency the CI machine brings to the team. We don't need a complex setup just to build, test, or upload to the store - a standard local machine can do all of that. What we really need is to ensure this process stays consistent across developers and environments.

If consistency is the main goal of CI, why not use it to make our **code itself** more consistent?

One of the processes that helps maintain high code quality is **linting**. Linting isn't a specific tool - it's a generic process that analyzes code to detect potential errors and style violations before it runs. The name comes from an old Unix tool called *lint*, which "picked out the lint" - small flaws - from C programs.

Based on my discussions with developers, most integrate a linting step into their CI pipelines to ensure the code being built is high quality. It's important to understand, however, that linting can either **check** or **fix** code. In CI, the machine isn't meant to modify the codebase - it's read-only. Developers apply fixes locally, and the CI step verifies that the result meets the standards. Think of it as a code review gatekeeper.

There are several reasons why teams run linting in CI:

- **Enforce Rules:** Developers can run SwiftLint locally - or forget to. SwiftLint is one of the most popular linters in the iOS ecosystem, but like any local tool, it depends on discipline. Running it in CI ensures that code violating the team's standards can't be merged. CI becomes the final judge.

- **Guarantee Uniform Standards:** Local environments may differ in SwiftLint versions or configurations. CI provides a single, consistent setup that defines the one true standard.

- **Enhance Code Reviews:** CI can post lint results directly into pull requests using inline comments or warnings. This automates stylistic feedback and frees reviewers to focus on logic, not formatting.

- **Build a Healthy Culture:** Beyond the technical side, linting contributes to engineering confidence. When developers see that satisfying "green check," they know everything - tests, builds, linting - went smoothly. That feedback reinforces trust in the process.

To see what this looks like in practice, here's a snippet from Vivino's SwiftLint configuration, which their iOS team runs as part of every CI build:

```
included:
  - App
  - Frameworks

disabled_rules:
  - line_length
  - function_body_length
  - file_length
  - cyclomatic_complexity
  - todo
  - identifier_name
  - large_tuple

custom_rules:
  deprecated_uiapplication_openurl:
    included: ".*\\.swift"
    name: "Deprecated UIApplication openURL"
    regex: "UIApplication\\.shared\\.open\\("
    message: "Avoid using openURL(_:); use open(_:options:completionHandler:)
instead."
    severity: error
```

This configuration tells a story of pragmatism. Instead of chasing perfect style scores, the team disables noisy or purely aesthetic rules and focuses on those that actually protect quality - such as flagging deprecated APIs. It also targets only first-party code (App and Frameworks), skipping external libraries and generated files to keep the pipeline lean and fast.

In other words, Vivino's **SwiftLint** file mirrors the philosophy behind their CI setup itself: **enforce what matters, ignore what doesn't.** The result is a consistent codebase, a faster review process, and a culture of confidence that extends from the first commit all the way to release.

And speaking of validation - once the linting process is done, we can turn to the next crucial stage, and the one many consider the heart of CI: **testing.**

Testing, Testing, and Testing

Testing again?

Didn't we already cover that in the previous chapter?

It's true - we just dedicated an entire chapter to testing.

But here's a little secret: this isn't the last time we'll talk about it.

That's because testing doesn't live in isolation. It's woven into the bones of iOS development - from how we design our architecture to how we release our apps.

Testing isn't a stage. It's a presence.

And once you start seeing it that way, you begin to notice how it shapes *everything*.

In Chapter 4, we explored how teams **build** tests.

Now, we'll explore how they **live** with them.

Defining the Tempo

What does *tempo* have to do with iOS development?

Have we ever thought of ourselves as musicians - or race-car drivers, balancing speed and control?

One of the most interesting insights from the interviews is that **every iOS team has a tempo**.

It's not about how fast developers type or how quickly they close tickets.

It's about how much they trust their automation - especially the testing process that drives it.

In other words:

> **A team's tempo is defined by the length of its feedback loop - the time between writing code and knowing it works.**

Remember what we discussed in the previous chapter: **unit tests are cheap.**

They provide *instant feedback* because they run fast, they're easy to automate, and there are plenty of them.

In the CI/CD world, they are the natural choice for continuous testing.

So, when we talk about **testing inside CI/CD**, we're actually talking about **two rhythms** running in parallel:

- The **inner circle**, where developers seek instant feedback on every change.

- The **outer circle**, where the team validates that the entire product is stable and ready for release.

Let's see an illustration of these two circles that many iOS teams follow - together, they form the **heartbeat** of the team (Figure 5-2).

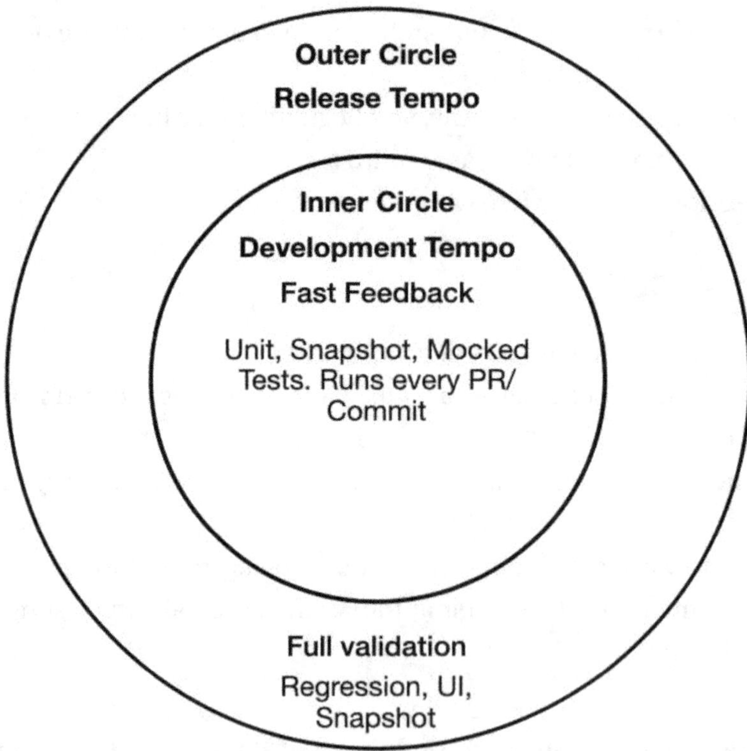

Figure 5-2. *The two development rhythms of iOS teams*

Figure 5-2 shows the inner circle (the "Development Tempo") and the outer circle ("Full validation"). To understand that, let's start with the inner circle.

The Inner Circle – Fast Feedback

The **inner circle** is built mainly from unit and snapshot tests, usually supported by mocks to keep them **consistent and stable**.

They run fast, often, and act as the team's *immediate pulse check*.

For example, **Monika Mateska** and her team at **Vivino** run **unit tests only on the affected module** for every PR.

That process isn't meant for release validation, but it provides *very fast feedback* that keeps the team moving confidently.

Similarly, **Zlatko Kuvendjiski** from **Axon** runs unit tests on every PR, using mocks to isolate functionality and keep CI fast.

And at **Deloitte Digital**, **Oliver Binns** and his team run **hundreds of unit and snapshot tests** on every PR still within minutes - proving that even a large suite can feel lightweight when architecture and CI are well structured.

Notice how all of these teams tie their **inner circle** directly to the **PR process**.

The CI doesn't just validate code; it participates in the review - it's a gate, a collaborator, and a confidence meter.

We'll dive deeper into the internal PR processes of different teams later in the book, but for now, it's important to understand that this **fast feedback loop** is an integral part of every modern CI pipeline.

The Outer Circle – Full Validation

While the inner circle is easy to digest, the **outer circle** is more complex.

Its goal is to take the codebase from "it builds" to **"it's ready for release."**

It runs slower - sometimes much slower - because it covers **the entire product surface**.

The outer circle consists mostly of **UI and integration tests**, layered on top of unit tests to test the app as a whole.

Remember that Vivino's team runs tests only on affected modules during the PR stage?

In the outer circle, they run **the full test suite** across the entire app.

Even this outer rhythm often has **two internal layers**.

The first runs **nightly** and focuses on UI tests - we can see this in the practices of **Vivino (Monika), Axon (Zlatko),** and **Headspace (Krzysztof).**

These nightly runs provide a broader view of the system once a day, revealing issues that fast loops can't always catch.

But nightly UI tests alone rarely make a product *release-ready*.

That's why most teams include another **outer layer** - often involving manual QA and exploratory testing - to verify the app end-to-end before release.

This is the slowest rhythm, but it's the one that turns confidence into certainty.

Now that we've talked about the different rhythms that set the tempo, let's understand how the app's architecture becomes the CI physics.

Architecture and Design Patterns: The Physics Behind the CI

One of the things we discover when we observe teams, developers, and apps is that different aspects of development are always connected. Nothing stands on its own.

We've already seen how the CI setup reflects a team's day-to-day work and release cycle. We've also seen how architecture and design patterns reflect a company's business and priorities.

The question is: can we find a relationship between architecture or design patterns and how the CI functions?

At first, we're not supposed to. One describes how we structure our app and connect its parts, and the other describes how we build it consistently.

But as we always find out, life finds its way.

Look at Figure 5-3.

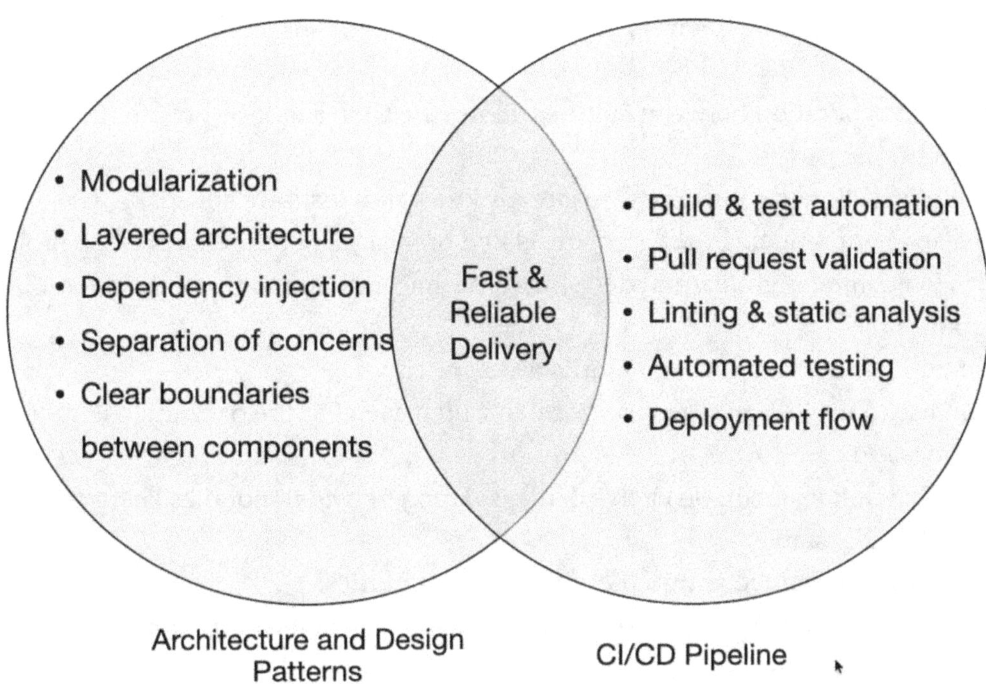

Figure 5-3. *The overlap between architecture and CI/CD is where teams achieve fast, predictable, and reliable delivery*

Figure 5-3 shows how these two domains (architecture and CI/CD) create a velocity "zone" that sets how fast teams can deliver new features and fixes. Let's talk about it.

Modular Architecture Leads to Modular CI

Let's start with modularity.

Think back to **Vivino's architecture** we discussed in Chapter 2.

Vivino's app is extremely modular and layered, composed of four distinct layers: **Features**, **Components**, **Foundation**, and **Data.**

Even though the team doesn't separate their project into Swift packages, the app is modular by design - features are clearly separated, the codebase is organized, and boundaries are well defined.

This architecture suits Vivino's needs perfectly. It allows them to scale their features and lets multiple teams work in parallel on the same app.

But there's another interesting result: **the same architecture makes Vivino's CI run faster.**

Because of their scale, Vivino's developers don't want the CI to run every test for every change.

The clear separation between features allows the CI to run tests only for the parts that actually changed.

It's not just about saving time - we already know unit tests are cheap.

It's also about reducing the risk of unrelated breakages in other parts of the project.

For Vivino, their architectural decisions are what let their CI stay both **fast and predictable**.

The same principle applies to **Zlatko** at **Axon**.

Axon uses a **multi-package structure**, in which each feature or domain is sufficiently isolated to stand on its own.

Even if all unit tests run on each PR, the isolation between modules keeps the CI process extremely stable.

Failures are contained within their module boundaries.

CI stability, in this sense, isn't only about speed - it's about **predictability**.

Design Patterns As Stability Features

We've said before that a *design pattern* is simply a common solution to a common problem.

But the patterns we choose - and how we use them - are what make our CI stable (or fragile).

Take **Krzysztof,** for example.

He puts great effort into setting clear boundaries between system components, such as time, network, and database, and the rest of his code.

These boundaries can be created in different ways - through **protocols** or **composition**.

For example, here's a simple protocol-based clock:

```
protocol Clock {
    func now() -> Date
}

struct SystemClock: Clock {
    func now() -> Date { Date() }
}
```

```
struct MockClock: Clock {
    var fixedDate: Date
    func now() -> Date { fixedDate }
}
```

For Krzysztof, using these kinds of abstractions doesn't just make the code clean and decoupled - it lays the foundation for a **stable CI process**.

Mocking gives him complete control over the parts that typically make tests flaky in CI: time, network, and database.

By isolating them, he removes randomness from the system, making every CI run deterministic and reliable.

Architecture defines how the app is built, and design patterns define how its pieces interact.

Together, they determine how **predictable** your CI can be.

A clean architecture gives CI clear boundaries to test, while good patterns remove the chaos that causes flakiness.

In that sense, architecture and design patterns are the **physics** of CI - they control how fast and how smoothly the entire system can move.

From Delivery to Deployment – The Last Mile

Most developers say CI/CD as if the last two letters mean the same thing. But they don't, and the small gap between delivery and deployment tells us everything about how much a team trusts its own automation.

Let's try to explain these two terms before we dive in and investigate a little more:

- **Continuous Delivery:** Automation up to a ready-to-release build

- **Continuous Deployment:** Automation that actually releases to users

In other words:

Delivery is where automation ends and people still make the call.

Deployment is where the machine presses the button for us.

If you've ever worked on (or with) server-side systems, you know that **continuous deployment** is common practice.

That's largely a result of how the server world operates.

A backend service is built almost entirely on logic and integrations - there's no visual interface, no App Store, no user device limitations.

Its quality can be verified through **unit and integration tests**, which are often the *only* way to ensure that code is ready to reach users.

That's why the server world has evolved a strong **testing culture**, and, naturally, a culture of **continuous deployment** has followed.

For iOS developers, however, the story is very different.

Most teams stop at **delivery** - usually uploading to TestFlight - and they do so for good reason.

First, an iOS app is a **user-facing product**.

Let me be even more specific: it's a *very* user-facing product.

We already saw that iOS developers today write more unit tests than ever before - something that wasn't common in the past.

But few teams go so far as to write full-scale UI tests.

And when they do, those tests usually cover only **critical business flows** (thank you, Vincent!).

There are also areas that make automation inherently difficult on mobile: camera access, GPS, multitouch, push notifications, sensors - features that are nearly impossible to simulate reliably inside a CI environment.

Even the best frameworks can't fully reproduce how real users interact with real devices.

And even if we overcome all of those challenges, we still end up facing **App Store Connect** - the unavoidable human checkpoint at the end of every iOS pipeline.

Real-World Experiences Toward True Deployment

When I spoke with **Oliver Binns** and **Monika** about CI/CD, I immediately felt something different from other interviewees.

For many developers, the CI/CD pipeline is just another task on their to-do list - something they have to set up as part of the workflow.

Sure, we talked about feedback loops, inner and outer circles, and how they reflect a team's heartbeat.

But for most, maintaining the CI/CD service is a tedious, sometimes boring, part of engineering life.

For Oliver and Monika, it's the opposite.

They see CI/CD as an exciting opportunity - a system that can constantly evolve, grow, and take on more capabilities with each iteration.

Every new automation is a small invention.

One of Oliver's goals is to end the process with a full deployment. Monika described a very similar setup at Vivino, where their pipeline can also build and submit the app to the App Store. In both teams, the CI/CD pipeline can push a release all the way to the store.

This is a rare aspiration - as we saw earlier, most iOS developers settle for continuous *delivery*.

But for Oliver, the process doesn't feel complete until the new version is actually *released* on the App Store.

It's important to note that going fully automated with deployment isn't just a technical decision - it's a **statement of trust**.

It reflects the high level of confidence Oliver and his team have in their CI/CD pipeline, a confidence that was earned through deliberate effort.

That trust is built on a foundation of **extensive test coverage** and a wide variety of test types - unit, integration, snapshot, and UI tests - that verify every layer of the product before it's shipped.

From a technical standpoint, however, true deployment is entirely possible using the **App Store Connect REST API.**

Using App Store Connect REST API

While few developers know it exists, the API can handle almost everything available in the App Store Connect interface, allowing teams to automate even the release step as part of their pipeline.

For Oliver, this is where his pipeline's journey truly ends - with the machine taking the final step on its own.

It's the point where automation stops waiting for human approval and simply acts with the same consistency and discipline the team built into it.

To use the App Store Connect REST API for full deployment, a developer needs to complete five main steps:

1. **Authenticate (JWT):** Before we can talk to the App Store Connect API, we need to authenticate using a **JWT (JSON Web Token)**.

   We generate an **API key** in App Store Connect, use it to mint the JWT, and include that token in every API request.

   This authentication model allows the pipeline to act on behalf of the team securely, without manual logins.

2. **Upload the Build**: Once we have authentication in place, we can upload the build to **TestFlight**.

   This step doesn't necessarily require the API - we can still rely on tools like **Fastlane** or **Transporter** to handle uploads.

   However, for teams pursuing a fully automated deployment, it's also possible to use the **App Store Connect API** directly for build uploads.

3. **Create the App Store Version**: This step might sound unusual to many iOS developers, because it's something we normally do manually.

   In continuous *deployment*, however, automation must also take care of creating a new **App Store Version** entry.

   Using the REST API, we can create or update the version object - specifying the version string, platform, release type, and linking it to the processed build uploaded in the previous step. This is the API equivalent of clicking "+ Version" in the App Store Connect interface.

4. **Submit for Review**: Creating a version isn't enough to keep the deployment flow moving - we still need to **submit it for review**, just as we do manually.

   Using the API, this is done with a simple POST request that creates a new **review submission object**, referencing the version we just created.

5. **Release the Version or on Demand:** Finally, we can decide how the release is triggered.

   When creating a version, we can configure it to **"release after approval,"** which means the App Store will automatically publish it once Apple approves it.

   If it's set to **manual release**, we'll need to perform one more step - sending a **release request** through the API. That final API call is what makes the difference between *delivery* and *deployment*.

Here's an example for what a POST request looks like when submitting for review:

```
POST /v1/reviewSubmissions
{
  "data": {
    "type": "reviewSubmissions",
    "relationships": {
      "appStoreVersion": { "data": { "type": "appStoreVersions",
      "id": "<APP_STORE_VERSION_ID>" } }
    }
  }
}
```

This request includes a single required property - the `data` object - which defines the submission type and the associated App Store version.

For teams managing multiple "flavors" of the same app, automating this step is an elegant way to avoid manual repetition.

Implementing a fully automated deployment flow isn't a trivial move.

It requires a solid CI/CD foundation, comprehensive testing, and strong team confidence in the process.

That's why most iOS teams still stop the automation at **delivery** - they prefer to monitor the version, validate analytics, and ensure everything looks healthy before the release goes live.

But as teams like **Oliver's** at Deloitte continue to push forward, the line between automated delivery and deployment grows thinner every year.

So, let's try to dig in in this line for a second.

Sticking with Continuous Delivery: The Human Checkpoint

Now that we understand why the line between delivery and deployment keeps getting thinner, let's look at why most teams still stop the machine before crossing it.

Oliver and his team at **Deloitte Digital** are chasing what many consider the holy grail of mobile CI/CD - a process that ends not in TestFlight, but in the App Store itself.

The dream is simple: finish a feature, press *Merge PR*, and watch the version appear in App Store Connect, already submitted for review.

Many teams imagine that future.

But high maintenance costs, complex testing environments, and smaller team sizes often make it difficult to reach.

That's why most teams, even highly mature ones, still include a **manual QA step** somewhere near the end of their release cycle - no matter how high their test coverage is.

Continuous Delivery doesn't eliminate QA - it makes QA predictable.

In a stable CI pipeline, every build arrives in the same state: tested, signed, and ready to review.

That consistency means QA can focus less on catching crashes and more on judging quality.

The pipeline doesn't remove the human checkpoint - it removes the chaos around it.

And that's where the most interesting question appears:

what is the role of QA today?

Because the real boundary isn't between *delivery* and *deployment* - it's between **automation and assurance.**

If QA's only purpose were to validate, then yes - we could automate that step.

Automated tests already confirm logic, validate flows, and catch regressions.

But QA, in most teams, isn't just testing *what* the app does - it's validating *how* the app feels.

After speaking with developers across multiple companies, it became clear that QA engineers wear different hats depending on the team's culture and maturity.

In smaller teams, they're the **testers**, running exploratory checks and verifying fixes.

In others, they act as **release gatekeepers**, stamping *Ready for Deployment* on builds that pass every check.

And in many mature organizations, they evolve into **quality managers** - reviewing the app from the user's perspective, asking the questions no unit test ever could.

The more mature the testing culture, the more QA shifts from execution to judgment.

Quality assurance becomes a shared effort - often split between QA engineers, product managers, and designers - yet in almost every case, QA still wears the **gatekeeper's hat**, ensuring that what reaches the App Store is good enough for users.

Take **Yazio**, for example.

Noam Efergan told me they invested enormous effort into testing - including UI automation - yet they still keep a manual QA step in the pipeline, and never considered removing it.

As Noam put it:

There's no such thing as 100% test coverage. We also run a lot of A/B tests, so we prefer a human to ensure the version feels stable.

At **Vivino**, where testing is deeply integrated in their development culture, QA focuses on validating each feature rather than each release.

Once a feature branch is merged into develop, QA manually verifies that specific change.

After QA signs off, the team triggers a build and submit pipeline. Jenkins (a popular CI/CD platform) runs the regression tests, builds the release, and submits the build to the App Store.

This workflow allows Vivino to rely on automation for integration and release, while still keeping a strong manual QA checkpoint for each individual feature.

The same is true at **Axon**, where every feature development ends with a QA review before it is merged.

Understanding the role of manual QA led me to an unexpected realization:

There are actually **two quality stages** - the **feature stage** and the **release candidate stage**.

Let's look at both and how they connect with the inner and outer circles we examined earlier.

The Development Life Cycle and the Quality Stages

If we thought the inner and outer circles made things complex, now it turns out there are even more "circles" - or rather, *stages.*

Let's zoom out for a second.

So far, we've talked about the pipeline - we prepare the environment, build, test, and then deliver or deploy.

But in practice, what we're really describing is what I call **the development life cycle.**

This life cycle touches on many other areas we'll discuss throughout the book, but from the continuous delivery perspective, it centers around **two primary quality stages**: the **feature stage** and the **release candidate stage**.

For many teams, this life cycle flows as follows:

- **For every change** (every "push to git"), the CI runs to provide immediate feedback based on fast, reliable unit tests. That's the **inner circle** we already discussed.

- **At night**, the CI runs heavier tests - UI, snapshot, and integration tests - to catch deeper issues. That's the **outer circle**.

- **When a feature is completed and merged**, teams usually trigger the **outer circle** again, followed by a **manual QA** that focuses on that feature only.

- **When a version is ready for release**, teams run the **outer circle** one last time, sometimes followed by a **manual QA** that reviews the entire app and stamps it as *ready for users*.

As we can see, **manual QA enters the process only when needed** - once at the feature level, and sometimes before launch.

Automation makes those human checkpoints more **predictable and efficient**, not redundant.

You can see this rhythm clearly in the teams we spoke to.

Vivino and Yazio showed how automation and human review don't compete - they reinforce each other.

And that's what led me to an interesting realization:

If every team still relies on human validation before a release, are we truly practicing **continuous** delivery?

Perhaps what we're really doing is maintaining a *continuous readiness* - a state where code can always move forward, but only once the right people, tests, and timing align.

Tools of the Trade

Let's try to picture our CI/CD pipelines as a workshop.

It has the basic working surface - like a **workbench** - which represents the actual machine that runs everything.

Then, there are the **essential tools** - the saws and drills - that do the core work, like **building and testing**.

And, of course, the workshop might also have some **gadgets** - small helpers that make life easier or refine our craft, such as **clamps** that hold things in place (like linting, signing, or dependency tools).

After all, in both cases, we're building a product.

And every woodworker has a different set of tools.

That set is never fixed: each product requires something different, and every team develops its own preferences - just like in a real workshop.

In this part of the chapter, we'll go over some of the most common tools iOS teams use to build their pipelines - from the essentials to the refinements that turn a good setup into a great one.

Now, let's begin with the workbench - the automation service.

The Automation Service

The automation service is our **workbench** - the machine that actually runs everything.

It's where our builds are compiled, our tests executed, and our delivery process begins.

I must say - I was a bit surprised to see how many different options and preferences came up in the interviews.

Because when we think about it, an automation service is just a machine.

To be specific, it's a Mac with Xcode installed.

And yet, the variety of setups I encountered shows how differently teams think about **control, cost, and trust**.

Control: How Much Power Do We Want Over the Machine?

The first factor that defines an automation service is **control**.

Some teams want to own every part of the process; others prefer a managed system that "just works."

Vivino, for example, runs a set of **Jenkins-based virtual machines** that trigger on every change.

Jenkins gives the team full flexibility to customize their build and testing environment - a true *industrial workbench* - but it comes at a cost.

It requires constant maintenance and dedicated attention, making it impractical for small teams or indie developers.

Bamboo, used by **Zlatko's team at Netcetera**, offers a similar level of control.

It integrates well with other Atlassian products like JIRA and Confluence, which makes it a good choice for teams already using those tools.

But it also demands operational effort - updates, agents, and monitoring - just like Jenkins.

Other teams choose lighter workbenches, where most of the control is handled by the service itself.

GitHub Actions, for instance, sits right inside GitHub's infrastructure.

It offers a modern, low-maintenance alternative that still allows flexibility through code.

Oliver Binns and **Stefan Blos** use it because it blends easily into their workflow - simple YAML files, automatic triggers, and fast setup, without the headaches of maintaining servers.

The more control you demand, the more responsibility you take.

And as I learned from these interviews, every team finds its own balance between flexibility and peace of mind.

Cost: How Much Are We Willing to Pay for Convenience?

Control isn't the only factor; **cost** plays an equally important role.

Since the automation service is a machine we intend to run often, the cost grows not only with money but also with **maintenance effort and scale**.

With **Jenkins**, the financial cost is minimal - the software is free - but the real price is in the hours spent keeping it alive.

For teams like **Vivino**, that operational cost is acceptable.

They can afford the infrastructure and people to maintain it.

For smaller teams, however, that investment makes little sense.

Bamboo, too, comes with licensing costs and maintenance overhead.

It fits mid-size companies that already use Atlassian tools, but it's overkill for lean mobile teams.

For smaller teams and indie developers, simplicity becomes the main currency.

Tools like **Bitrise** and **Xcode Cloud** are designed for ease of use.

They require almost no setup and no infrastructure management.

Mikaela Caron, for instance, uses **Xcode Cloud** for her personal projects.

It's integrated directly into Xcode and free for the first 25 build hours each month for Apple Developer Program members.

Beyond that, Apple charges about **$14.99 for each additional 25 hours** - which makes it a cost-effective option for individuals or small teams.

But at larger scales, those build hours add up quickly, and the convenience starts to fade.

Vincent's team followed a similar journey with **Bitrise**.

They initially adopted it because it was effortless and affordable.

As the team grew and the number of builds increased, the cost scaled rapidly.

Eventually, they decided to move to a **local Mac mini** to save money - trading convenience for control.

In short, every automation service has a price tag, even if it isn't printed on a bill.

Jenkins costs in maintenance, Bitrise in usage, Xcode Cloud in scale.

Teams don't just choose a service; they choose **what kind of cost** they're willing to pay.

Choosing an automation service is never just about technology.

It's about the balance between **control and cost**, between the freedom to shape the system and the comfort of letting it run itself.

Jenkins and Bamboo give full control, but demand time and care.

GitHub Actions and Bitrise reduce friction but limit flexibility.

And Xcode Cloud - simple, polished, and tightly integrated - is perfect for one-person workshops, but less so for busy factories.

In the end, the best workbench is the one that fits your scale, your craft, and how much of the machine you're willing to maintain yourself.

So, if the automation service considered to be the "basis," what can we add more?

Enriching the Instruments

Theoretically speaking, having a machine (a Mac with Xcode) should be enough to build, test, and upload a new version to TestFlight (and even deploy it, as Oliver aims to do).

But in practice, you'll rarely find a CI/CD pipeline without additional tools that make the process more efficient and insightful.

Let's begin with Static Analysis and Code Quality.

Static Analysis and Code Quality

We already covered **SwiftLint** earlier in the *Building Our App* section as one of the most popular linting tools in the iOS ecosystem.

We even looked at a real SwiftLint script from **Vivino** and analyzed it together.

Not every team mentioned SwiftLint explicitly, but most perform some kind of linting as part of their workflow, and SwiftLint is often the default choice.

Still, there are tools that go beyond simple linting.

One example is **SonarCloud**, which **Oliver Binns's team** at Deloitte uses as part of their CI pipeline.

SonarCloud doesn't just check for formatting or syntax violations - it performs **deeper static analysis.**

It looks for **code smells, duplicated logic, potential bugs, and complexity patterns** across the codebase.

In a way, SonarCloud performs an **automated code review**, generating a health report after every build.

But a good human reviewer doesn't just evaluate a single pull request; they notice **trends** - how code quality evolves over time.

SonarCloud does the same.

It tracks metrics like **code duplication**, **test coverage**, and **security hotspots**, giving teams visibility into whether their codebase is improving or quietly degrading.

For Oliver's team, SonarCloud acts as a **quality checkpoint** before any pull request can be merged.

It integrates seamlessly with **GitHub**, posting results directly into the PR view so developers can see and fix issues before merging.

It's important to remember that SonarCloud doesn't replace testing - it **complements** it.

Tests verify *what* the app does, while SonarCloud ensures that *how* it's built will hold up over time.

It's not an essential tool for every workshop, but for teams that value maintainability and visibility, it's one of the best instruments to keep the craft clean and sustainable. But do you want to talk about an essential tool? Let's talk about Fastlane.

Gluing Everything with Fastlane

For new iOS developers, the idea of **Fastlane** can feel confusing.

What is it, exactly? Does it replace Jenkins? Or Xcode's built-in CI tools?

Fastlane is a unique tool - on one hand, it doesn't replace anything. On the other hand, it **glues everything together.**

If our CI/CD workshop is full of tools, then Fastlane is the **electricity that powers them.**

But there's another thing that makes Fastlane so special:

you might assume that since it doesn't replace any other tool and simply sits on top of them, it's just a "nice-to-have" helper that makes life easier.

But in reality, almost every team I interviewed mentioned Fastlane at some point. This little "helper" has quietly become a **foundational tool** in the iOS CI/CD world.

It's now hard to find a team that hasn't installed Fastlane - even teams without a full CI/CD pipeline rely on it.

To understand why, let's go over a few of the everyday challenges that Fastlane solves:

- **Code Signing:** This isn't one of the most frustrating parts of iOS development - it's *the* most frustrating.

  Every developer, machine, and environment needs the right certificates, provisioning profiles, and entitlements.

  Manually handling them causes constant issues, and the problem becomes even worse when setting up CI.

  Fastlane's `match` command centralizes all signing assets in a shared, encrypted Git repository so everyone - and every machine - stays in sync.

- **Manual Build and Upload:** Building and uploading an app from the command line can easily go wrong.

  Fastlane's `gym` and `pilot` lanes take care of that, producing consistent builds and uploading them to TestFlight automatically.

- **Testing and Feedback Integration:** Running tests manually is easy; running them consistently in automation isn't.

  Fastlane's `scan` makes test execution part of the workflow, collecting results and feeding them back into the pipeline seamlessly.

These are just a few of the headaches Fastlane eliminates.

I haven't even mentioned release asset management, metadata uploads, consistent configuration across developers, or the fact that none of the automation services we discussed - Jenkins, Bitrise, GitHub Actions, Bamboo, Xcode Cloud - actually *know* how to build or test iOS apps without it.

At the end of the day, iOS development is full of tiny, painful steps that don't belong in our era - code signing, archiving, uploading, testing, managing screenshots.

These steps consume our time, attention, and energy, pulling us away from what we actually love to do: **writing code.**

Fastlane gives that time back.

It turns frustration into flow, and that's why it powers nearly every iOS workshop today.

Best Practices from the Field

Managing a CI/CD pipeline and deploying versions is never easy.

Listening to other developers can make our lives easier - which is, in fact, the whole idea of this book.

Before we move to the next chapter, I want to summarize some of the things I've learned from the teams I spoke with - lessons that deserve to be highlighted.

Automation Should Be Practical, Not Perfect

Both **Zlatko** and **Monika** described a pragmatic approach to automation.

You don't need to run every test on every commit. It's not only a matter of cost - it's a matter of *time*.

Remember the feedback loops - the **inner** and **outer circles**?

That's exactly the point. Practical automation means building pipelines that fit the way your team works, not the other way around.

Optimize for Cost and Scale

This best practice is closely related to being practical, but from a different angle.

A service that works beautifully for an indie developer might not fit a small startup, and what fits a startup might not fit an enterprise.

Cost isn't just about money - it's also about **time, maintenance, and flexibility**.

Each team has different needs.

On one end, there's **Mikaela**, who uses Xcode Cloud solely to upload her projects to App Store Connect.

On the other, **Oliver** wants everything in one place - 90% test coverage, automatic reviews, and even deployment.

Vincent's team moved from Jenkins to Bitrise, then left Bitrise once their scale changed - and that's completely normal.

Choose tools that match our team's current size and evolve as we grow.

Don't adopt enterprise-grade solutions too early just because *"that's what we used in my previous company."*

Adapt Tools to Our Team Rhythm

Every team has its own rhythm - and if you don't know yours, that's the first thing to define.

When do we release a version to QA or to the App Store?

When and where do tests run?

What's the QA team's role in the process?

Once we understand that rhythm, we should adapt our tools to match it.

These tools drive our pipeline, and they should work in harmony with our workflow, not against it.

For example, **SonarCloud** is a great tool, but it might not be relevant for **Yazio**, whose team works in a trunk-based model with multiple merges a day.

In general, "finding our rhythm" might be the most valuable lesson from this chapter - because it influences every decision we make about tools, processes, and releases.

Automate What Hurts the Most

Automation should remove pain - not become a new one.

As we saw, we can automate almost everything: environment setup, builds, tests, reviews, signing, uploads, even deployment.

But every automated step introduces maintenance overhead, and automation can become flaky if not nurtured.

Monika said, "Jenkins provides full control, but it requires constant maintenance."

And she's right. **Fastlane** became popular for the opposite reason - it's a lightweight set of tools that target the most painful, repetitive parts of iOS development.

Start small. Automate the biggest friction points first - building, signing, and uploading - and only then expand to other areas.

Make the Pipeline Runnable Locally

Krzysztof pointed out something that many developers overlook.

Too often, pipelines exist only on remote machines - Jenkins, GitHub Actions, Bitrise - and that makes maintenance complex and debugging slow.

If developers can't run the pipeline locally, they stop fixing issues, stop improving it, and sometimes even give up on CI/CD altogether - going back to manual uploads from Xcode.

Krzysztof's advice is simple but powerful:

"The same commands that run in CI should run locally."

That's how we keep our pipeline **trusted, debuggable, and alive**.

This reflects Krzysztof's broader mindset: invest in methods, infrastructure, and tools that save time in the long run.

Spend a day or two building a solid foundation - and gain months or even years of higher productivity.

That's what builds lasting success.

Final Takeaway

Successful iOS teams don't chase perfect automation - they build **trust** in their process.

They automate where it saves time, test what truly matters, and stay pragmatic about cost.

Jenkins is perfect for **Monika**, but not for **Mikaela** - and both made the right choice.

In every case, a team's CI/CD setup mirrors its **culture**, its **rhythm**, and what it truly values.

Summary

Personally, the topic of CI/CD was a big surprise for me.

I had always looked at it from a purely technical point of view - how do we make everything work without problems?

But through these conversations, I discovered it's so much more than that.

Simple YAML scripts tell the story of a team's workflow, rhythm, priorities, and even dynamics.

This chapter showed that what might seem like a "boring" technical topic - CI/CD - can actually reveal the human patterns behind how iOS teams collaborate and ship software.

In this chapter, we explored the human side of automation, the methods of building pipelines, the tools teams use, and the best practices that emerged from their experiences.

Our next chapter makes a big shift from automation to **design, UI, and styling** - the visual language that brings an app to life.

CHAPTER 6

Styling, Theming, and Design

Too many modifiers mean your design system is broken.

—Vincent Pradeilles

Introduction

In the previous chapter, we explored the big engine that powers our app all the way from a Git commit to the App Store: continuous integration and deployment. Now we're taking a sharp turn and climbing back to the very top of the stack - the user interface.

Almost every iOS developer builds user interfaces. Every developer has worked closely with designers at some point. And yet, most examples we see in blogs, tutorials, or even Apple's documentation don't reflect the messy, scaled, real-world apps we build. SwiftUI made creating beautiful screens more enjoyable than ever, but building a *good* UI system, one that grows, evolves, and survives multiple designers, is still a complex challenge that demands planning and discipline.

In this chapter, we will

- Talk about design systems

- Discuss how and when to reuse UI components

- Understand the difference between view modifiers and components

- Explore what it really means to work with designers

- Dive into tools like Inject and RocketSim and how they shape our workflows

© Avi Tsadok 2026
A. Tsadok, *Real-World iOS Development*, https://doi.org/10.1007/979-8-8688-2815-7_6

We'll see why UI is much more than placing a title on the screen, and we'll see it through the eyes of the developers in this book.

And as always, we'll begin with a story.

This time, we start with Mikaela.

Going Native

When **Mikaela Caron**, an indie developer from the United States (you've met her before), opens Xcode, she doesn't reach for Figma tokens, Slack threads full of color approvals, or a dedicated design-system repository.

It's just **SwiftUI and a blank screen.**

For many developers, that might look unusual. *No design system?*

Well, not exactly. I didn't say Mikaela has no design system at all - I said she doesn't use a *special* one.

Because in a way, Mikaela's apps already rely on one of the most mature design systems in the world: **Apple's own.**

Her apps support light and dark modes, Dynamic Type, and accessibility right out of the box.

The "designer" behind those rules is the Apple Human Interface Guidelines. Look at Figure 6-1.

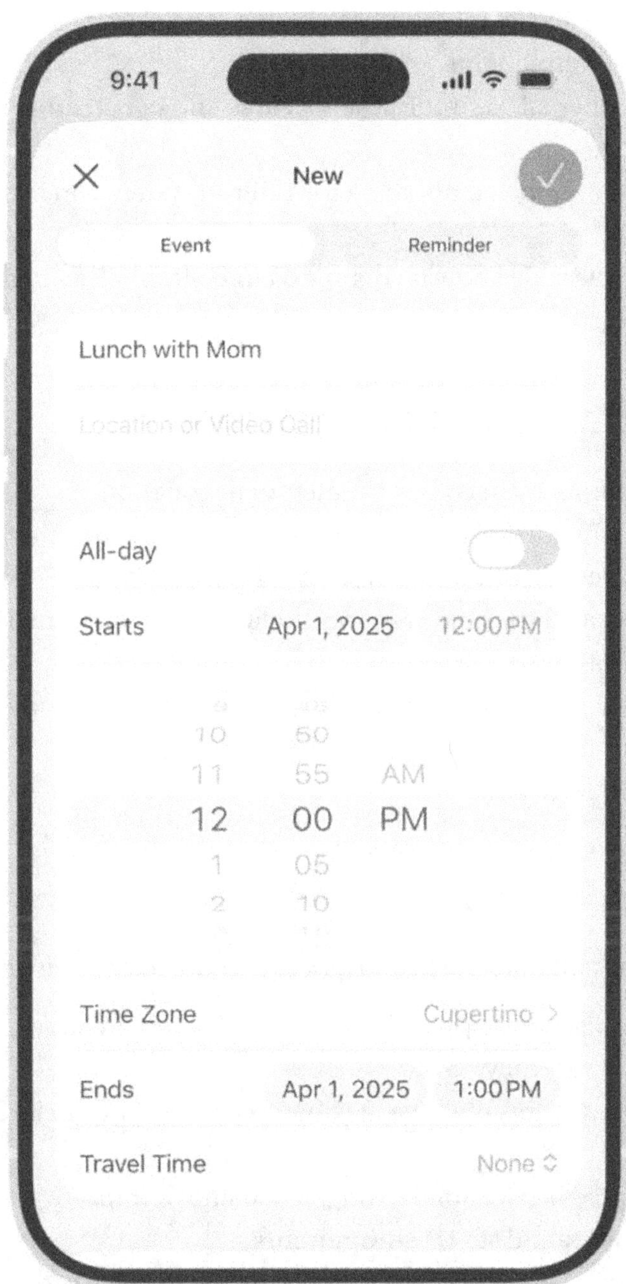

Figure 6-1. *The Add Event screen from the Calendar app, taken from Apple.com website*

Figure 6-1 shows a clear, complex screen with a special design - based on Apple's guidelines and native components.

A design system, after all, is simply a set of **rules and constraints** that control how things look and behave.

And for an indie developer, embracing the built-in system can be the smartest possible choice.

Mikaela - who we already know favors **speed and simplicity** - lets her design philosophy reflect exactly that.

When Simplicity Turns to Negotiation

But as teams grow, simplicity becomes a matter of negotiation.

What used to be straightforward becomes a web of dependencies: colors turn into tokens, fonts into shared libraries, and every pixel gains an owner.

It's no wonder Mikaela sticks with Apple's defaults - she can smell that complexity of alternatives from miles away.

At first glance, design may look like a thin layer on top of our code.

In practice, it runs much deeper.

Teams face hard questions:

- How do we organize our design tokens?

- Can we reuse components?

- How do we collaborate with designers without losing velocity?

If we don't plan ahead, our app will evolve in awkward directions, struggling to support new features gracefully.

But investing too early in a massive, flexible design system can be an even bigger gamble.

Done right, it enables scale; done wrong, it becomes a trap.

That same tension extends to **UI components**.

In most of her apps, Mikaela relies on standard SwiftUI views for a reason – accessibility, dynamic sizing, and automatic light/dark support.

Sometimes, trusting Apple's system isn't a shortcut; it's **good engineering**.

Why Build Your Own System?

So why do developers build their own design systems and components?

Are they over-engineering?

Well... not exactly.

The UI layer is critical.

It's the part of our app that presents our creative and business ideas to the world, communicates with users, and, at the end of the day, it's our **art.**

It's such a central piece of our work that it naturally develops its own **language** - a design language.

That language helps us stay consistent across different screens and, just as importantly, consistent within the app itself.

It ensures that all components communicate with each other and live in harmony.

Think I'm exaggerating?

Try designing an app from scratch - dozens of screens that evolve over time - and then translate that vision into color tokens, fonts, and UI components such as text labels, buttons, tabs, and menus.

It's not just a task; it's a **philosophy.**

And representing that philosophy in code is anything but simple.

From Apple to Everyone Else

Now that we understand why Mikaela relies on Apple's design system, the question is - what do other developers do?

Most teams eventually build a design system tailored to their own apps.

The key difference is that they have a **designer.**

Let's be clear: a design system isn't a technical concept.

It's a **collection of components, standards, and guidelines** that help create a consistent, effective interface.

In the context of development, our code must reflect that system, but the designer owns the definitions.

And that, of course, adds another layer of complexity - **working with designers.**

(A challenge that Mikaela, or even Danijela in her indie work, doesn't have to deal with.)

In this chapter, we'll dig deeper into how maintaining a design system is actually done.

But before we move on, it's worth breaking another myth - one that every developer faces sooner or later:

The **reuse myth.**

The Reuse Myth

This book isn't just about what developers say on different topics - it's also about **breaking myths** and seeing iOS development for what it really is.

One of those myths is about **reusability**.

Every iOS developer dreams of reusable code.

The idea that we can *build once and use everywhere* is irresistible.

It makes us genuinely excited - sometimes even more than a beautiful sunset in autumn.

But the reality is far more complicated.

Many developers struggle to reuse their UI components "everywhere."

Sure, there are ways to do it.

We already discussed **Swift Package Manager** in Chapter 2 as one way to share code.

Technically, reuse is possible.

The problem is that reusability isn't really a **technical** challenge - it's a **contextual** one.

The deeper causes come from **business goals and design decisions**, not from engineering limitations.

So, before we can talk about where engineering ends and where design and business begin, let's talk about what it means to build a design system.

Building a Design System

By now, we already know a few key things about what a **design system** really is.

Every team has one, even if it isn't formally defined, and designers rather than engineers usually manage it.

We also know that a design system is a **set of rules** that define how an app looks and behaves - not a technical constraint.

In this part, we'll explore the **main components** of a design system and see how they appear in real life.

We'll also understand why a design system is almost always **tailored to a specific app** - and why it rarely makes sense to reuse it elsewhere.

Let's start from the bottom layer and climb our way up.

Fifty Shades of Gray (or Tokens)

Here's a personal story (yes, I'm also an iOS developer - not just the interviewer).

I once worked on an app that had been in the App Store for about a decade.

You can probably imagine the layers of legacy that came with it.

One of the oldest and most complex areas was, unsurprisingly, the **design system**.

Over the years, several designers had contributed to the project, each with their own ideas of how the app should look and feel.

So yes, technically, we had a design system - but in reality, it reflected every visual philosophy that had ever passed through the company.

Some things stayed consistent: the app's tint color hadn't changed, and neither had the corner radius.

But other things... evolved.

The biggest offender? **Gray.**

Every few months, a new shade of gray appeared.

A slightly different background here, a subtly darker border there.

Each one came with its own token and component because none of the existing ones were "just right."

As a developer, I eventually found myself managing a palette so enormous I started calling it *"50 shades of gray."*

That experience taught me something important:

For developers, a design system isn't static - it's the team's messy mirror.

Without shared understanding and discipline, even the most elegant system will slowly dissolve into a gradient of good intentions.

So, one of the first questions I asked the developers I interviewed for this book was:

How do you manage your design systems?

Almost all of them use some kind of **token system** to store their color constants.

Most developers define them directly in code, but Vincent (for example) took it one step further and uses the **Asset Catalog** to store colors and ensure type safety.

Assuming we have a color set in the Asset Catalog named `CustomColor`, not only is it easy to preview and manage across light/dark modes, devices, and even localizations - it's also simple to use in code:

```
Text("Hello, world!")
    .foregroundStyle (.custom)
```

Notice how Xcode generated a type-safe constant for us called `.custom` - and even removed the "Color" suffix.

Using an asset catalog was one of Vincent's tips, and it shows how we can enjoy both worlds: clarity and type safety.

This definition of a color is called a **token**, and it's the smallest brick in a design system.

A token isn't only a color - it can represent spacing, corner radius, animation duration, or any value that affects how the app looks and feels.

Tokens in Practice

The next question is: **what's the naming principle behind tokens, and how do they look in practice?**

Monika from Vivino sent me a snippet of their color definitions:

```
enum Assets {
    static func color(named name: String) -> Color {
        return Color(name)
    }
}

public let blue200 = Assets.color(named: "blue200")
public let gray700 = Assets.color(named: "gray700")
public let red500  = Assets.color(named: "red500")
```

Vivino's palette looks like a painter's toolbox - numeric and structured. Vivino defines these colors in the Assets Catalog (Figure 6-2).

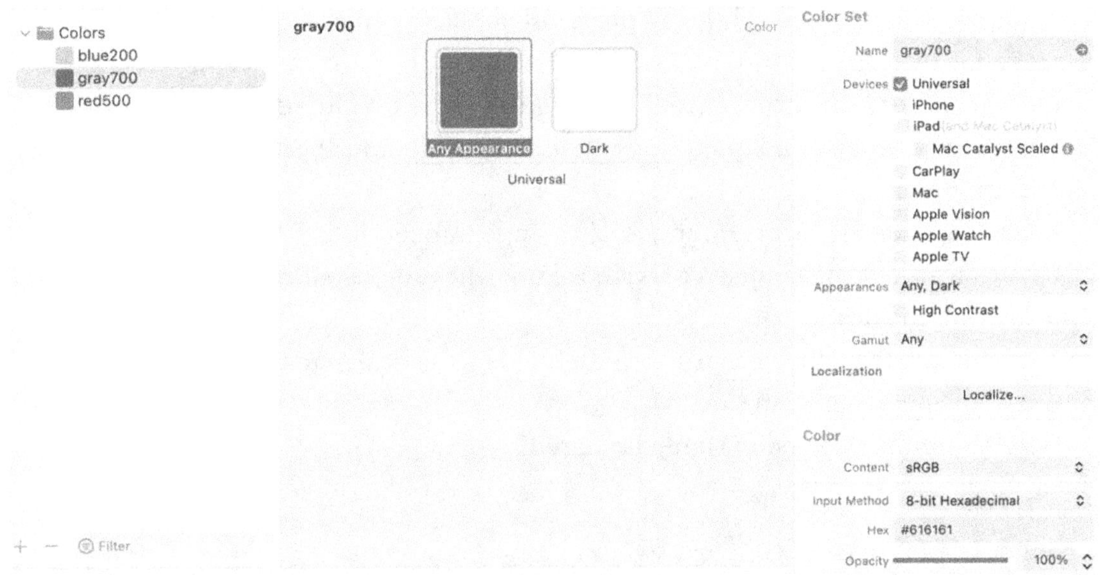

Figure 6-2. *The Assets Catalog*

The Assets Catalog is an Xcode tool that allows developers to define colors and fonts with an easy and simple user interface.

Vivivon's colors definition is clear, predictable, and aligned with their brand.

But it's also static.

The names describe how the color *looks*, not what it *means* - there's no `primary` or `error`.

For Vivino, that makes perfect sense: from a **branding** perspective, consistency matters more than flexibility.

Now, let's look at a different example from **Zlatko's** personal project:

```
// MARK: - UI -
static var accent: Color { Color("accent", bundle: .module) }
static var brand: Color { Color("brand", bundle: .module) }
static var background: Color { Color("background", bundle: .module) }

// MARK: - Text -
static var text = Color.white
static var headerAndFooterText: Color { .text.opacity(0.6) }
```

Here, the color names describe their **role** in the interface rather than their hue.

accent, brand, background, and text each express purpose.

There's also something subtle but powerful here: every derived color is based on a base token.

Look at `headerAndFooterText` - it's a variation of `text`, tailored to a specific use.

That means we could adapt to a new theme (like a rebrand) without rewriting a single component.

Zlatko's approach reflects **intent**, not just appearance.

Finally, let's look at Danijela's previous team, where ownership of the design system sat firmly with the designers.

The code reflected the design system defined by the design team - including the naming conventions in Figma.

Here's a simplified version Danijela shared:

```
enum Theme {
    enum Dimensions {
        case extraSmall, small, medium, large, extraLarge
    }

    enum Color {
        case white100, white200, red150, backgroundLight, backgroundDark
    }
}
```

It's not the exact version they used, but close enough to capture the structure.

The key idea wasn't the syntax - it was the **naming alignment** between design and development.

The design team decided on the names; developers just ensured they stayed consistent in the code.

That might sound like a small detail, but it represents the real power of a mature design system:

It's not about control - it's about **ownership**.

When a developer can build a new screen without asking, "Which color should I use here?" or "What spacing does this component have?", that's when **design and development truly speak the same language.**

Implementing Themes (Like Light and Dark)

We just buried 50 shades of gray, and that's the first step toward building a complete theming system.

Earlier in this chapter, I mentioned a popular principle for naming colors: **name them by what they mean, not by how they look.**

Imagine we have a title component that looks like this:

```
Text("Welcome!")
    .foregroundStyle(.lightRed)
```

Now Imagine:

```
Text("Welcome!")
    .foregroundStyle(.pageTitle)
```

There's no argument about the clarity of that code. But what happens when we decide to change the app's theme?

Not just switching between light and dark, but introducing new design directions, accessibility modes, or even user-defined color themes?

The lightRed ties use to how it looks, and pageTitle? It just works.

That brings us back to something we discussed earlier in *When Simplicity Turns to Negotiation*: our code should reflect the **philosophy behind the design system**.

This isn't a technical issue - it's about communication and intent.

Just as with naming functions or classes, **naming colors brings clarity**.

But here, good naming also brings flexibility.

And yes - just like every other topic in this book - even naming reveals something about a team's **culture and workflow**.

And that culture brings us to the next layer of our design system - **themes**.

Perhaps the most recognizable example of a theme is supporting **light and dark modes** in our apps.

Apple introduced Dark Mode back in **iOS 13**, along with first-class tools for developers.

Every color asset can now include two values - one for light and one for dark appearances - and the Asset Catalog even provides previews for both.

So, technically speaking, supporting dark mode is no longer a challenge.

And if we look across the developers I interviewed for this book, most of them do support both light and dark modes - in their teams and even in their personal apps.

However, there are two interesting exceptions: **Vivino** and **traditional banks**.

We've already met both Vincent and Monika, and we know how their teams think about architecture and technology.

So why are these two examples different?

Vivino, for example, supports only **light mode**.

The product is about wine, and wine lives in color.

A light interface better represents real-world lighting: the warm tone of a tasting room, the brightness of a restaurant table, the glow of a wine label under light.

Their brand depends on warmth, authenticity, and color fidelity.

Dark mode would make the product feel cold and distant - a digital experience instead of a sensory one.

Even Vivino's website follows the same rule: no dark mode, by choice.

Vincent's example of **traditional banks** comes from a completely different angle, but the logic is similar.

For a bank, especially a large one, the most essential qualities are **trust and transparency**.

Dark mode can introduce a sense of opacity or informality - not ideal for an audience that values stability and familiarity.

Branding plays a significant role, too.

Imagine a customer who's been logging into the same light-themed banking website for years suddenly downloading a dark-mode version of the app.

They might question whether it's even the official one.

When it comes to finance, trust and familiarity are everything.

These are two very different cases, yet both lead to the same conclusion: **Supporting dark mode isn't a technical decision – it's a brand one.**

As Vincent put it:

Consumer apps should support dark mode – it improves retention.

For lifestyle and consumer products, dark mode is part of modern user expectations.

But for brands built on warmth or trust, staying light-only can be just as intentional - and just as strategic.

Support for additional themes leads us to the next layer of our design system (Figure 6-3).

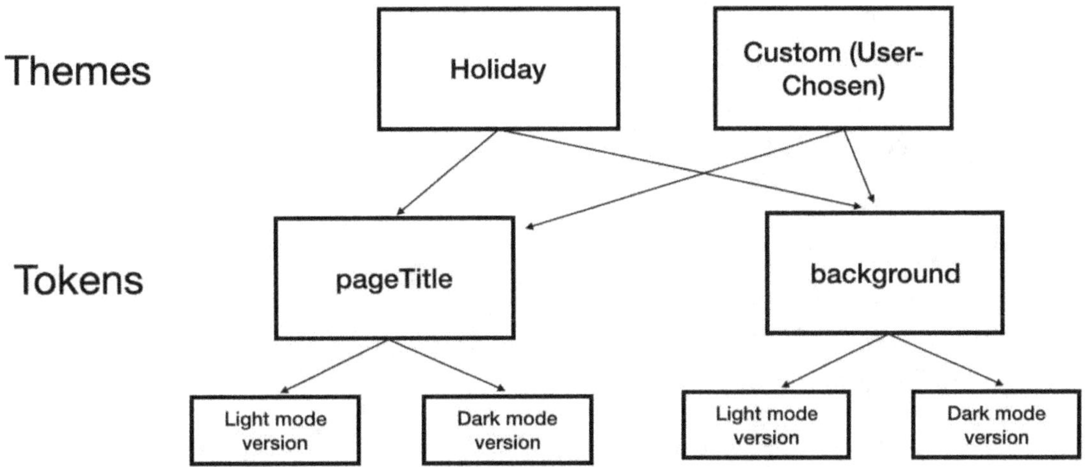

Figure 6-3. *Themes define how tokens are used together*

I think Figure 6-3 perfectly illustrates where we currently stand in building our design system.

Each token describes the color or value for a specific role in the interface - such as a page title or background.

For each token, we can define a **light** and **dark** variant.

This isn't the case for Vivino and some traditional businesses, but it is for most consumer apps.

Above that, a **theme** defines a set of token values that work together.

Switching to a new theme - whether for a holiday campaign, a user-selected skin, or even a business rebranding - should then be as simple as replacing that grouping.

Perhaps surprisingly, the most challenging part of building a design system is defining the **tokens** themselves.

Once we have a clear and consistent set of tokens, creating a theme is just a matter of grouping them.

Let's take Danijela's Theme Enum from the previous section and extend it to create a concrete theme instance:

```
import SwiftUI

struct Theme {
    let colors: Colors
    let dimensions: Dimensions
```

```swift
    struct Colors {
        let pageTitle: Color
        let background: Color
        let accent: Color
    }

    struct Dimensions {
        let small: CGFloat
        let medium: CGFloat
        let large: CGFloat
    }

    static let `default` = Theme(
        colors: Colors(
            pageTitle: .primary,
            background: .white,
            accent: .blue
        ),
        dimensions: Dimensions(
            small: 8,
            medium: 12,
            large: 16
        )
    )
}

extension Theme {
    static let holiday = Theme(
    colors: Colors(
        pageTitle: Color("pageTitleHoliday"), // maybe a gold accent
        background: Color("backgroundHoliday"), // soft red or
        green tone
        accent: Color("accentHoliday") // festive highlight color
    ),
    dimensions: Dimensions(
        small: 8,
        medium: 12,
```

```
        large: 16
    )
)

static var currentTheme: Theme {
    let m = Calendar.current.component(.month, from: Date())
    // Example: December = Holiday theme
    return (m == 12) ? .holiday : .default
  }
}
```

Danijela's previous team grouped their theme tokens using an **Enum**, which is an elegant way to keep the system type-safe and predictable.

In the example above, we extend the Enum to create a new instance, `holiday,` and add a `currentTheme` property that returns the appropriate theme based on the current month.

Of course, this is only an example, but it shows how easy it can be to adapt an existing system to seasonal or brand-specific themes.

Does our design system end here? Well, not exactly, we have more levels to climb. Let's continue!

View Components As Part of the Design System

We discussed tokens (colors, dimensions, spacing) and themes, and we might think we've already covered what a design system is.

But a design system is much more than that.

Remember: a design system is a **set of rules that defines how the UI looks and feels**.

So, our next level is view components and view modifiers - code structures that describe how different UI elements should appear and behave.

View components can be controls, texts, images, banners - anything that represents a reusable piece of UI.

The design system defines how a page title appears, what color a confirm button should be, and how spacing between elements behaves.

When I planned the book and prepared the interview questions, this was one of the sections I was most curious about.

As developers, building view components is where our creativity meets design - it's the part that makes apps beautiful and engaging.

I wanted to understand how real teams build them.

My first question was simple:

What is the difference between a view modifier and a view component?

And when should we use one over the other?

View Modifiers or Views?

If there's one pattern that consistently emerged from the interviews, it's this:

> ***Most teams rely on view modifiers to style their UI rather than custom components.***

It's not that developers don't use custom views - they absolutely do.

But they **apply their design system through view modifiers**.

Here's a tiny example.

Let's say we have a page title and want to apply our design system style.

```
PageTitle("Settings")
```

Or we can do:

```
Text("Settings")
    .pageTitle()
```

Both produce the same result on the screen.

The difference is in how the styling is applied: either encapsulated within a component or used through a modifier.

So... which one is the "right" approach?

Let's make this even more confusing.

Earlier, in the "Implementing Themes" section, we talked about color tokens based on roles.

Imagine we have a color token called `pageTitle`.

Now we have

- A **color token** called **pageTitle**

- A **view modifier** called **pageTitle()**

- A **component** called **PageTitle**

It looks like three different elements are competing for the same responsibility.

So how do we untangle this?

The Three Layers of Responsibility

Here's the clear separation between the layers:

- **Token – the value**

  "What color should a page title use in this theme?"

- **View Modifier – the style**

  "Apply the page title styling: font, weight, spacing, color token."

- **Component – the identity**

  "This is what a Page Title is in our app."

A **token** is just a value: no fonts, no padding, no behavior.

A **modifier** is a styling recipe. It decides how something should look visually.

A **component** is a standalone UI element. It has structure, can combine multiple views, and can include behavior and accessibility traits.

To make it clearer, here's a healthy PageTitle component:

```swift
import SwiftUI

struct PageTitle: View {
    @Environment(\.theme) private var theme
    let text: String

    var body: some View {
        Text(text)
            .pageTitleStyle(using: theme)
            .accessibilityAddTraits(.isHeader)
    }
}

struct Theme {
    static let `default` = Theme()
}
```

```swift
private struct ThemeKey: EnvironmentKey {
    static let defaultValue: Theme = .default
}

extension EnvironmentValues {
    var theme: Theme {
        get { self[ThemeKey.self] }
        set { self[ThemeKey.self] = newValue }
    }
}

struct PageTitleStyle: ViewModifier {
    let theme: Theme

    func body(content: Content) -> some View {
        content
            .font(.title)
            .foregroundColor(.primary)
    }
}

extension View {
    func pageTitleStyle(using theme: Theme) -> some View {
        self.modifier(PageTitleStyle(theme: theme))
    }
}
```

This component doesn't hardcode spacing or colors.

It uses tokens (through the theme), applies a style (via a view modifier), and wraps it inside a semantic component.

Notice that in the context of a design system, there's a clear distinction between a "component" and just a "view." Both are indeed SwiftUI structures – but they mean different things in terms of their roles in the app and whether we can reuse them across screens.

Another thing to remember about components is that they don't have to be small.

Sometimes an entire screen can be part of your design system.

Settings screens, for example, almost always include a title, a subtitle, and a list of options.

That entire pattern can be componentized.

It's just a more abstract component that requires tighter collaboration between designers and developers. Sounds simple, right?

Well… mostly in user-interface blogs (and in other books).

Now, the Reality

While reviewing my notes for this chapter, I re-read something Vincent said:

"Too many modifiers mean your design system is broken."

Immediately, I thought back to my "50 shades of gray" incident, and the illusion that design systems are straightforward.

The theory always sounds simple:

Take the tokens, themes, and components your designers define and apply them in code.

What could go wrong?

Vincent's comment stayed with me because, unlike many books that stick to theory, I wrote this book based on voices from real teams.

I have zero intention of painting iOS development as a clean theoretical playground.

And Vincent is absolutely right.

The hard part of a design system isn't building it – it's **keeping it healthy over time**.

It doesn't matter if we use the Asset Catalog or enums for tokens.

It doesn't matter if themes are injected through @Environment or (God help us) through a Singleton.

Those are implementation details.

The real challenge – and the part you won't find in tutorials – is **maintenance**.

Why?

Because it's incredibly easy to **add** to a design system.

A new background layer?

Just throw in a new color.

Another title?

Add a slightly different font size.

Another designer joins the team?

Welcome to shade number 51.

It takes discipline to stop and ask:

- *Should I reuse an existing token?*

- *Is this new shade essential?*

- *Should we adjust the current components rather than create new ones?*

- *Is the design system drifting?*

Each time we take the "easy" path and introduce a new token, we push our design system one step closer to entropy.

In that sense, Mikaela and Danijela – who rely on Apple's built-in design system – actually have simpler lives.

The system is already maintained, disciplined, and enforced.

They get all the benefits without any maintenance burden.

Now let's talk about a topic you won't find in iOS development books, but we all know (not you, Mikaela!), closely - working with designers.

Bridging the Gap: Working with Designers

If you've read the previous chapters, you already know one of the book's recurring themes:

The tools and processes developers use always reflect their team's culture.

And nowhere is that more visible – or more sensitive – than in how developers work with designers.

In *Inside Apple (2012, John Murray publisher)*, Adam Lashinsky describes how product development often begins with design, and how Apple places design at the very front of its priorities.

Apple might be an extreme case, but we all agree on one thing:

The user interface is the window through which users experience our code.

An app is, first of all, a user interface. And that simple fact can create tension among developers, product managers, and, of course, designers.

Tension is not inherently bad – it's part of building products.

But each team needs to find its own way to manage that tension, and the way they do so tells us a lot about the underlying culture.

For indie developers like Mikaela and Danijela, having no designer is both a dream and a trap.

It's peaceful – until they realize they *are* the designers.

Every spacing decision, every color, every hierarchy is suddenly their responsibility.

In teams, collaboration with designers reveals a lot about the environment:

- How decisions are made

- How organized the product process is

- How much ownership developers really have

- How "negotiable" design rules are

Now let's break these dynamics down by scale and see how they evolve as teams grow.

Scaling Up: Collaboration to Negotiation

Many things change when a team – or a company – scales.

Their DNA (yes, even small teams have one) determines how they behave as they grow, and the industry and brand shape that evolution as well.

Imagine a tree growing in a specific environment – the soil, the light, the humidity.

All of those conditions influence how the tree looks years later.

The same goes for product teams.

Indie developers like Mikaela, Danijela, and even Zlatko in his personal projects take full responsibility for their design decisions.

This is partly why they rely on Apple's built-in design system – it is already proven, consistent, and stable.

In small teams, we typically have one designer sitting close to one or two developers.

The collaboration is direct, the communication is simple, and the design system – if it exists at all – is mostly implicit.

Design evolves naturally through conversation, not documentation.

But as the team grows, something changes.

Design stops being a friendly collaboration and slowly becomes a negotiation. This is the point at which the design system becomes a natural sibling of the developer toolbox.

Also, the term "Pixel Perfect" enters the team's jargon. And that's a good opportunity to say a few words about it.

Perfecting the UI

Let's start with a definition.

Developers – and mostly designers – use the term *pixel-perfect* to describe the effort of making the final product identical to the design in every visual detail: colors, margins, spacing, font sizes, corner radius, and more.

In theory, if we put the implemented screen half-transparently on top of the design file, we should get one clean image.

Of course, several challenges immediately appear.

The most obvious one is: *What do we do with multiple screen sizes?*

And beyond that, most screens contain dynamic content – text that wraps differently, images of different proportions, even colors that change across themes.

How can we possibly guarantee pixel-perfect output when the content itself varies?

On top of those challenges, pixel-perfect work is notoriously tedious.

It requires constant back-and-forth adjustments, comparisons, tweaks, reviews, and tuning until everything falls precisely into place.

So naturally, when I began the interviews, I had one question in mind:

How common is pixel-perfect in the iOS developer community today?

Before answering that, I want to share the hypothesis I brought into this chapter.

Logically, if a designer defines a strong design system and developers implement it faithfully in code, pixel-perfect rendering should happen automatically.

Spacing, font sizes, corner radius, padding, tokens – all defined in Figma and translated one-to-one into the design system.

If everything is codified, why would we need to compare the final screen to the design?

That was my expectation, but the interviews surprised me.

Pixel-perfect work is actually **much more common today** than I anticipated.

In fact, most developers I spoke with perform some form of pixel-perfect process – either strict, visual, or hybrid.

I didn't find a contradiction between having a strong design system and doing pixel-perfect checks.

If anything, I found the opposite:

Teams with robust design systems tend to be the same teams that enforce pixel-perfect visual quality.

In other words, pixel-perfect isn't an alternative to a design system – it's part of the same cultural mindset that leads to having a design system in the first place.

Vivino is a great example.

They have a rich, structured design system represented in a shared UI library used across all features.

That level of attention to detail naturally extends into pixel-perfect expectations.

Yazio follows a similar pattern: strong visual identity ➤ strong incentive to get the visuals exactly right.

Pixel-perfect has indeed become a more popular technique over the years, but I suggest there's another reason for that trend, and that's SwiftUI.

Speaking with Designers Through SwiftUI

For many years, UIKit was the go-to framework for building user interfaces in iOS apps. In fact, UIKit is still present in many apps today, especially legacy codebases and even modern apps that rely on UIKit for navigation (we'll talk about that later in the book).

But SwiftUI has largely replaced UIKit as the default UI framework – and the two can live side by side quite happily.

SwiftUI didn't just make building beautiful screens simpler – it made UI *declarative*. You don't have to be an iOS developer, or even a developer at all, to look at a basic SwiftUI view and understand what's happening.

But SwiftUI has another surprising benefit: **it makes working with designers easier** by aligning designers and developers around a shared vocabulary.

Unlike UIKit, SwiftUI speaks a language designers naturally understand – stacks, spacing, padding, layers, tokens.

Just open Figma and see for yourself. Designers think in vertical and horizontal stacks, frames, alignment, spacing, padding, and components.

In SwiftUI, developers think in terms of `VStack` and `HStack`, `.frame`, `spacing:`, `.padding`, and `View` components.

That shared language simply doesn't exist in UIKit. UIKit lives in a different universe – constraints (remember Auto Layout?), hugging and compression resistance, layout guides, and `UIView` hierarchies. These concepts are powerful, but they're foreign to most designers.

SwiftUI makes building UI feel much closer to how designers *design* it.

And SwiftUI previews push that alignment even further. Building a screen often feels like designing directly in Figma, just with code: instant visual feedback, multiple device previews, Dynamic Type simulation, and automatic light/dark switching.

You can even find teams where a designer sits next to the developer, and together they tweak SwiftUI code until the preview matches the desired look. This kind of collaboration simply wasn't practical with UIKit.

SwiftUI isn't a design tool any more than Figma is a coding tool – but they finally speak the same language. That shared language makes collaboration smoother, faster, and far more enjoyable.

Design systems give us the rules, but tools are what make those rules usable. Let's look at the tools developers rely on to bridge the gap between design and implementation.

Tools That Shape the UI

I started coding more than 30 years ago as a kid playing with *Turbo Pascal* and *BASIC*, and 20 years ago with *PHP* for the early web. Later, when the iPhone came out, I moved to UIKit. Despite the decades between Pascal and UIKit, the way we refined UI never really changed very much. Developers would receive a design, implement it, adjust it, go back to the designer, fix it again, and repeat. That rhythm stayed untouched for years.

But in the past decade, something shifted. New tools appeared that didn't just make UI development faster – they changed how designers and developers collaborate. Today, the tools we use **shape the design system** itself and reveal something about the team behind it.

And the first tool that captures this shift is **SwiftUI Previews.**

Instant Feedback with SwiftUI Previews

When Apple announced SwiftUI, it was clear from the start that this wasn't simply another framework. The move to declarative UI changed how we thought about state, structure, and layout. But SwiftUI brought something much more immediate to our workflow: instant visual feedback.

Previews sit next to your code and update as you type. Change a color token, adjust spacing, switch between light and dark mode, and move a component, and the screen reacts instantly. For developers who spent years building UIKit screens, running the simulator, tapping through the app, and repeating the cycle dozens of times a day, this felt revolutionary. Every developer I interviewed relies on SwiftUI Previews daily (with one curious exception that we'll touch on later). Many even described it as "Figma inside Xcode," which captures the feeling surprisingly well.

But like many magical features, SwiftUI Previews come with their own limitations. As soon as the codebase grows, the experience begins to change. What once loaded instantly now takes a few seconds. Occasionally, previews fail to appear altogether, hanging with an eternal "Updating…" message or producing an error no one understands. This is something developers often mention – and Vincent, in particular, emphasized that previews simply don't scale well in very large projects.

To understand why, we need to look at what's happening under the hood.

Previews Secretly Build "Too Much"

SwiftUI Previews give the impression that Xcode compiles only the file we're editing. It feels like Previews watches our view code and redraws it instantly. In reality, Xcode has to build the entire module the view belongs to, link all its dependencies, start a hidden "preview app" process, and inject the view into that environment. When our project is small, this work is trivial, when our project is extensive – with dozens of Swift files, multiple layers, networking SDKs, analytics, feature flags, Core Data, and everything else that sums up in a mature product – that "small" build becomes a miniature version of a complete app build.

This is what Vincent was getting at. In large-scale apps, the cost of building these modules repeatedly becomes too high. You start losing the very thing that made previews special: immediacy.

The architectural solution many developers arrive at independently is the same one we discussed in Chapter 2 of the book: modularization. When we break the UI into more minor Swift Packages, Previews only need to build those units. This dramatically improves speed and stability. Previews work well when the module they operate on is small, isolated, and focused.

But architecture alone isn't the whole story.

Views Are Too Coupled to the "Real App"

SwiftUI Previews work beautifully when a view is self-contained, receives its data explicitly, and avoids unnecessary side effects. Something like:

```swift
import SwiftUI

struct ProfileView: View {
    let model: ProfileViewModel

    var body: some View { ... }
}

// MARK: - ViewModel
struct ProfileViewModel {
    let name: String
    let role: String

    static let mock = ProfileViewModel(
        name: "Avi Tsadok",
        role: "iOS Developer"
    )
}

#Preview {
    ProfileView(model: .mock)
}
```

The code above is idealized. The view is simple; we mock the data, and the preview environment is stable.

Real-world apps, however, rarely behave this way. In many teams, views reach into singletons like `SessionManager.shared`, trigger network requests in `onAppear`, assume the existence of a complete dependency graph, query persistent storage, or depend on environment objects that aren't available in the preview context. Previews operate in a small, sandboxed environment that doesn't behave like the real app, and anything that relies too heavily on the real world may cause strange crashes, timeouts, or weird failures.

The instability of Previews is why Stefan Blos reuses the exact same mock data for both testing and previews – the view sees predictable, controlled input regardless of whether it's being tested or previewed. Zlatko uses the `swift-dependencies` library for similar reasons, allowing his views to swap real services for mock ones effortlessly.

The more isolated our view is and the more predictable its dependencies are, the more reliable SwiftUI Previews become. In fact, Previews loves clean architecture almost as much as unit tests do. That connection isn't accidental, and just like Unit Tests – Previews punish tight coupling.

To summarize that part, SwiftUI Previews is the go-to tool for most developers when developing a SwiftUI-based UI. Now, I mentioned twice that there's one developer with a different approach and promised I would talk about it. Now it's time to keep the promise.

Live Reloading with Inject

SwiftUI Previews work by creating a tiny, isolated version of your app and recompiling it every time you change a file. That model is powerful, but it also explains why previews slow down or break as soon as a view becomes complex or tightly coupled. And if we go back a few years, this kind of instant visual feedback didn't exist in UIKit at all. Even today, UIKit previews are essentially UIKit wrapped inside SwiftUI, so they can still suffer from the same SwiftUI preview flaws.

The important point is that SwiftUI Previews **belong to Xcode**. They function inside the development environment, using the development toolchain. They are not part of the running app. Developers instinctively understand this: to preview a view, we need to launch something that behaves like the app.

Krzysztof Zabłocki understood the same thing, but instead of building a better preview engine, he took a completely different approach. He asked: What if instead of building a miniature app, *we changed the real one*? What if instead of recreating our UI from scratch, we simply updated the running code?

That question became the foundation for **Inject**, a tool he released in 2020.

Inject gives developers something SwiftUI Previews cannot: **true hot reload** inside the running app. And it does it astonishingly fast. Changes apply in less than a second, regardless of whether the app uses Core Data, networking, feature flags, or anything else. In a way, Inject fills the exact gap Apple left open. As Krzysztof told me in our interview, Apple never fully exploited the dynamic nature of the Objective-C runtime – the part of the system that allows method swizzling, runtime symbol replacement, and dynamic code loading. Inject embraces that dynamic world completely.

It is, by every definition, an extremely clever tool.

Let's take a look at how it actually works.

Explaining How Inject Works

Unlike SwiftUI Previews, Inject does not try to rebuild your entire application. The mechanism is almost the opposite. When we modify a Swift file and hit save, Inject detects the change using a companion macOS helper app that runs in the background. Instead of triggering a complete module rebuild, Inject takes **only the changed file**, compiles it into a small dynamic library (`.dylib`), and loads it directly into the running process using `dlopen()`.

Once the new library is inside the app, Inject extracts the updated symbols and replaces the old implementations in memory. The process resembles method swizzling in Objective-C, but adapted to Swift's more static, mangled symbol world. Inject rewires function pointers, updates Swift method bodies, and then signals the active UI to re-render – for SwiftUI, this is done through `ObjectWillChange`, and for UIKit by re-triggering layout or appearance callbacks.

The entire app continues running as if nothing happened. Navigation stays exactly where it was. View models keep their state. Environment objects still hold the same data. Only the changed code is replaced. It feels like plugging a new circuit board into a machine while it is running – the machine never stops, but its behavior instantly updates.

Here's a simple example of how a SwiftUI view integrates with Inject:

```swift
import SwiftUI
import Inject // https://github.com/krzysztofzablocki/Inject

struct ProfileView: View {
    @ObservedObject private var iO = Inject.observer

    var body: some View {
        VStack {
            Text("Hello!")
                .font(.largeTitle)

            // Try changing this line during runtime:
            Text("Updated with Inject")
                .foregroundStyle(.secondary)
        }
```

```
        .padding()
        .enableInjection()
    }
}
```

The `@ObservedObject` subscribes to Inject's internal publisher, which fires whenever a new `.dylib` is loaded. This forces SwiftUI to re-run the view's body. The `.enableInjection()` modifier registers the view with Inject so it can be refreshed when an injection occurs. One listens for changes; the other triggers a re-render. Together, they make SwiftUI behave like a live, interactive canvas inside the running app.

Inject transforms SwiftUI into something much closer to a visual editor. There's no simulator relaunch, no navigation reset, no tedious tapping through screens just to see a small layout change. You edit, you save, and the UI updates instantly – in place.

Now that we understand how Inject works, the natural question is: how does it influence the way we build apps? And what does the workflow look like when hot reload becomes part of the development routine?

That's what we'll explore next.

Adopting Inject

To understand how Inject influences the way we build apps, it helps to look at our daily workflow as developers:

- We begin by writing a new view or adjusting an existing component, and the first place we refine that UI is inside SwiftUI Previews. Previews let us load mock data, simulate a simplified navigation stack, and quickly validate the visual side. But even at their best, previews show a *version* of our screen – not the real thing.

- Eventually, we still need to build and run the app. Only then do we see our view in the real world: the full navigation stack, the actual data flows, and the unpredictable device state that reveal how the UI behaves in practice. And inevitably, something behaves differently than in the preview.

- We jump back to Xcode, make adjustments, and see them in SwiftUI Previews. Again, with mock data and an isolated state.

- We repeat the flow by running the simulator, and hope we land in the right spot on the right screen.

It's a cycle every iOS developer knows too well.

This back-and-forth doesn't only cost time. It shapes how we think. When we rely heavily on mock data previews, we design our UI for a synthetic world that doesn't fully match the product we're actually shipping. We tweak spacing and colors within a bubble rather than in the live app users' experience. The workflow becomes fragmented – half real, half simulated.

Inject changes that model completely. With Inject, we can run our app on a device or simulator, navigate through it as an end user would, and modify the UI of any screen while the app stays alive. State and navigation are preserved, and we're adjusting the interface inside the product itself rather than next to it. Let's remember – this isn't limited to SwiftUI – we can hot-reload UIKit as well, something SwiftUI Previews never truly solved.

Once we experience that workflow, the question naturally arises: why isn't this part of Xcode?

The answer has less to do with technical capability and more to do with philosophy. Inject doesn't follow the rules that define Swift and iOS. It performs real runtime mutation – loading dynamic libraries, rebinding functions on the fly, and updating the running app without restarting it. Apple prioritizes safety, determinism, and static guarantees, which is why their tools focus on sandboxed previews rather than patching live code. Inject lives in a space Apple deliberately avoids, and that's precisely why developers embrace it so enthusiastically.

Pixel Perfect with RocketSim

Back in the old days (yes, I was younger once), I tried to figure out how to achieve pixel-perfect screens. I was tired of getting endless comments from designers, and I wanted my code output to match the design exactly. My secret weapon at the time was Photoshop. I would take a screenshot from the simulator, drop it into Photoshop, overlay the design at 50% transparency, draw rulers, measure every spacing, adjust the opacity again, switch back to Xcode, change a few points, take another screenshot... and repeat. Eventually, I moved to something lighter like Pixelmator, but the core workflow remained the same: slow, manual, repetitive, and painful.

Long story short, pixel-perfect used to be much harder. But today, things are very different. Modern tools like *RocketSim* make pixel-perfecting not only easier, but surprisingly enjoyable.

RocketSim: A Modern Pixel-Perfect Tool

The reason I used Photoshop or Pixelmator wasn't that they were great for pixel-perfect – it was because there was no other option. There were a few tiny utilities that let you stack two images on top of each other with transparency, but they were extremely limited.

Luckily, things evolved. RocketSim (`https://www.rocketsim.app`), created by *Antoine van der Lee*, has become the tool many developers rely on to polish their UIs. Monika from Vivino uses it daily. Noam from Yazio uses it as part of his pixel-perfect routine. Even Vincent, who doesn't use it himself, immediately recognized the name. RocketSim has become the go-to simulator companion for developers who want to skyrocket their visual quality. (Rock ➤ Rocket ➤ RocketSim. Yes, I did that on purpose.)

When I asked Antoine van der Lee how RocketSim came to be, he told me it started in 2019 as a personal productivity hack: a few small utilities he built to speed up his own apps. Over time, it snowballed into the powerhouse it is today, packing more than 30 features the default simulator never had. Antoine says the feedback he gets most often is that developers are now roughly twice as fast when polishing UIs, and honestly, once you've tried it, that claim feels conservative.

So, let's take a deeper look at what RocketSim gives us.

RocketSim As a Pixel-Perfect Engine

Tools like Photoshop forced me to constantly jump between windows, manually align images, re-export, and check again. RocketSim eliminates all of that and brings the entire workflow **directly into the Simulator**. We can import a Figma design, place it on top of our running app, adjust its opacity, and instantly see where things don't match. Misalignments, spacing issues, off-by-one errors – everything becomes visible in seconds.

RocketSim doesn't stop there. We can add rulers, verify color accuracy, compare multiple designs, and even keep a library of screens to switch between as you test. It feels like putting QA glasses on top of the Simulator – the ones Apple never gave us.

All these features blend seamlessly into a typical development workflow. We build the app, run it, and immediately evaluate how close you are to the design. Pixel-perfect stops being a Sisyphean work and becomes part of the process.

But how does RocketSim manage to do this? Apple doesn't allow plugins in the simulator, so what exactly is happening underneath?

Let's enter the nerdy part.

Understanding How RocketSim Works Underneath

Many developers assume RocketSim is some kind of simulator plugin, but Apple doesn't allow that. There are no public APIs for extending the simulator, and App Store apps are not permitted to modify or inject code into other processes.

Instead, RocketSim takes a much more innovative approach. It runs as a separate macOS app and simply **watches the Simulator window** from the outside. It tracks which device is running, reads the window's dimensions and scale, and synchronizes its coordinate system with the simulator's. macOS allows apps to query window size, position, and scale, which is precisely how RocketSim aligns its overlays perfectly with the Simulator.

For pixel-perfect results, RocketSim **captures screenshots** using Apple's public screen-capture APIs, processes them internally, and draws rulers and overlays directly on the Simulator. It doesn't hack anything. It simply observes, analyzes, and adds a transparent layer above the simulator window.

The way it works is what makes RocketSim safe, stable, and allowed in the App Store.

RocketSim also handles practical tasks, such as simulating push notifications, deep links, and location updates. These don't require any tricks – they just use Apple's official command-line tools (`xcrun simctl push`, `openurl`, `location`, and so on). RocketSim simply wraps those commands in a clean UI that makes them far easier to trigger.

To summarize, RocketSim doesn't modify the simulator in any way. It watches the simulator, captures its output, and draws whatever you need on top. And that simplicity is exactly why it works so reliably.

If you're thinking what I'm thinking by now – yes, RocketSim and Inject actually complete each other. RocketSim lets you see what's wrong. Inject enables you to fix it on the spot. Let's sit back and enjoy that moment of discovery.

Final Thoughts and Takeaways

This chapter made me rethink what we call a design system. It reminded me of my early iOS days and those infamous "50 shades of gray" that somehow kept multiplying. There aren't many areas in iOS development that are so easy to start, and yet so easy to ruin over time.

So, what should we actually do?

It's tempting to believe there's a universal answer. A perfect token library. The ultimate component architecture. A structure that works for every team, every app, every designer.

But the truth is messier, because this topic is everything *but* coding.

If we want the best design system for our app, we should invest in our relationship with our designer. Invest in our workflow, communication, and the team's discipline. And understand these three brutal truths:

- **Most design systems fail because we built them too early, not because we chose the wrong tool.**

  Mikaela is the perfect example. Sometimes the most innovative system is no system at all.

- **The best design system is one we could delete in two years without anyone noticing.**

  We should build for flexibility, and remember Vincent's warning: *too many modifiers mean your system is broken.*

- **Our goal isn't a perfect system – it's shipping features without losing our mind over spacing and colors.**

  UI development needs to be predictable enough to let us focus on what users actually care about. Designers will always add grays – our job is making their chaos codable. Inject and RocketSim can help get us there faster.

These truths point to one conclusion:

The answer to a good design system isn't in the code. It's somewhere else entirely. Turns out, we've been holding it wrong the whole time.

Summary

When I planned the outline for this book, it was obvious that UI and design deserved an entire chapter. We build iOS apps not only because of the engineering challenges, but because design is the most immediate expression of our work – the part users actually touch. It's where code becomes experience.

In this chapter, we explored how teams create and maintain design systems, how tokens and themes shape consistency, and how components and view modifiers bring that system to life in code. We also examined collaboration with designers, the tension between simplicity and scale, and the reality behind tools like SwiftUI Previews, Inject, and RocketSim.

Design is fun to look at, and with SwiftUI, it's also fun to build. But as enjoyable as the visual layer is, great apps depend on more than their looks. In the next chapter, we move from the visible world to the invisible one – monitoring, logging, and understanding what really happens inside our apps once they're in the hands of users.

CHAPTER 7

Navigation and Routing

Coordinator was a good technique, but once you learn about swift-navigation, it's so good, you don't want to go back to UIKit.

—Zlatko Kuvendjiski

Introduction

In the previous chapter, we talked about design – a discipline that demands long-term thinking, consistency, and restraint. Navigation belongs to the same category, but we often treat it very differently. It sits at the intersection of UI, animations, and application logic. At scale, it quickly becomes one of the most complicated problems to get right.

Most experienced iOS developers eventually reach the same conclusion: navigation in iOS is still not solved. Apple has iterated on APIs, renamed types, and introduced new abstractions – yet teams continue to build their own solutions on top of them. The real question is not *whether* navigation is broken, but *where* it breaks, and *how* teams choose to fix it.

In this chapter, we will

- Walk through the evolution of navigation frameworks and patterns in iOS – and expose the uncomfortable truths behind them

- Examine a state-driven coordinator built by the Yazio team

- Review an imperative, UIKit-based coordinator used at Vivino

- Explore a tree-based navigation approach using the swift-navigation framework at Axon

159

© Avi Tsadok 2026
A. Tsadok, *Real-World iOS Development*, https://doi.org/10.1007/979-8-8688-2815-7_7

As with the rest of this book, this is not a *"how to navigate in SwiftUI"* chapter. Instead, it is a deep dive into real production systems, real constraints, and real trade-offs. Different teams made different choices for good reasons.

But before we get there, we need a bit of context. So, grab a pen and paper – it's time for a short history lesson.

Navigating Through Frameworks and Patterns

Imagine it's 2014. We're building an exciting new iOS app using UIKit - the framework we all know by heart. We begin with Storyboards, Apple's magical drag-and-drop interface builder introduced just three years earlier. It feels modern, visual, even fun... until it doesn't. Storyboards don't play nicely with the rising MVVM pattern, which promises cleaner separation and testability. So, like many teams, we abandon Storyboards and go "full code," wiring everything manually through `UINavigationController`.

But there's a tension: the view controller pushes the next screen, while the view model is supposed to decide *when* to push. Where does navigation logic really belong? We try moving it into the view model - and suddenly the view model grows large, awkward, and strangely aware of UIKit internals. It feels wrong.

And then, a new pattern enters the community: **the Coordinator**.

For iOS developers at the time, the Coordinator pattern felt like a revelation. Elegant. Decoupled. Testable. The perfect engineering solution we had been waiting for (well, that and a better IDE). Coordinators became a badge of architectural maturity. We wrote blog posts, presented the approach at meetups, and congratulated ourselves: finally, we nailed navigation.

Fast-forward to 2019. Apple introduces SwiftUI - a declarative UI framework that rewrites the rules. Navigation is no longer something we *perform*: it's something our *state* describes. `NavigationView` arrives, and with it, unsettling questions. Should we stay with UIKit? Should we move to SwiftUI? Should we build hybrids? And what does declarative navigation mean for MVVM - or for our beloved Coordinator? New blog posts emerge claiming MVVM is dead, Coordinators are obsolete, and no one is quite sure whether to believe them.

Then 2022 arrives. Apple ships `NavigationStack`, a brand-new model that promises to fix the problems of `NavigationView`. And suddenly, almost quietly, the Coordinator pattern resurfaces. Developers rediscover the need for explicit navigation decisions, flow orchestration, and separation from the UI layer.

What about MVVM? That's a story for later.

But if you've been an iOS developer for seven or eight years or more, you already know what this opening is hinting at:

iOS navigation has been a problem for more than a decade. And even in 2025, it's still not solved.

Let's dive in.

The Sad Truth

When I look back at the history of iOS development, I can't think of any area that has reinvented itself as often or as painfully as navigation. SwiftUI transformed how we build UI. Core Data morphed into SwiftData (well... sort of). But navigation? Navigation has shape-shifted more times than any other part of the framework.

Earlier, I said navigation doesn't have a solution, but that isn't entirely true. It *does* have a solution - just not the one any of us expected. Figure 7-1 illustrates the pattern most production apps rely on today: the **hybrid navigation solution**.

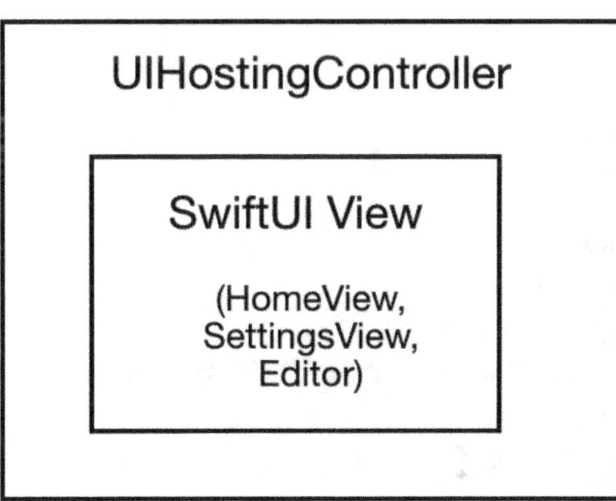

Figure 7-1. *Using UIHostingController for a hybrid navigation solution*

Figure 7-1 shows how we can navigate SwiftUI views using UIKit, what I call the **hybrid navigation solution**.

Let this sink in for a moment:

> *In late 2025, the most common navigation stack in shipping iOS apps is still* UINavigationController *- an 18-year-old imperative class - with SwiftUI views wrapped inside a* UIHostingController*.*

This phrase isn't a theoretical workaround or a niche trick. It's the production reality in banks, fitness apps, photo editors, global consumer products, and even apps from companies with hundreds of engineers. It's the default solution in the real world. And by the end of this chapter, we'll see why this sad truth becomes even more heartbreaking.

But before diving into all the ways SwiftUI and UIKit collide, let's first understand a simple question:

> *Why, after 18 years of iOS, is navigation still so complicated?*

The NavigationView Approach

When Apple unveiled SwiftUI in 2019, they sold us a dream: that navigation would finally be **declarative**. Just wrap your views in a NavigationView, use NavigationLink, and you're done.

```swift
struct UsersView: View {
    let users: [User]

    var body: some View {
        NavigationView {
            List(users) { user in
                NavigationLink(
                    destination: UserDetailsView(user: user)
                ) {
                    Text(user.name)
                }
            }
            .navigationTitle("Users")
        }
    }
}
```

At first glance, this looks perfectly reasonable. We present a list of users, and tapping one navigates to a `UserDetailsView`, passing the selected user. Looks innocent, right?

Now look closely at this line:

```
NavigationLink(
    destination: UserDetailsView(user: user)
)
```

This single line explains why so many developers struggled with SwiftUI navigation. It's a trap.

- The view knows exactly **which screen comes next** and what data it needs.

- The navigation decision lives **inside the list cell**.

- Deep linking requires **recreating the exact view hierarchy** or introducing hidden NavigationLinks.

- Testing? **Good luck** with that.

The core problem is that navigation is a side effect of rendering a row, not an explicit piece of state. That might be acceptable for demo apps and tutorials - but it doesn't scale to serious applications.

Want to navigate only after an API call completes? Welcome to invisible navigation links and zombie state flags:

```
struct UsersView: View {
    let users: [User]
    @State private var selectedUser: User?
    @State private var isActive = false

    var body: some View {
        NavigationView {
            List(users) { user in
                Button(user.name) {
                    loadUser(user)
                }
            }
            .background(
                NavigationLink(
```

```
                        destination: UserDetailsView(user: selectedUser),
                        isActive: $isActive,
                        label: { EmptyView() }
                    )
                )
                .navigationTitle("Users")
            }
        }

        private func loadUser(_ user: User) {
            Task {
                let fullUser = await fetchUser(user)
                selectedUser = fullUser
                isActive = true
            }
        }
    }
}
```

In this example, we fetch the user information and navigate to the new user details screen only afterward. Now, when a user tap triggered navigation, it is somehow ok and natural. However, the moment navigation becomes conditional or a function of external events, it forces us to fight the framework rather than sing with it. For three years, Apple let us suffer with that. Then, in iOS 16, they quietly admitted and shipped **NavigationStack**.

NavigationStack As a Turning Point

NavigationStack introduced a completely new navigation system. It wasn't just a name change – it was a totally new approach, which was different not only from SwiftUI's NavigationView but also from UIKit's UINavigationController. In the old NavigationView, we responded to user actions (and somewhat hacked it for other cases). In NavigationStack, we decouple the navigation state from the views, moving toward a data-driven approach. Instead of pushing views, we push data objects into a NavigationPath:

```swift
import SwiftUI

struct User: Identifiable, Hashable {
    let id = UUID()
    let name: String
}

struct UserDetailsView: View {
    let user: User

    var body: some View {
        Text("Selected user: \(user.name)")
            .navigationTitle(user.name)
    }
}

struct UsersView: View {
    let users: [User]
    @State private var path: [User] = []

    var body: some View {
        NavigationStack(path: $path) {
            List(users) { user in
                Button(user.name) {
                    path.append(user)
                }
            }
            .navigationTitle("Users")
            .navigationDestination(for: User.self) { user in
                UserDetailsView(user: user)
            }
        }
    }
}
```

While this code snippet appears more cumbersome than the previous
NavigationView example, it is more intuitive: upon user tapping, we add the user object
to the NavigationPath and, based on the object type, navigate the user to the appropriate

screen. This approach allows programmatic navigation, multiple types of destinations, and easier (much easier!) deep linking. More importantly, this design is much more type-safe and flexible.

So, are all our problems solved? For indie apps and small teams, often, yes. For scaled apps with multiple squads and millions of users? Far from it.

NavigationStack is excellent, but it still *ties navigation tightly to individual views*. In large codebases, we want the same centralization we already apply to UI components and design systems (remember the previous chapter?). Instead, navigation logic remains scattered: every view decides how to push, present, or animate.

That's acceptable for small apps, but for larger apps and teams, it just doesn't scale.

Apple gave us powerful tools to standardize buttons, colors, and typography across an app. For navigation? We're still on our own.

The current Navigation situation is why the Coordinator pattern, and its modern hybrids, remain alive and well in 2025. Let's look at real examples from the teams I interviewed.

Navigation in Reality

In practice, navigation looks very different depending on the app's size and the team behind it.

Among indie developers, it was surprisingly hard to find anyone still using the Coordinator pattern. **Mikaela**, for example, says she avoids it altogether, preferring to stick with `NavigationStack` and keep her apps simple. And it's not a matter of awareness - **Danijela** used coordinators extensively in her previous team, but as an indie developer today, she also chose to rely on pure `NavigationStack`. **Oliver** follows the same approach in his personal projects.

The reason is straightforward: the Coordinator is a robust solution, but to a problem that doesn't always exist. It's like buying a $400 cast-iron pan when all you're making is a fried egg. It works perfectly, looks great on Instagram, but the overhead isn't worth it when a $10 nonstick pan gets the egg on the plate just as fast.

Once an app grows to dozens of screens, multiple squads, and complex user flows, the story changes completely. To see what that looks like in practice, let's turn to **Noam** and the Yazio team to see how they handle navigation in a 100-million-download app.

A Real 2025 Coordinator: Yazio's First Session Flow

Noam and his team at Yazio use NavigationStack for internal routing, navigating between SwiftUI views. However, at their scale, they cannot settle for having the NavigationStack managed directly inside SwiftUI views. For a team of their size, navigation state needs to live elsewhere - or more precisely, inside a coordinator.

Let's look at how they approached this, starting with MealFirstSessionNavHost:

```swift
struct MealFirstSessionNavHost<StartContent: View>: View {
    @StateObject private var coordinator: FirstSessionFlowCoordinator
    @ViewBuilder private let startView: StartContent

    init(coordinator: FirstSessionFlowCoordinator, startView:
StartContent) {
        self._coordinator = .init(wrappedValue: coordinator)
        self.startView = startView
    }

    var body: some View {
        NavigationStack(path: $coordinator.routes) {
            startView
                .navigationBarBackButtonHidden()
                .navigationDestination(for: FirstSessionFlowCoordinator.
                Route.self) { route in
                    Group {
                        switch route {
                            case .landing:
                                MealFirstSessionLandingScre
                                en(viewModel: coordinator.
                                mealFirstSessionLandingViewModel)
                            case .add:
                                MealFirstSessionAddScreen(viewModel:
                                coordinator.mealFirstSessionAddViewModel)
                        }
                    }
```

```
                    .navigationBarBackButtonHidden()
            }
        }
    }
}
```

The code above is not the Coordinator itself, but a SwiftUI view that *hosts* a NavigationStack and resolves routes into screens using navigationDestination.

I assume you're familiar with how NavigationStack works (if not, Apple's docs are excellent). The interesting part is how it's driven from outside the view hierarchy.

One way to think about MealFirstSessionNavHost is as Noam's SwiftUI equivalent of UIKit's UINavigationController: it owns the navigation stack and is responsible for pushing new screens. The difference is that instead of pushing view controllers, it reacts to route values.

This view depends on two components: the coordinator (FirstSessionFlowCoordinator) and a starting view. The coordinator holds both the navigation path and the view models for the flow, while the NavHost is responsible only for executing navigation. Splitting into two components is a clear separation of concerns: routing and state live in the coordinator, while NavigationStack remains a purely declarative UI construct.

If that feels abstract, Figure 7-2 shows the same structure visually.

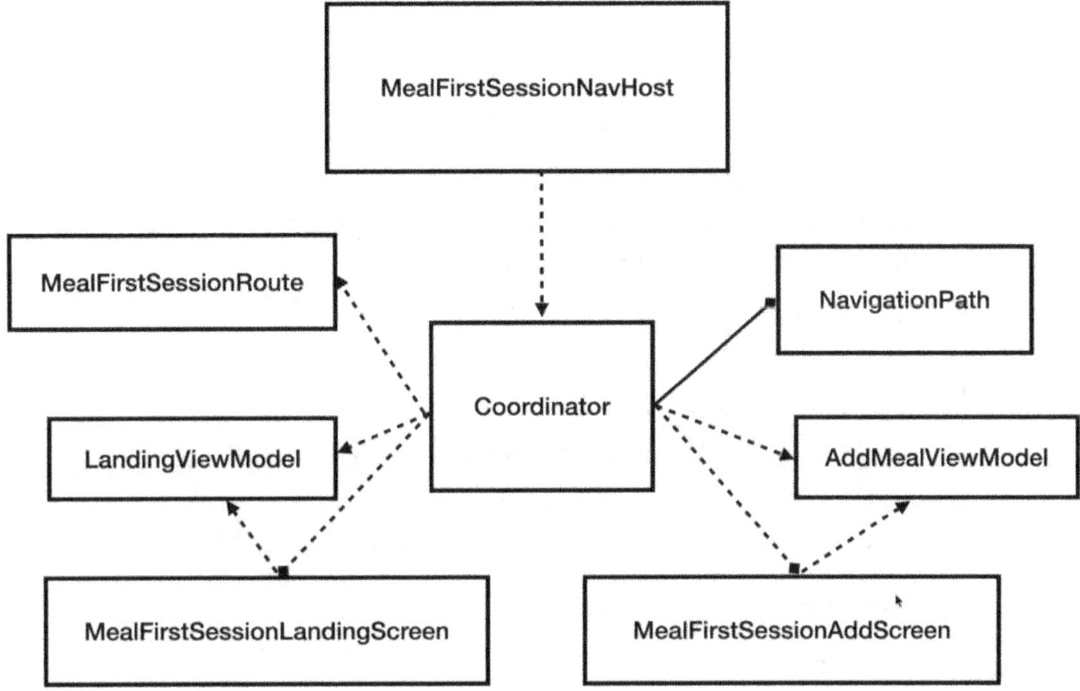

Figure 7-2. *UML diagram of Noam's flow-scoped coordinator pattern*

As the diagram in Figure 7-2 shows, the coordinator acts as a central hub: it owns the navigation path, creates the view models, and injects them into the screens. It is also a dependency of `MealFirstSessionNavHost`, which hosts the `NavigationStack`.

What's important here is the scope: this coordinator represents a *single flow*, not the entire app. This keeps navigation logic local, avoids a global routing bottleneck, and allows teams to reason about flows independently.

To better understand how this works in practice, let's look at the actual coordinator implementation.

```swift
public final class FirstSessionFlowCoordinator: ObservableObject {

    public enum OnFinish {
        case diary
        case addFood(foodtime: SharedCode.FoodTime)
    }

    enum Route {
        case landing
```

```
    case add
}

@Published var routes: [Route] = .init()

@Injected(\MealFirstSessionModule.
mealFirstSessionLandingViewModelFactory) private var
mealFirstSessionLandingViewModelFactory
@Injected(\MealFirstSessionModule.mealFirstSessionAddViewModelFactory)
private var mealFirstSessionAddViewModelFactory

lazy var mealFirstSessionLandingViewModel =
mealFirstSessionLandingViewModelFactory.creator(WeakRef(self))
lazy var mealFirstSessionAddViewModel =
mealFirstSessionAddViewModelFactory.creator(WeakRef(self))

let onFinish: (OnFinish) -> Void

public init(
    onFinish: @escaping (OnFinish) -> Void
) {
    self.onFinish = onFinish
}

public func start(_ mealFirstSession: SharedSwift.
MealFirstSessionVariant) -> UIViewController {
    let view = MealFirstSessionNavHost(
        coordinator: self,
        startView: start(mealFirstSession)
    )

    let viewController = UIHostingController(rootView: view)
    viewController.modalPresentationStyle = .fullScreen

    return viewController
}

private func start(_ mealFirstSession: SharedSwift.
MealFirstSessionVariant) -> some View {
    Group {
```

```
        switch mealFirstSession {
            case .variantB:
                MealFirstSessionAddScreen(viewModel: self.
                mealFirstSessionAddViewModel)

            default:
                MealFirstSessionLandingScreen(viewModel: self.
                mealFirstSessionLandingViewModel)
            }
        }
    }
}

extension FirstSessionFlowCoordinator: SharedCode.
MealFirstSessionNavigator {
    public func close() {
        onFinish(.diary)
    }

    public func navigateToAddFood(foodTime: FoodTime) {
        onFinish(.addFood(foodtime: foodTime))
    }

    public func navigateToMealFirstSessionAdd() {
        routes.append(.add)  // Internal navigation via @Published array
    }

    public func navigateToMealFirstSessionLanding() {
        routes.append(.landing)
    }
}
```

In this (quite long, I admit) code example, we can see Yazio's coordinator implementation. There are a few things worth highlighting.

First, the coordinator is based on an enum called Route. Each case represents a screen (or step) in this flow, and routes is the current navigation state - the stack of route values. In other words, it plays the same role as NavigationPath, but instead of storing a NavigationPath, Yazio binds NavigationStack directly to routes:

```
NavigationStack(path: $coordinator.routes) {
```

Once the `routes` array is observable, the NavHost has a direct link to coordinator state. Appending a new route immediately updates the SwiftUI navigation stack.

Second, the coordinator exposes intent-focused navigation methods, for example:

- `navigateToMealFirstSessionAdd()` appends `.add` to `routes`, effectively pushing the next step in the flow.

- In other places, the coordinator may call an `onFinish(...)` callback to hand control back to the parent flow.

Finally, notice the two `start()` functions:

```
public func navigateToAddFood(foodTime: FoodTime) {
      onFinish(.addFood(foodtime: foodTime))
   }

public func navigateToMealFirstSessionAdd() {
      routes.append(.add)
   }
```

The private `start()` function constructs the initial SwiftUI view for the flow. The public `start()` function wraps that view in a `UIHostingController` and returns a UIKit view controller. This is the bridge that allows Yazio to keep a `UINavigationController` above SwiftUI flows (Figure 7-3).

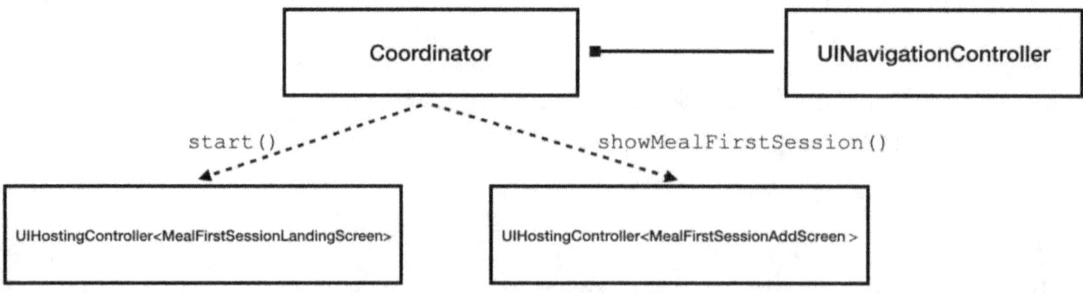

Figure 7-3. *The coordinator's public `start()` bridges SwiftUI into a UIKit navigation stack*

This hybrid approach is not accidental. At Yazio's scale, it brings several advantages:

- **Explicit Lifecycle and Entry Points:** UIKit navigation is imperative and explicit, which makes flow ownership and debugging more deterministic. SwiftUI's state-driven model is powerful, but harder to reason about at the boundaries of large flows.

- **Cross-Technology Navigation:** A root `UINavigationController` provides a single navigation model across UIKit and SwiftUI screens.

- **SwiftUI Limitations:** Custom transitions, resets, and debugging are still easier to control in UIKit than in pure SwiftUI navigation.

- **Gradual Adoption:** Teams can move one flow at a time to SwiftUI without rewriting the entire app shell.

Even with the progress in `NavigationStack`, many teams still keep UIKit navigation at the top level. Next, let's look at a different coordinator style from Vivino.

UIKit-Based Coordinator

What stood out in Yazio's example is the clear separation between **internal flows**, which are handled by `NavigationStack`, and **larger, cross-feature flows**, which UIKit still manages.

The example Monika shared from Vivino approaches the problem from a different angle - and as a result, looks very different.

At Vivino, UIKit handles navigation. The coordinator is built on UIKit's navigation system and has two primary goals: **standardize navigation actions** (such as push and present) and **explicitly manage the lifecycle of navigation flows**.

Before diving into the implementation details, it's essential to understand that this coordinator is not a lightweight helper. It is core infrastructure. Let's move to the BaseCoordinator class.

The BaseCoordinator

We begin by looking at the foundation of Vivino's navigation system: the BaseCoordinator base class. This class serves as the backbone for all navigation flows in the app.

```swift
@MainActor
open class BaseCoordinator {
    /// The parent coordinator, typically the one who initiated this
        coordinator.
    weak private(set) var parent: BaseCoordinator?

    /// List of child coordinators initiated by this coordinator,
        representing nested flows.
    private(set) var childCoordinators: [BaseCoordinator] = []

    /// A collection of Combine subscribers used within the coordinator.
    open var subscribers = Set<AnyCancellable>()

    /// A publisher signalling the completion of this coordinator's
        lifecycle.
    public let coordinatorDidFinish = PassthroughSubject<Void, Never>()

    /// The navigation controller used for managing the coordinated flow.
    public var navigationController: UINavigationController

    private var started: Bool = false
    ...
}
```

By introducing a shared base class, Vivino enforces not only a standard **navigation policy** but also consistent **behavior** across teams. Earlier in this chapter, we saw why indie developers like Mikaela and Danijela often avoid coordinators - they simply don't need this level of structure. For a product at Vivino's scale, however, alignment is critical.

The BaseCoordinator encapsulates navigation state (started), lifecycle signaling (coordinatorDidFinish), ownership of a UINavigationController, and hierarchical relationships between parent and child coordinators. In other words, a coordinator in Vivino's system represents a **flow** that lives within a broader hierarchy of other flows.

We saw a similar concept in Yazio's example, but Vivino takes it a step further. Looking at the apps themselves helps explain why: Vivino's navigation experience is deeper and more branched, spanning millions of wines, social interactions, and e-commerce journeys. Managing these paths without explicit flow ownership would be extremely difficult. For Vivino, hierarchical coordinators are not a nice-to-have - they are essential.

Now, let's move and try to understand what each Coordinator is capable of.

Exploring Coordinator Actions

If the purpose of Vivino's coordinators is centralization and lifecycle control, the navigateTo function is where that intent becomes concrete:

```swift
open func navigateTo(viewController: UIViewController, action:
NavigationAction) {
    switch action {
    case .push(let animated, let navBarHidden):
        guard started else {
            startByPushing(viewController: viewController, animated:
            animated)
            return
        }
        navigationController.setNavigationBarHidden(navBarHidden,
        animated: false)
        navigationController.pushViewController(viewController,
        animated: animated)

    case .present(let style, let animated, let navigationBarHidden):
        guard started else {
            startByPresenting(viewController: viewController,
            style: style, animated: animated, navigationBarHidden:
            navigationBarHidden)
            return
        }
        viewController.modalPresentationStyle = style
        navigationController.present(viewController, animated:
        animated)

    case .presentInBottomSheet(let config, let animated):
        guard started else {
            startByPresentingInBottomSheet(viewController:
            viewController, config: config, animated: animated)
            return
```

```
        }
        let bottomSheet = instantiateBottomSheet(viewController:
        viewController, config: config)
        navigationController.present(bottomSheet, animated: animated)
    }
}
```

At first glance, the navigateTo function appears to be a wrapper for navigation actions. However, the most crucial detail is actually the started flag we mentioned earlier.

Before a Coordinator starts, it treats the navigation actions as **flow initialization**. Once the Coordinator is active, the same actions simply push or present screens on the existing stack. This distinction might seem odd at first, but it gives Vivino specific control over entry points.

Entry points are vital in a complex navigation system, and they define the boundaries between the different flows, or in our case, different coordinators. Notice that the Coordinator doesn't decide what happens, but rather how it happens.

Now, let's see the dual-start logic.

Understanding the Start Logic

At this point, it is too early to understand why entry points are so important in Vivino's Coordinator pattern. Let's review the present action from the navigateTo() function:

```
case .present(let style, let animated, let navigationBarHidden):
    guard started else {
        startByPresenting(viewController: viewController,
        style: style, animated: animated, navigationBarHidden:
        navigationBarHidden)
        return
    }
    viewController.modalPresentationStyle = style
    navigationController.present(viewController, animated:
    animated)
```

Based on the code, if the Coordinator hasn't started yet, it calls a private function called startByPresenting(). Let's see how this function looks:

```swift
func startByPresenting(viewController: UIViewController, style:
UIModalPresentationStyle, animated: Bool, navigationBarHidden: Bool
= true) {
        if let alertViewController = viewController as? UIAlertController {
            // If the view controller is an alert controller, present it
                directly
            presentAlertController(alertController: alertViewController,
            animated: animated)
            return
        }

        let presentedNavigationController = BaseNavigationController(rootVi
        ewController: viewController)
        presentedNavigationController.modalPresentationStyle = style
        presentedNavigationController.setNavigationBarHidden(navigationBarH
        idden, animated: false)
        presentedNavigationController.onDidDisappear.sink { [weak self] in
            PersistedLogger.general.log("Modally presented coordinator: \
            (String(describing: self)) did disappear")
            self?.onFinish()
        }.store(in: &subscribers)

        // Check if something is already presented else present on the
            origin navigation controller.
        if let presentedVC = navigationController.presentedViewController {
            presentedVC.present(presentedNavigationController, animated:
            animated)
        } else {
            let originNavigationController = navigationController
            originNavigationController.present(presentedNavigation
            Controller, animated: animated)
        }
        navigationController = presentedNavigationController
        started = true
    }
```

Vivino's `navigateTo` function isn't pretty - and that's precisely the point. It's long because UIKit navigation is full of edge cases that Apple never fully centralized.

This single function performs several critical tasks: it starts a new coordinator modally, ensures the flow runs on a fresh navigation stack, manages lifecycle completion, and updates the coordinator so that it now controls the presented navigation controller. In short, it starts a new flow by presenting a brand-new navigation controller modally and explicitly handing control over to the coordinator.

Earlier in the chapter, I mentioned that coordinators often exist to compensate for gaps in Apple's navigation APIs - and this function is a perfect example. What happens when we pass in a `UIAlertController`? What if another view controller is already being presented? How do we consistently log navigation events to make debugging easier? Vivino doesn't leave those questions to chance. They handle them centrally once and enforce the same behavior across the entire system.

This is what coordinators still do better than `NavigationStack` in 2026: they wrap Apple's incomplete APIs in one place, so no team has to solve the same problems twice.

Now that we've explored some of the coordinator's most important responsibilities, let's visualize this behavior (Figure 7-4).

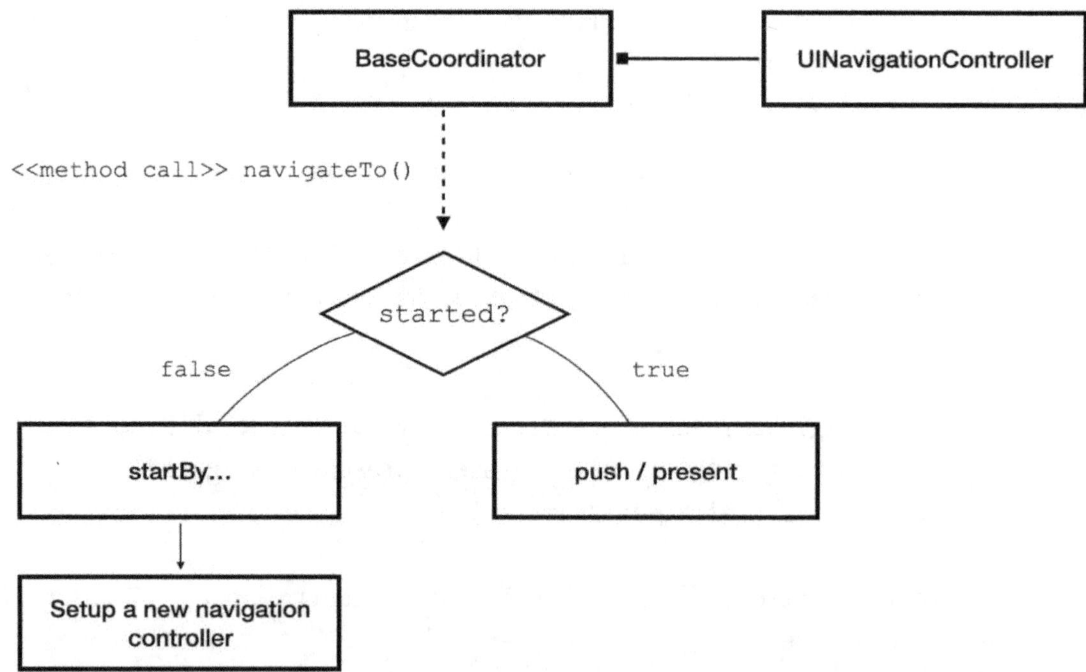

Figure 7-4. Vivino's Base Coordinator starting logic

Figure 7-4 illustrates the core control flow of Vivino's coordinator pattern. It shows how the coordinator behaves differently when a flow is already active versus when we start it for the first time. More importantly, it highlights how Vivino addresses some of iOS's long-standing shortcomings in navigation, though, as we'll see, not without trade-offs.

At this point, you might be wondering: where does SwiftUI fit into all of this? We already know that Vivino uses SwiftUI extensively.

To answer that, let's look at their hybrid solution.

Including SwiftUI Views

In Yazio's example, we saw how Noam and his team centralized the creation of UIHostingController, enabling a hybrid approach that combines UINavigationController with NavigationStack. Vivino takes a different path. Even though they chose not to rely on SwiftUI's navigation system, they still provide a clean way to integrate SwiftUI views into their UIKit-based coordinator.

Here's how they do it:

```
open func navigateTo(view: some View, action: NavigationAction,
configuration: HostingControllerConfiguration = .default) {
        let hostingController = view.toHostingController(configuration:
        configuration)
        navigateTo(viewController: hostingController, action: action)
    }
```

Vivino's approach is based on a technique called **method forwarding**. This overload of navigateTo accepts a SwiftUI View, wraps it in a UIHostingController, and then forwards the call to the original UIKit-based navigateTo method we examined earlier.

For Vivino's developers, this means that navigating to a SwiftUI screen is a straightforward, first-class operation without duplicating navigation logic or leaking UIKit concerns into the view layer.

When we look at Yazio's and Vivino's coordinators, we can clearly see two different navigation philosophies.

Vivino's coordinator is **imperative**. It is built on top of UINavigationController, navigation is expressed as explicit commands, and the flow lifecycle is clearly defined through start and finish points. Control is centralized, predictable, and deliberately explicit.

Yazio, on the other hand, takes a **state-driven (or stack-oriented)** approach. Navigation is modeled as a state using SwiftUI's `NavigationStack`, and the UI reacts automatically when that state changes. There are no explicit push or pop commands; navigation is a consequence of state mutation.

Both approaches are valid, proven, and widely used in production apps.

But this raises an interesting question: **is there a third way?**

In Chapter 2, Zlatko mentioned a set of tools created by Point-Free that rethink common architectural problems through state and composition. One of those tools focuses specifically on navigation: **swift-navigation.**

So far, every solution we've seen has focused on improving navigation. **swift-navigation** asks a different question: What if we *constrain* navigation instead? Let's explore how it approaches navigation and what problems it tries to solve.

Tree-Based Navigation with Swift-Navigation

Imagine looking at our app's navigation as a decision tree rather than a stack of screens. At any point, the app is in a specific node of that tree, and from that node, there's a closed set of possible destinations. This might sound very intuitive at first, but that's not precisely how SwiftUI or UIKit navigation works. In classing iOS navigation, we push (or present) screens on top of each other, adding them to a "stack." The stack is our navigation "history," so we can also pop them back and "go back in time." But a tree-based navigation is fundamentally a different mental mode.

In other words, stack-based navigation answers **"What was the previous screen?",** while tree-based navigation answers **"What are the valid next states?".** Notice these are entirely different questions.

It's worth noting that swift-navigation is not limited to tree-based navigation. As Zlatko pointed out during our conversation, the framework also supports traditional stack-based navigation. In practice, this means teams can mix both approaches depending on the problem they're solving. For example, an onboarding flow might naturally follow a stack-based sequence of screens, while the main product experience might benefit from the stricter structure of tree-based navigation. The framework allows both models to coexist in the same app.

To understand tree-based navigation better, let's look at Figure 7-5.

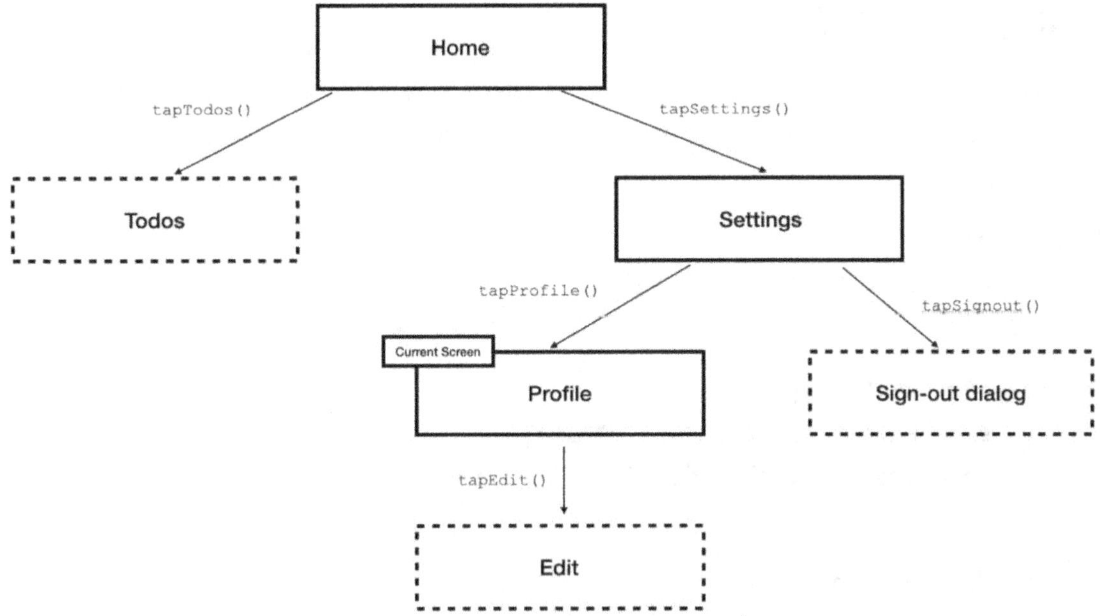

Figure 7-5. *An example of a tree-based navigation diagram*

Figure 7-5 shows a (partial) tree-based navigation map of a typical mobile app. The user starts on the Home screen and has only two possible paths: either navigate to the Todos screen or to the Settings screen. From Settings, the user can continue either to the Profile screen or open a Sign-out dialog. If the Profile screen is active, the user can then navigate further to the Profile Edit screen.

This navigation map should feel very familiar - there is nothing unusual or exotic here. What *is* interesting, however, is that at every screen the set of possible navigation actions is strictly limited. From Home, we can only go to Settings or Todos. There is no way, by design, to jump directly to Profile or Edit.

At a small scale, this constraint may feel obvious. At a large scale, enforcing it - *even at compile time* - becomes critical.

One of the core strengths of tree-based navigation, and of the swift-navigation framework specifically, is its ability to encode these constraints directly into code. Let's see how that looks in practice.

Reflecting the Tree in an Enum

When demonstrating navigation code, we usually start with the UIKit or SwiftUI layer. In this case, we'll start somewhere else entirely: the view model. More specifically, with an Enum.

```swift
@Observable
final class HomeViewModel {

    @CasePathable
    enum Destination {
        case settings(SettingsViewModel)
        case todos(TodosViewModel)
    }

    var destination: Destination?

    func goToSettings() {
        destination = .settings(SettingsViewModel())
    }
}
```

This example is intentionally partial, but it already contains the most important piece of the navigation system: the Destination Enum.

This Enum defines not only the *possible* navigation routes from the Home screen, but also the *only* ones. Home can navigate to Settings or Todos, and nothing else. That limitation is not enforced by convention, documentation, or discipline; it is enforced by the type system.

Now look closely at the goToSettings() function:

```swift
destination = .settings(SettingsViewModel())
```

This single line performs the navigation. Assigning a value to the destination variable activates a branch in the navigation tree. SwiftUI reacts to this state change and presents the corresponding screen (we'll see how in the next section).

At this point, you may be asking: **Where is the coordinator?**

Here's the answer: **the enum *is* the coordinator.**

Let's break that down.

Enum As a Coordinator

We usually think of a Coordinator as an Object. But that thinking is, how do I put that? A little rigid. Because "an Object" is an implementation detail. A Coordinator is a role, not (necessarily) a class.

At its core, a coordinator is responsible for three things:

- Defining the allowed navigation routes

- Owning the currently active route

- Controlling the lifecycle of a navigation flow

In our ViewModel, the Enum (and the `destination` variable) clearly fulfill these three responsibilities. The Enum lists every screen the Home is allowed to navigate to, the destination property holds the current active child flow, and notice it is also an optional – that signals if the flows started. If the destination property is nil, the flow ended.

So now we understand this part of the equation – the view model. But how does setting the destination property perform the actual navigation? It's time to turn to SwiftUI.

Using a Special NavigationDestination

We've just learned how a simple Enum declaration and a variable can become a Coordinator. But I must admit, you won't find any special magic in the SwiftUI part as well (honestly, I find this extreme simplicity magical, but that's me).

So, let's have a look at the `HomeView` structure:

```
NavigationStack {
    Button("Go to Settings") {
        viewModel.goToSettings()
    }
    .navigationDestination(item: $viewModel.destination.settings) {
    settingsVM in
        SettingsView(viewModel: settingsVM)
    }
}
```

We can see that `HomeView` is still built on a familiar SwiftUI `NavigationStack`, using the `navigationDestination` view modifier. However, this is *not* the standard `navigationDestination` most SwiftUI developers are used to. This variant comes from the **swift-navigation** framework.

This version:

- Accepts a Binding<**Optional**<Value>>

- Shows the destination only when the binding is non-nil

- Automatically dismisses the screen when the binding becomes nil.

Accepting a `nil` value is a crucial detail. It's what allows the Enum to act as a coordinator - activating and dismissing screens purely through state changes.

Now look closely at this line:

```
item: $viewModel.destination.settings
```

Remember the @CasePathable macro from the view model? This is what makes it possible to "zoom in" on a specific enum case and extract its associated value *only* when that case is active. Without it, this style of navigation would be significantly more verbose and error-prone.

As I said earlier, simplicity can be powerful.

But this approach doesn't stop at simple navigation. It also addresses one of the most fragile parts of mobile apps: deep linking.

Deep Linking Done Right

Deep linking tends to be flaky for the same reason many other systems become flaky: we often implement different logic for different entry points. This problem frequently occurs in testing (especially UI testing), but it's just as common in navigation.

If deep links follow a different code path than regular user interactions, inconsistencies are almost guaranteed.

Because swift-navigation uses a tree-based approach, it enforces valid navigation paths at compile time. In fact, deep linking becomes nothing more than state construction.

Here's how we can navigate directly from the Home screen to the Profile Edit screen, automatically creating the Settings and Profile screens along the way:

```swift
func goToProfileEditScreen() {
    destination = .settings(
        SettingsViewModel(destination: .profile(
            ProfileViewModel(destination: .editProfile(
                EditProfileViewModel()
            ))
        ))
    )
}
```

This function works by *chaining view models together*, setting the destination for each level of the tree. The result is an entirely constructed navigation path, without manually pushing screens, mutating stacks, or risking invalid transitions.

So, we saw how swift-navigation navigates a tree-based approach and handles complex tasks like deep linking in an elegant, straightforward way. But is there a downside to using swift-navigation framework? So, let's talk about flexibility for a second.

Flexible Trees...?

So far, tree-based navigation looks elegant, safe, and expressive. But those same strengths can also turn into real-world constraints.

By defining a closed set of destinations, we intentionally limit flexibility. In many cases, that's exactly what we want, but not always.

Think back to the A/B testing chapter. What if we want to experiment with multiple onboarding flows? Or dynamically reorder steps? Tree-based navigation assumes structure and locality: main flows leading to sub-flows, which lead to deeper sub-flows.

In reality, many apps also require *cross-cutting navigation*:

- "From anywhere, open the paywall"

- "If the session expires, force login and return"

- "Open support chat regardless of current flow"

These aren't edge cases - they're standard product requirements.

Tree-based navigation can support these scenarios, but not without additional abstraction. At some point, the strictness that gives us safety can start working against us.

swift-navigation is powerful, but it is not a silver bullet.

And that leads me to final thoughts about navigation.

Final Thoughts

By now, one pattern should be clear: there is no single "correct" way to handle navigation.

Indie developers like Danijela and Mikaela are pleased with the pure `NavigationStack`. Vivino relies on a UIKit-based coordinator for explicit lifecycle control. Yazio uses a hybrid approach. Axon adopts swift-navigation and treats enums as coordinators.

Each solution reflects the scale, constraints, and priorities of the team behind it.

Navigation is a complex problem that sits at the intersection of product needs, engineering discipline, and long-term maintainability. SwiftUI improved the situation, but it didn't fully solve it.

Will Apple ever ship a `NavigationStack 2`? Maybe. Until then, iOS developers will keep doing what they've always done: building their own abstractions around one of the most fundamental parts of every app.

Summary

Navigation sits at the heart of every iOS app, touching user experience, architecture, and long-term maintainability. In this chapter, we explored why it remains one of the most challenging problems to solve at scale - and why no single API or framework fully addresses it.

We looked back at the evolution of navigation in iOS, examined two production-grade Coordinator implementations from Yazio and Vivino, and explored a fundamentally different, tree-based approach using the swift-navigation framework. Each solution reflects a different philosophy: state-driven, imperative, and structural. None is universally correct, but each is correct in the proper context.

The key takeaway is not which navigation system to choose, but *why* teams choose differently. Navigation decisions are architectural decisions, and they must align with team size, product complexity, experimentation needs, and long-term ownership.

In the next chapter, we move down the stack to another area where similar trade-offs emerge: data management. As with navigation, the challenge is not learning the APIs, but designing systems that survive real-world complexity.

CHAPTER 8

Data Management and Persistence

The best user experience comes from interacting with a single, centralized data store. If you structure it with a store and sync, it's not that complicated. Most interactions should be optimistic - waiting for the server only matters in rare cases.

—Krzysztof Zabłocki

Introduction

If navigation moves users between screens, data moves truth **through the app** - and truth is what users actually trust. Get it wrong, and no amount of polish saves the experience.

Which data is the source of truth? How many copies of that truth are acceptable? And how much inconsistency are we willing to tolerate in exchange for simplicity, performance, or speed?

These are not abstract questions. They shape offline behavior, synchronization bugs, user trust, and how confidently a team can evolve its codebase months or years later.

In this chapter, we will

- Explore **what "truth" really means** in a mobile app - and why every copy is already a little outdated

- Uncover the tension between **simplicity and responsibility** - and when one must win over the other

A. Tsadok, *Real-World iOS Development*, https://doi.org/10.1007/979-8-8688-2815-7_8

- Examine **different levels of persistence** and their real costs - from zero ownership to complete control

- See how teams **choose the right tools** - not as a starting point, but as the consequence of earlier decisions

To understand data reliability, we first need to step back from Core Data versus SwiftData debates and examine the underlying trade-offs teams are actually making. Data isn't just bits on the device - it's the **truth users rely on**. This chapter is about deciding how much of that truth we're willing to own.

The Importance of Data

At this stage of the book, we've discussed architecture, design, testing, and navigation. But most apps ultimately revolve around data. Without it, they're just collections of buttons, screens, and titles - no matter how elegant the design or clean the navigation. *Vivino* provides wine information, *Yazio* tracks food, *Axon* stores recordings, and banking apps guard financial records. Strip the data away, and these apps become practically useless. Because data is so valuable, users care about one thing above all else: **reliability**.

But what do we actually mean when we say *"reliable data"*? Are we talking about crashes? About *Core Data* versus *SwiftData*, *Realm* versus *GRDB*, *CloudKit*? No - those are implementation details - important ones, but not the real question. To understand data reliability, we need to step beyond frameworks and tools - and look at truth itself.

What Is the Truth?

In many apps, the backend is considered the source of truth. A single database shared across users and services represents the "final" version of the data. At least, that's the assumption.

Now imagine what happens when we perform a network request and fetch some of that data into the app. We parse it into models, store it in memory, and treat it as accurate. But in that moment, we've made a copy - and with data, copies have consequences.

While our app is working with its local data, the backend may already have changed. Another user, another device, or another service may have modified the same record. So, the question becomes uncomfortable: Are we still showing reliable information to the user?

The ancient Greek philosopher **Heraclitus** famously said:

"You cannot step into the same river twice."

What he meant was that reality is in constant motion. Any snapshot of it is already outdated the moment it exists.

In this metaphor, the backend is the river. Our app state is a cup of water taken from it. The copy isn't wrong - we didn't fetch it incorrectly. It's simply that the truth has already moved on.

And fetching data from the network and presenting it is only the simplest version of this story. In real apps, data rarely takes such a short, clean path. In real life, data items *go through a journey*, so let's reveal the journey of our data.

The Journey of Our Data

When I talk about a "journey" for data, you might first think of the trip from the backend to the device. And yes - that is a journey. But it only takes time; it doesn't change the data itself.

It's the path data takes after it lands on the device, from the moment we parse it from a network response to the point where we present it to the user or use it to drive a business decision inside the app.

That journey is far more interesting - and far more dangerous.

Let's make this concrete.

Imagine a straightforward app that displays a list of recipes. We store the recipes in a backend service, and the app performs a GET request to fetch them. The response is parsed into a straightforward data model:

```swift
import Foundation

struct Recipe: Identifiable, Codable {
    let id: UUID
    let title: String
    let ingredients: [String]
```

```
    let instructions: String
    let preparationTimeMinutes: Int
}
```

In the simplest case, we could display this array of `Recipe` objects directly using a *SwiftUI List*. That would be a very short journey: backend ➤ parsed model ➤ UI.

But in practice, working with this raw model directly in SwiftUI is often uncomfortable.

For example, `preparationTimeMinutes` isn't formatted for presentation, and an array of ingredients isn't ideal for display inside a list cell. So, we introduce another model, one that better fits the needs of the UI:

```
Import Foundation

struct RecipeViewModel: Identifiable {
    let id: UUID
    let title: String
    let ingredientsText: String
    let preparationTimeText: String
}
```

And we add an explicit transformation between the two:

```
Import Foundation

extension RecipeViewModel {
    init(recipe: Recipe) {
        self.id = recipe.id
        self.title = recipe.title
        self.ingredientsText = recipe.ingredients.joined(separator: ", ")
        self.preparationTimeText = "\(recipe.preparationTimeMinutes) min"
    }
}
```

This transition is small, intentional, and harmless. The data hasn't really changed - only its shape and presentation. But at a larger scale, each step adds logic, formatting, and context, until the UI data looks nothing like the original.

Can we still call it "the truth"?

And more importantly, do we even need to?

These are not purely technical questions. They're product decisions. In some industries, such as banking, maintaining a tight connection to the source of truth is critical. In others, such as consumer or creative apps, the user experience matters far more than strict fidelity to the original data snapshot.

This journey, how far data travels, how many shapes it takes, and how loosely it remains connected to its origin, is at the heart of data management. And just like everything else in this book, the "right" answer depends on the product, the industry, and the scale of the team.

Now, it's a good way to learn how different teams tackle layers of data.

Negotiating with the Truth

In the previous section, we tried to define what "truth" means when dealing with data in our apps. We saw why moving away from the original model we fetched from the backend makes it harder to treat that data as entirely true. And sometimes, that's perfectly fine.

Being strict about constantly working with the original backend model comes with a cost. There's the cost of additional network requests, as well as a cost to the user experience. Reloading data every time introduces latency and makes the app feel less responsive - a little closer to a website than a native application.

However, there's another price we pay when we work directly with backend data models, and that's something I call **developer experience**.

Backend developers rarely design models with SwiftUI Lists or collection views in mind. Their structure usually reflects the needs of multiple clients and services, and they're often optimized for smaller payloads and faster network responses. From an iOS developer's perspective, this can make them inconvenient to work with when it's time to present data on screen.

In other words, staying very close to the "truth" can make life harder once those models reach the UI layer, and this is where negotiation begins.

Every team ends up negotiating between truth, user experience, and developer experience. How much data do we fetch? How often do we refresh it? How far are we willing to reshape it to fit our UI and codebase, knowing that each transformation moves us a little further away from the original source?

We'll start by looking at our two indie developers - *Mikaela Caron* and *Danijela Vrzan* - and see how they choose to negotiate with the truth, and just as importantly, what costs they deliberately refuse to pay.

Keep It Simple

By Chapter 8, one thing has become clear: indie developers tend to optimize for simplicity - sometimes aggressively so. Should we expect four or five layers of data models, a full-featured persistent store, and sophisticated caching strategies? Probably not.

Let's start with the interesting example of *Mikaela Caron*.

Server-Side Swift

Mikaela builds and maintains her own backend service, giving her complete control over the data's shape. This full control is a common reality in indie development and directly affects how data flows through the app.

On the client side, she starts by parsing the network response using a DTO (*Data Transfer Object*). When that DTO isn't ideal for presentation, she converts it into a view model - similar to the transformation we saw earlier in *The Journey of Our Data*.

That conversion is intentionally the **only** transformation step in her data flow.

Mikaela deliberately avoids local persistence. There is no database, no offline support, and no syncing logic to maintain. By doing so, she avoids an **entire class of problems**: migrations, stale data, conflict resolution, and long-term maintenance.

One remaining challenge of relying solely on the backend is API evolution. Over time, responses change, and the client must handle these changes carefully. Larger teams often address this through formal API versioning, treating the API as a long-lived public contract.

Mikaela takes a simpler approach. When a breaking change is needed, she creates a new endpoint. It's a form of versioning - just not a formal one. For an indie developer who owns both sides of the wire, this trade-off keeps the system easy to reason about and cheap to maintain.

Another thing to note here - because *Mikaela* controls both sides (backend and client), she uses the same model structure and shares the same DTO with her backend service (***Vapor***, for that matter). This alignment results in fewer translations and fewer mismatches. When talking about "being close to the truth," this is a strong example of how simplicity and low scale are actually an advantage.

Now, let's turn to an even more straightforward approach: iCloud Syncing.

Using SwiftData and iCloud Syncing

Mikaela made a conscious effort to control both the backend and the client, resulting in strong alignment between the two. The data types defined on the backend closely match those she uses in her apps. By keeping that alignment tight, she avoids many of the usual transformation and sync problems that come with local persistence.

Yet other indie developers take a different path.

Danijela Vrzan chose a very different approach, combining *SwiftData* and iCloud syncing. Not many iOS developers are aware of this, but Apple provides a built-in way to sync a local *SwiftData* (or *Core Data*) store with the user's iCloud account via **CloudKit** - no custom backend required. The local store provides fast reads and offline access, while CloudKit propagates changes across all devices signed in with the same Apple ID.

Is it perfect? No. Developers have minimal control over how the sync behaves, debugging user data is difficult, and perhaps most importantly, it only works within Apple's ecosystem. For teams like *Vivino* or *Yazio*, these limitations are deal-breakers. For *Danijela*, they are acceptable trade-offs that dramatically simplify her workflow.

At first glance, the difference might seem mostly about tooling: custom backend versus *CloudKit*. In reality, they represent two fundamentally different philosophies for indie data handling - one prioritizing total control and simplicity, the other accepting delegation for speed and a seamless offline experience.

In a way, both *Mikaela* and *Danijela* live in the tough-but-limitless world of indie development, where they practically can make choices that suit their needs perfectly. Now, let's step up our observation and see how *Vincent* tackles that issue.

Fintech and the Truth

At the time of writing, *Vincent Pradeilles* works at *Photoroom*, but years before that, he worked in the fintech industry, developing apps for banks. If you've read the book up to this point, you already know this, and you also know that fintech apps come with special requirements.

One of those requirements is ***accuracy***. When it comes to data, fintech apps must stay as close to real values as possible. Earlier, we talked about *"being close to the truth,"* but in the fintech world, that idea carries far more weight. If an app shows the wrong number of likes on a post, the consequences are usually negligible. But showing incorrect information about a transaction or an account balance is a very different story.

Because of that, when working on banking apps, *Vincent's* team deliberately ***avoided using a persistent store***. Their goal was to reduce the risk of displaying outdated information. This might sound contradictory, especially after I opened the chapter by arguing that any copy of data fetched from the network is, in some sense, already outdated. But that argument was meant to illustrate a concept, not to suggest that all copies are equally problematic.

In practice, *Vincent* and his team did everything they could to stay as close as possible to the backend, their single source of truth. And that brings us to an interesting question: if truth is not that critical, what do teams actually gain by moving it closer to the app? Let's see how *Vivino* tackles that and how it relates to the architecture chapter.

Truth at Scale – Vivino's Layered Approach

If we go back to Chapter 2, we can see the multi-layered architecture Vivino chose for its app. That decision wasn't the result of watching YouTube videos about "how to build the perfect app" - it came from careful thinking about how the architecture should serve the team's needs over time.

The same pragmatic thinking shapes how Vivino models its data. Rather than relying on a single model type, the team chose a layered approach, introducing multiple model types to keep responsibilities clear and boundaries explicit.

These are the data types *Vivino* uses in the app:

- **DTOs (Data Transfer Objects):** Lightweight structures used to fetch and parse data from the backend. This use of DTOs is similar to what we saw with Mikaela in the *Server-side Swift* section. DTOs help separate backend parsing concerns from the rest of the app and are a common practice in larger teams.

- **Realm Objects:** Vivino uses Realm as its persistent store. When an app relies on local persistence, it's usually a good idea to isolate database-specific models from the rest of the system. Realm objects serve that purpose and never leak into business logic or UI layers.

- **Raw Data Models:** After data is fetched from the backend via DTOs and stored locally using Realm objects, Vivino still needs a representation of the data that is not tied to either the backend schema or the persistence layer. Raw data models fill that role. They represent the core data in a decoupled form that Vivino can use freely throughout the codebase. You can think of Realm objects here as "internal DTOs," while raw data models are the first truly app-owned representation of the data.

- **App Models:** Vivino heavily modularized their architecture around features, and working directly with raw data models in business logic or UI code is often too limiting. To address this, the team introduces App Models. These models may share properties with raw data models, but they can also include computed values and feature-specific logic. Because they are explicitly separated, each feature can shape its own models without affecting the rest of the system.

At first glance, this list of model types can feel overwhelming. We already know that every transformation moves us further away from the source of truth. But for a team operating at *Vivino's* scale, this layering is not overengineering - it's the price of stability. Each layer adds distance from the original backend response - but also reduces risk, coupling, and coordination cost across teams.

To make this more concrete, Figure 8-1 illustrates the whole flow from backend to UI.

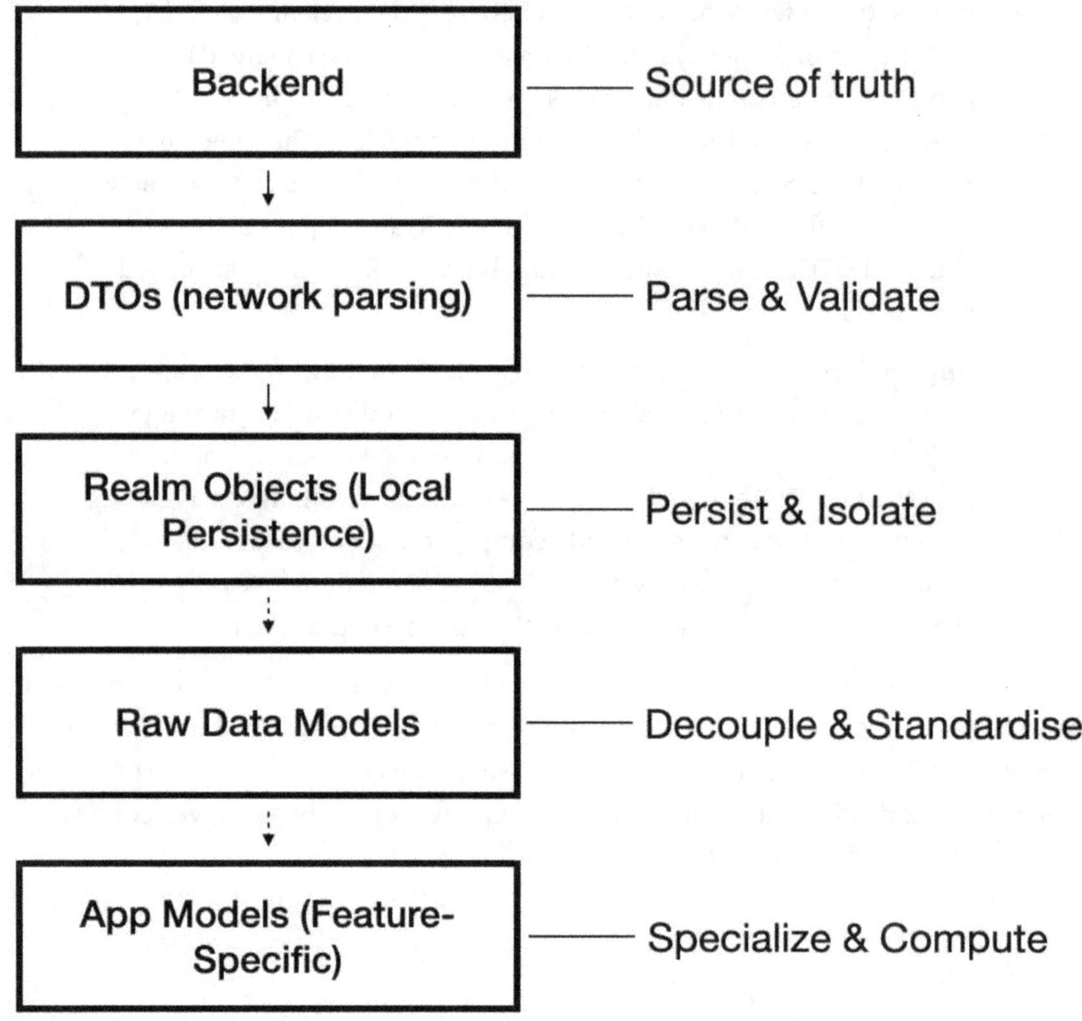

Figure 8-1. *Each layer represents an increasingly app-owned view of the data*

Figure 8-1 shows how the data flows from the backend to the UI. Remember, at the end, we are working on a mobile application. It means we need to represent the data to the user somehow, and as we move along the funnel, the data becomes more business- and UI-centric. This is what we call "truth at scale."

At this point, we've seen how different developers and teams think about "the truth." We saw how much it varies across industries, team sizes, and levels of experience.

But truth doesn't exist in isolation. At some point, it has to live somewhere.

That brings us to another topic where these differences become even more concrete: persistence. So, let's take the next step and talk about what it really means to make data persistent.

Persistence – Where Truth Is Allowed to Stay

If we look back at Vivino's model layers, we can see that some data is saved locally in Realm. We'll save the Realm versus Core Data debate for later, but it's worth asking a simpler question first: **why persist at all?**

When we store something locally, we're implicitly saying we might load it before - or even instead of - a network response. And that raises an uncomfortable point: doesn't persistence move us even further away from the source of truth?

Yes. This tension between persistence and truth shows up across many teams, and in some industries, it carries real security and legal implications. Vincent's banking experience is the clearest example.

Vivino's use of Realm is a great case study in balancing that tension. So, before we talk about tools, let's understand the strategy: does Vivino aim for full offline mode? And if not, what is the actual goal of persistence in their case?

Selective Persistence at Scale – Vivino

Before going further, let's clarify what we mean by *offline mode.* Offline mode relies on a local source of truth to function without a network. Caching, by contrast, stores data temporarily for performance, but the backend remains authoritative.

Despite using Realm as part of its structured, layered data pipeline, Vivino does **not** support offline mode in its iOS app. Opening the app without an internet connection results in a familiar message: *"Sorry, we couldn't load the page."* And yet, Realm is clearly there under the hood.

That's because Vivino uses Realm primarily as a cache. Its purpose is to avoid "spamming" the backend with API calls for information that is mostly static and reused throughout the app. In practice, this includes data such as wine details, vintage, region, and grape type. Persisting this data locally reduces backend load and noticeably improves performance, without committing the app to offline behavior.

Crucially, Vivino doesn't treat Realm as the primary source of truth. A source of truth is authoritative - its data is considered final, and other systems must reconcile to it. In Vivino's case, the backend retains that authority. The data stored in Realm is replaceable and refreshable; if it becomes outdated, it can be safely overwritten without conflict resolution or reconciliation logic.

More dynamic data tells a different story. Ratings, reviews, and other user-centric or screen-specific content remain strictly online-first. Vivino behaves much like a social network where freshness matters more than availability: feeds, reviews, following relationships, and profile screens all depend on fresh data fetched per screen. The result is a deliberate balance of local persistence for high-reuse, low-volatility data, and close, continuous coordination with the backend for everything else.

On a much smaller scale, persistence can serve a very different purpose and be implemented in very different ways.

Delegated Persistence – Danijela's Two Stores

We already mentioned earlier that Danijela uses SwiftData with CloudKit. Now it's worth slowing down and looking more closely at what that actually means in practice.

Danijela relies on **two local data stores**, each serving a very different purpose.

The first is a **read-only, preloaded local database** that ships with the app. This store contains static reference data that does not change during the app's lifetime. Because the data is immutable, there is no need for syncing, conflict resolution, or runtime migrations beyond app updates. It is always available, fast to read, and entirely predictable.

The second store is a **mutable SwiftData store synced via iCloud using CloudKit**. This store holds user-generated or user-specific data. SwiftData provides local persistence and offline access, while CloudKit propagates changes across the user's devices that are signed in with the same Apple ID. From the app's perspective, the local store serves as the source of truth, while syncing is entirely delegated to the platform.

What's notable here is not just the tooling, but the **distribution of responsibility**. Danijela does not control how conflicts are resolved, when sync happens, or how data is merged. She pushes those decisions down to the system. In exchange, she avoids the cost of building and maintaining custom sync logic.

Figure 8-2 shows what Danijela's pattern looks like.

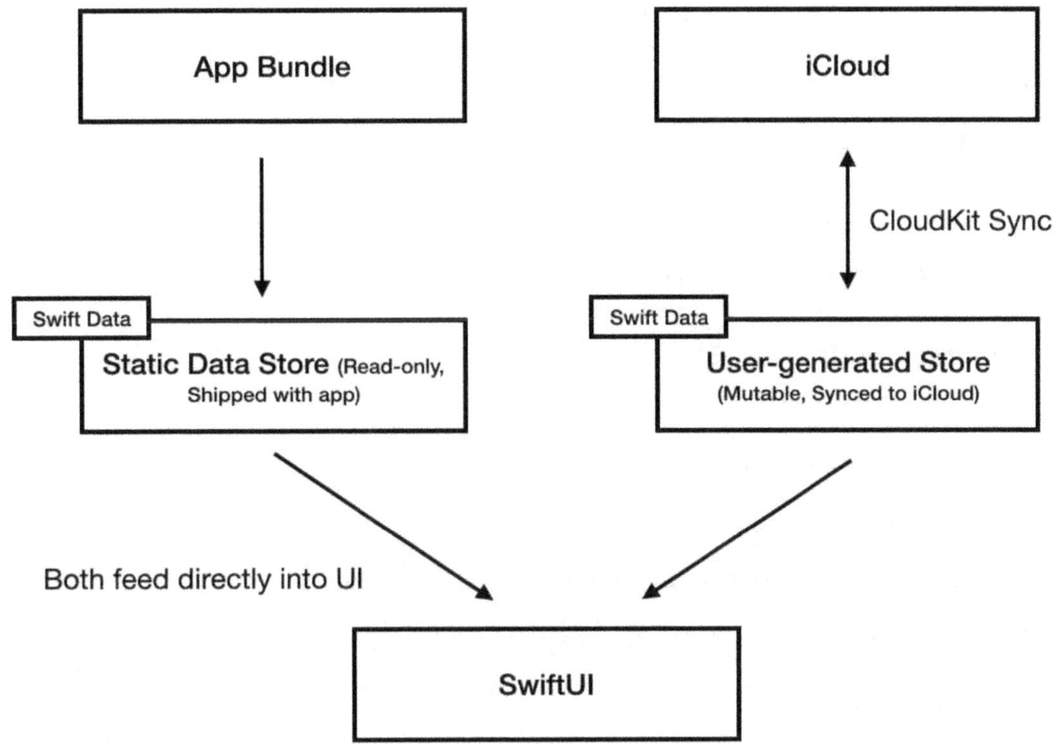

Figure 8-2. *Danijela's Dual SwiftData Setup – Bundled Static Data + CloudKit-Synced User Data*

Figure 8-2 shows how *Danijela* takes advantage of SwiftData's ability to work with multiple stores, in addition to syncing with iCloud.

This pattern of separating static reference data from dynamic user data is not unique. Apple itself demonstrates similar approaches in sample projects and documentation, where bundled datasets coexist alongside mutable, user-owned stores. The difference is that *Danijela* deliberately **applies this pattern as a product strategy**, not just as a technical convenience.

Compared to *Vivino*, the contrast is sharp. *Vivino* persists selectively and keeps the backend firmly in control. *Danijela* allows truth to live locally and delegates consistency to the platform. Neither approach is *better*. Each reflects a different tolerance for complexity, control, and risk.

One pattern that keeps resurfacing throughout these examples is the use of DTOs. Most teams parse network responses into DTOs and then quickly transform them into domain models or persistent objects.

The DTO mirrors the backend payload:

```
Import Foundation

struct RecipeDTO: Codable {
    let id: String
    let title: String
    let ingredients: [String]
    let instructions: String
    let preparationTime: Int
}
```

Notice the differences:

- id is a String (as often returned by APIs)

- preparationTime uses a different naming convention

Then, we transform the DTO into our app model:

```
Import Foundation

extension RecipeDTO {
    func toRecipe() -> Recipe {
        Recipe(
            id: UUID(uuidString: id) ?? UUID(),
            title: title,
            ingredients: ingredients,
            instructions: instructions,
            preparationTimeMinutes: preparationTime
        )
    }
}
```

This extra step might feel redundant at first, but it gives us an important advantage: We control how external data enters our system.

In general, this is a logical and widely adopted approach. However, *Zlatko* offers a slightly different perspective on when this extra layer is actually worth the cost.

Pragmatism Over Purity

If we look again at how *Vivino* implements different data types for different layers, it's hard not to think about the number of transformations involved. *Noam* from *Yazio* mentioned that the team isolates Core Data objects in the data layer, and *Oliver* described a similar approach. Many teams operating at scale follow this approach: clear boundaries, explicit layers, and strict separation of concerns. Data modeling, in this mindset, should serve clarity, not ceremony.

Zlatko, however, takes a more pragmatic stance. In his view, DTOs can become **over-engineered** when they closely resemble the models used in the app's business logic. If the server response already matches what the app needs, introducing an additional layer of types increases cognitive load without adding real safety. DTOs, he argues, make sense when responses are significantly more complex than what the app requires, or when meaningful transformation is needed to make the data usable.

As he put it: *"So as always, the answer is: it depends."*

It's a familiar phrase, but in this context, it's worth unpacking. In many apps, the server response is already structured in a meaningful way. We parse it into DTOs, then into data models that may look identical. From there, we transform it into app models, which again may carry the same properties. Sometimes this pattern continues all the way into UI-specific models. The result can be four or five different types, all mirroring each other, created in the name of architectural purity rather than necessity.

Zlatko's point is that this similarity often results in **unjustified overhead in data modeling**. When the server response changes, we must update every layer. One practical tip *Noam* shared in this context was keeping DTO properties optional, which can increase resilience to backend changes without introducing additional layers.

This pragmatic mindset extends naturally into persistence as well. For small or simple apps, *Zlatko* doesn't rush to introduce a full-fledged data store. In many cases, *UserDefaults* or local files are sufficient. More complex solutions are reserved for cases that truly demand them. Once again, the guiding principle remains the same: **it depends**.

Paying the Price for Owning the Truth

Up until now, every approach we've seen shares one common trait: most teams stop short of making the device the primary source of truth. They either avoid persistence altogether, treat it as a cache, or delegate it to iCloud as *Danijela* does. However, some products can't afford that.

When the app must remain responsive regardless of network connection, we must accept user actions immediately; waiting for the backend is not an option. Everything we talked about changes. Persistency is no longer optimization for speed – it becomes a commitment. Let's cross the line together with *Krzysztof*.

The Decision to Cross the Line

Krzysztof strongly believes in offline-first design. As mentioned earlier, offline-first is not caching, nor is it simply the ability to display some data without a network connection. It represents a fundamentally different type of application, and a radical shift in how we define where truth lives.

Choosing this approach means redefining authority. The local store is no longer a convenience or a performance optimization; it is allowed to be correct, even when the backend is unreachable. Compared to every approach we've discussed so far, this is a clear break.

It is also an expensive choice. But this is the moment where the app stops waiting for the server's permission.

Offline-First in Practice

Offline-first means the app must continue to function correctly without a network connection. That requirement introduces challenges that simply don't exist in online-first systems.

- **Clock Synchronization**: When an app performs changes locally and later syncs them to a backend, conflicts become inevitable, especially when multiple devices can modify the same data. In collaborative systems like Google Docs, deciding which change "wins" requires more than comparing timestamps. We cannot trust local device time, so aligning the actual order of changes across devices becomes a complex problem. This is what Krzysztof refers to when he talks about clock synchronization.

- **Partial Sync**: Offline-first does not necessarily mean syncing everything every time. To be efficient, the system needs to track entity versions and fetch only the changes since the last successful sync. That requires careful versioning strategies and backend support for incremental updates.

- **Correct Ordering of Inserts**: Finally, there's the problem of ordering. Changes can arrive from different devices in unpredictable sequences, and data often has dependencies. For example, a sports team must exist before its players can be inserted or updated. Handling these dependencies correctly at scale requires deliberate design and deep planning.

All of these challenges grow significantly in collaborative or real-time applications. And they exist for one reason only: we decided that local storage is allowed to be the truth.

Optimistic UI: Always Assume Success

Developers like *Krzysztof* don't choose offline-first just for no-network access. After all, it's reasonable to expect users to be connected most of the time. But for an app to truly benefit from offline-first design, it almost always needs to adopt another strategy as well: *Optimistic UI*.

So, what is Optimistic UI?

Optimistic UI is a UI strategy where the app updates immediately in response to a user action, assuming the operation will succeed, without waiting for backend confirmation.

The impact on user experience is dramatic, and so is the effect on the engineering effort behind it.

Allowing users to add, modify, or delete data and continue using the app without waiting for a server response means that

- We must trust (*be optimistic*) that the **operation will succeed** when it eventually syncs to the backend.

- The app needs **on-device business logic** that mirrors backend rules. Validation and constraints must behave consistently on both sides.

- All relevant data must be **available locally**, as the device now serves as the source of truth.

- In multi-device scenarios, we must **detect conflicts and resolve them** when they occur.

Optimistic UI is not a UX trick. It is a foundational architectural decision, one that requires careful design, deep system understanding, and a willingness to accept complexity. It delivers a fluid, responsive experience, but it also introduces risks and challenges that are not always suitable for indie developers or small teams.

Let's see how an Optimistic UI framework works in a typical app (Figure 8-3).

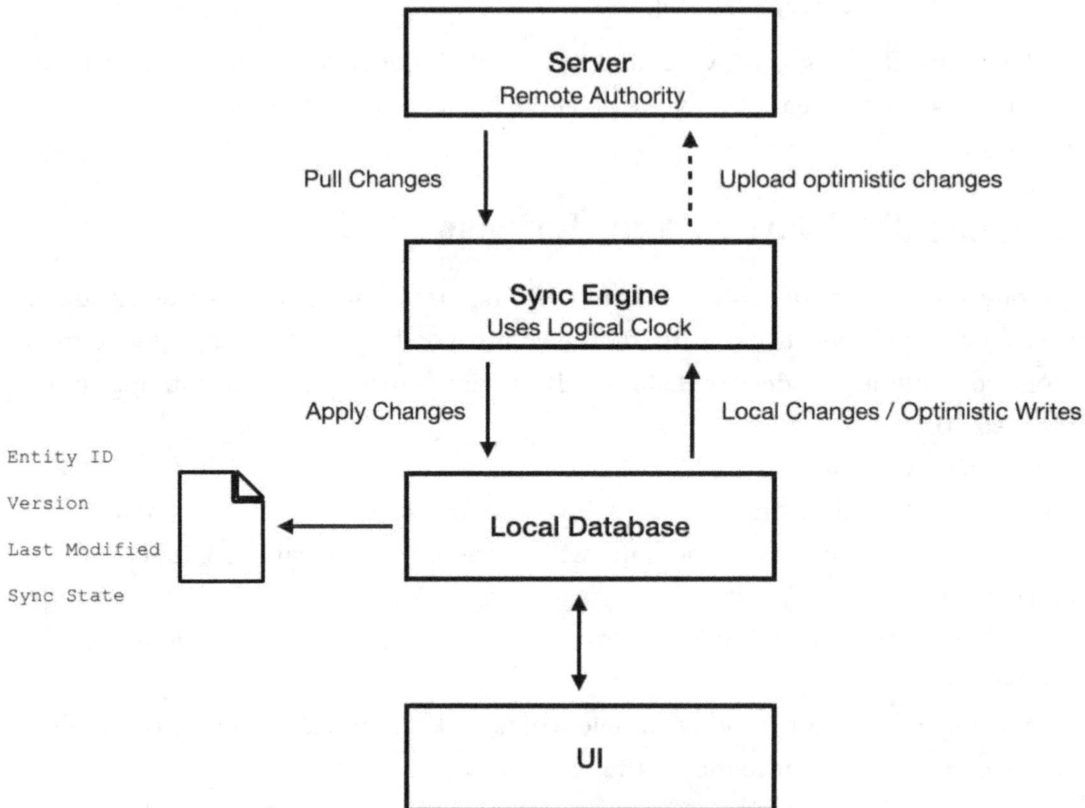

Figure 8-3. *Offline-first sync engine with Optimistic UI*

Figure 8-3 shows the three primary components of a sync mechanism that ensure the UI remains responsive and fluid:

- **The Local Database:** This can be any type of persistent store. Its role is to act as the primary source of truth for the app, unlike in online-first architectures. It stores entities locally and ensures each entity has a stable ID (to match records during sync), a version (to detect and resolve conflicts), and a sync state. The sync state allows the app to mark local entities as "pending sync," so we can later upload them to the backend as part of the Optimistic UI flow.

- **The Sync Engine**: The sync engine pulls changes from the server and applies them to the local database. It is also responsible for querying local changes and uploading them back to the backend. To perform these tasks, the sync engine typically tracks a logical timestamp or version marker locally, which it uses to request only incremental changes from the server and to determine which local entities still need to be synced.

- **The Server**: In an offline-first architecture, the server's responsibility goes far beyond simply serving data. It must maintain entity versions, expose APIs for incremental sync, and often participate in conflict resolution. These are non-trivial problems; conflict resolution, in particular, requires a clear strategy and careful design to ensure consistency across devices.

As we can see, Optimistic UI comes with a high price tag, but one that buys a significantly more responsive and resilient user experience.

So, the question now remains: what strategy should we choose for our app?

How Much Truth Should We Own?

This is not an easy question, because it's not really about tools at all; it's about strategy. Data modeling and persistence are not decisions between *SwiftData* and *Core Data*; After all, both tools sit in the same spot – persistent, abstract frameworks that manage an object graph and support Apple ecosystem features. But Data modeling and persistence are responsibility decisions.

They are about correctness, conflicts, migrations, and long-term maintenance. More than anything, they reflect how we choose to treat *truth* inside our app. Recall the river metaphor from earlier in the chapter: every step away from the backend river means the app absorbs more of its flow-and with it, more responsibility.

The good news is that by now we've seen multiple teams and developers confront this challenge in very different ways. Together, these examples form a spectrum of truth ownership. Let's examine that spectrum and step back to see the bigger picture.

The Truth Ownership Spectrum

If you've read the previous sections carefully, you've probably noticed the same pattern: different developers arrive at very different answers to the question of how they should handle data. The solutions range from strictly online-only apps on one end to fully offline-first systems with Optimistic UI on the other.

Let's try to visualize that range (Figure 8-4).

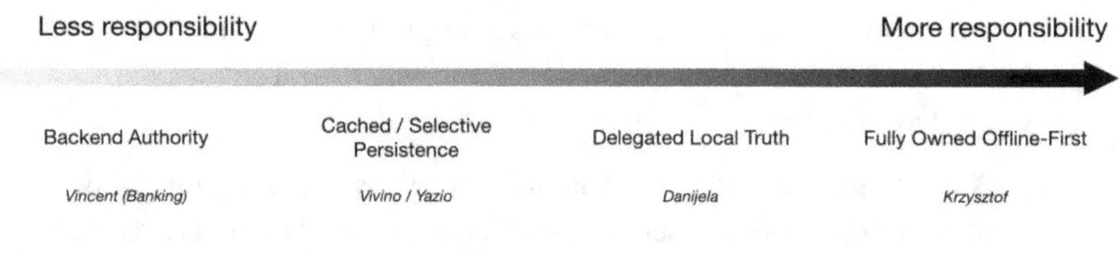

Figure 8-4. *The truth ownership spectrum*

Figure 8-4 illustrates the truth ownership spectrum we discussed in the previous section, moving from minimal responsibility for data correctness to wholly owned local truth. Importantly, moving right on this spectrum does not mean *better* or *worse*. It simply reflects how much responsibility a team is willing to take on and how high a price it is willing to pay in complexity, maintenance, and long-term ownership.

With this spectrum in mind, we can now ask a more practical question: what factors actually push teams along it? Let's break down the key questions that tend to move a product from one position to another.

Questioning Ourselves About Our Position in the Spectrum

When I asked developers why they chose their data approach, many couldn't point to a single *original* reason. That didn't surprise me.

Developers rarely make these decisions in isolation. Some were taken on long before they joined the team; others evolved gradually into patterns that "just worked."

Yet these are heavyweight decisions. They not only influence the user experience, but also how close the app stays to the truth. They must align with the app's architecture (as we saw with *Vivino*), and they are notoriously hard to change later. Most apps present their UI directly on top of data models, and in large-scale systems, changing how those models are structured is a sensitive and risky move.

To reason about our place on the spectrum more deliberately, here are some questions worth asking:

- **The Nature of Truth:** Who owns the data at this exact moment? If a user is on a plane, is the data they see considered "true," or is it merely a cached snapshot? Recall Vincent's work on banking apps - does checking your balance make sense without an internet connection? On the other end of the spectrum, Krzysztof described the power of Optimistic UI. But what happens when a user edits the same data from both an iPad and an iPhone at the same time? What is our strategy for deciding which version is "true"?

- **The Importance of Persistence**: Do we need the data to exist on the device without a network connection? For a calculator or a train schedule viewer, probably not. For a productivity app, almost certainly yes. Vivino's and Danijela's examples show that this is rarely an all-or-nothing decision. Some data may be worth persisting for performance or convenience, while other data remains online-only. And what happens when the user deletes and reinstalls the app? How much pain do they experience?

- **Architectural Overhead**: *Zlatko* raised an important concern: Are we over-modeling? If we maintain five layers of models that all contain the same `id`, `name`, and `date` fields, are we gaining safety, or just adding friction? Consider this: when backend developers add a new field tomorrow, how many files must we touch before that field appears in the UI?

- **The Offline Experience:** This is not the same question as "who owns the truth." Is the app read-only when offline? Can users navigate previously loaded data? Can they create or modify content? We've seen compelling approaches here, but they come with significant complexity. How much are we willing to pay to make the app usable offline?

- **Data Sensitivity and Security**: iOS devices are well protected, but the safest place for sensitive data is often still the server. What happens if a device is compromised? For *Vivino*, wine preferences are low risk. For *Yazio* or *Axon*, this could already be a privacy concern. For fintech apps, it can be catastrophic. This doesn't mean we can't store sensitive data locally, but it must be a conscious decision.

These questions help frame data management decisions more clearly. And as we've seen throughout this book, they don't exist in isolation. Many of them intersect with testing strategies, CI/CD pipelines, and architectural choices. That interconnection is one of the defining challenges - and rewards - of building real-world apps.

Now that we have a clearer sense of how much truth we're willing to own, choosing the right tools becomes far more obvious.

So, let's talk about the tools.

Choosing the Right Weight for the Job

If we ask Apple what we should use to manage data, the answer is simple: *SwiftData*. But when I looked across the interviews in this chapter, the picture was far more varied. *Vivino* chose Realm as its database, while *Krzysztof* builds directly on top of the *GRDB toolkit*. At first, this might seem inconsistent. In reality, it reflects how different teams think about data and what role the app plays in managing it.

This reflection leads to a significant shift in perspective. Tools and frameworks do not define the architecture we use - where the truth lives does. From a technical point of view, we could manage a small app using *SQLite*, or even build a large app using something far less sophisticated. The framework itself is rarely the deciding factor. What really matters is how much responsibility the app takes for data correctness, syncing, and long-term consistency. Frameworks are just a means to support that decision.

With that framing in mind, we can map the tools used by our interviewees based on how they treat truth ownership:

- **Online-First/Cached**: *Zlatko* uses `NSCache` and `UserDefaults` to keep a lightweight, temporary state. The backend remains the source of truth, and the app focuses on speed and responsiveness rather than durability.

- **Selective Persistence**: *Core Data* and *Realm* sit in the middle. These frameworks are widespread in production apps, and we saw *Oliver, Monika, Noam, Stefan*, and *Zlatko* rely on them. They allow teams to store essential data locally without fully owning it, and they strike a good balance between convenience and control.

- **Delegation**: *SwiftData*, especially when combined with *CloudKit*, represents a more delegated approach. As *Danijela* described, she handed much of the responsibility for syncing and consistency to Apple's infrastructure through the SwiftData–CloudKit integration.

- **Fully Owned Offline-First**: Developers like *Krzysztof* and *Stefan* choose *GRDB* when they want complete control over their data. This approach gives them clear queries, predictable behavior, and better visibility into what happens under the hood, but it also means taking on more responsibility.

All of these tools help teams reach different goals when managing data. It's also worth calling out that persistence is only one part of what data frameworks do. Their role is not just to save data between launches, but to help model data, manage relationships, run queries, and observe changes across the app. Saving data for later is just one feature among many.

With that context in place, we can move on. Let's start with the tools commonly used in online-first apps.

Online-First: Lightweight Tools, Explicit Limits

Let's return to the river metaphor from the *"What Is the Truth?"* section. We cannot step into the same river twice, which means that, in many cases, the backend remains our source of truth, and we should be careful about copying data to the device. *Vincent's* banking apps are a good example of this approach. At the same time, staying close to the backend does not mean we must avoid all local optimizations. We can still use lightweight tools to improve performance and responsiveness, as long as we are clear about their limits.

In this model, there is no database, no migrations, and no long-lived local models. That decision directly affects the architecture and the patterns we use for observation and state management. The tools we choose must make it challenging to treat local data as authoritative by accident.

One of the most effective tools for this approach is NSCache. Surprisingly, many developers are not very familiar with it, even though it fits online-first apps extremely well. Both *Zlatko* and *Mikaela* mentioned using it in their apps, so let's see how it works.

NSCache is an in-memory, system-managed cache designed for temporary data. The most important thing to understand about it is that it is **explicitly temporary**. Not only does NSCache avoid writing to disk, but it also does not guarantee that cached objects will remain in memory. The system is free to evict data at any time, without warning. This makes it impossible to treat cached values as authoritative, which is precisely what we want in an online-first approach.

Here's a minimal example:

```swift
import Foundation

final class Recipe {
    let id: UUID
    let title: String

    init(id: UUID, title: String) {
        self.id = id
        self.title = title
    }
}

final class RecipeCache {
    private let cache = NSCache<NSString, Recipe>()

    func recipe(id: String) -> Recipe? {
        cache.object(forKey: id as NSString)
    }

    func store(_ recipe: Recipe) {
        cache.setObject(recipe, forKey: recipe.id.uuidString as NSString)
    }
}
```

At first glance, NSCache may look like a simple dictionary wrapper. The difference is that the app owns the dictionaries in full, while the system manages NSCache. We don't control when the system removes the data, and we aren't notified when it does. In other words, NSCache is a performance tool without ownership, and that constraint is precisely what makes it safe to use in online-first architectures.

NSCache represents the safest possible boundary in an online-first app: data may disappear at any moment, forcing the app to recover by asking the backend again. But not all local states are that disposable. Some information is small, stable, and not worth re-fetching or recomputing every time the app launches, and this is where another tool often comes into play. Many teams turn to UserDefaults for this kind of state. Unlike NSCache, UserDefaults persists data across app launches, but that persistence does not automatically make it a source of truth. Used carefully, it allows apps to remember preferences, flags, and lightweight configuration without taking on responsibility for real domain data. The risk, as we'll see next, is how easily this convenience can slide into accidental ownership.

The usage of UserDefaults is extremely simple:

```
UserDefaults.standard.set(true, forKey: "hasSeenOnboarding")
let hasSeenOnboarding = UserDefaults.standard.bool(forKey:
"hasSeenOnboarding")
```

In this example, UserDefaults stores a simple flag that helps the app remember whether it already shown the onboarding flow. This flag is exactly the kind of problem UserDefaults was designed to solve: small, stable pieces of state that should survive app restarts but do not represent domain data.

UserDefaults ease can lead to abuse - storing complete records feels like a shortcut, until it becomes a shadow database:

```
Import Foundation

struct Recipe: Codable {
    let id: String
    let title: String
    let ingredients: [String]
}
```

```
let recipes: [Recipe] = fetchRecipes()

let data = try JSONEncoder().encode(recipes)
UserDefaults.standard.set(data, forKey: "recipes_db")
```

In this example, UserDefaults is used to store a list of recipes for a recipe-collection app. None of the developers I interviewed uses UserDefaults this way, but for some, it can feel like a reasonable shortcut compared to setting up a local data store.

The problem is that this turns UserDefaults into a serialized database, without a schema or any real ability to evolve. There are no queries, no versioning, no partial updates, and no protection against unbounded growth. Every small change requires rewriting the entire dataset. This is often the moment when a convenient tool quietly becomes a source of truth.

So yes - UserDefaults *can* store data. That does not mean it should.

Selective Persistence with Realm and Core Data

Now that we understand how problematic UserDefaults is for storing all the data, let's identify the leading candidates for managing data entities. Their goal is not to provide a whole offline-first experience, but to make data fast and reliable, with low latency and high reuse, without constantly hitting the backend. But – why do I call that "Selective Persistence"?

Why Selective Persistence at All?

There are actually two related questions here. The first is why manage entities in a store at all, whether that store is persistent or not. The second is: once we introduce a store, why do many teams choose to make persistence selective? The answer to the first question builds directly on the limitations we saw with UserDefaults.

A proper store provides tools that simple key–value storage does not: schemas, relationships, queries, delete rules, indexing, and migrations. Yes, introducing a store comes with setup costs and a learning curve, but at larger scales, avoiding a structured store usually leads to even more complexity over time.

The reason persistence becomes *selective* is more interesting. When teams decide to persist data locally, they rarely persist everything. Instead, they choose to store only certain kinds of data - typically stable, high-reuse entities - while leaving dynamic, user-centric content strictly online-first. Developers use persistence primarily to improve performance and user experience, not to claim ownership of the truth. For data that changes frequently or is sensitive to freshness, many teams still prefer fetching from the backend every time to avoid the cost and complexity of synchronization.

Selective persistence, then, is rarely about offline support. It is about scale and polish.

With that context in place, let's look at the first framework most teams reach for when they decide to introduce structured persistence: Core Data, as seen through the eyes of our interviewees.

Core Data: Structured Persistence for Scale

When lightweight caching (NSCache, UserDefaults) starts to feel limiting, many teams reach for their first real structured store: Core Data. Its primary role is not just persistence, but structured data management, defining entities, modeling relationships, querying efficiently, and evolving schemas over time. Persistence is part of that picture, but it is not the only reason teams choose it.

Among the developers I interviewed, Core Data was the most commonly used framework for structured data management. *Noam, Oliver, Stefan,* and *Zlatko* all use (or have used) *Core Data* in production apps. There are good reasons for this. *Core Data* is a native Apple framework, which means long-term platform support and no external dependencies. It handles complex object graphs and relationships well, includes built-in support for versioning and migrations, and integrates naturally with the rest of Apple's ecosystem.

Here's the typical shape of *Core Data* in action:

```
import CoreData


let persistentContainer = NSPersistentContainer(name: "Model")
persistentContainer.loadPersistentStores { _, _ in }

@objc(RecipeMO)
class RecipeMO: NSManagedObject {
    @NSManaged var category: String?
}
```

```
let context = persistentContainer.viewContext

let request: NSFetchRequest<RecipeMO> = RecipeMO.fetchRequest()
request.predicate = NSPredicate(format: "category == %@", "Dessert")

let recipes = try context.fetch(request)
```

This fetch pattern is where *Core Data* feels most natural. The framework handles persistence, relationships, and querying behind the scenes, while the app focuses on higher-level behavior.

Core Data also demands discipline. It enforces strict rules around object lifecycles, concurrency, and ownership, and teams need to respect those rules to use it safely. For that reason, most larger teams isolate *Core Data* models inside the data layer and never expose managed objects directly to business logic or UI code. That isolation prevents persistence concerns from leaking into the rest of the system.

This combination of power and constraint makes *Core Data* a good fit for teams operating at scale. Its verbosity, concurrency model, and overall heaviness can feel restrictive to teams looking for a lighter abstraction. But when used well, Core Data's maturity often means fewer surprises in production and better integration with Apple's tooling.

For teams looking for a lighter, less rule-heavy persistence layer, *Realm* is often an appealing alternative.

Realm – Core Data Third-Party Alternative

Realm surprised me at first - I expected *Core Data* everywhere - but once I saw how teams use it, the choice made sense. So, I took a step back and tried to understand what *Realm* offers, and why it still shows up in production apps.

Realm emerged in the early 2010s as a response to the friction many teams experienced with *Core Data*. It aims to provide a simpler, lower-boilerplate way to persist and query objects. If we look back at the *Core Data* fetch example from the previous section, the equivalent query in Realm looks like this:

```
let realm = try Realm()

let recipes = realm.objects(RecipeRO.self)
    .filter("category == %@", "Dessert")
```

Notice what's missing: no context and no fetch request. The code opens the store and returns a **live collection** of matching objects with minimal infrastructure. Even in Objective-C, the same idea remains relatively compact, which helps explain why *Realm* appealed to teams that wanted structured persistence without Core Data's ceremony:

```
RLMRealm *realm = [RLMRealm defaultRealm];

RLMResults<RecipeRO *> *recipes =
    [[RecipeRO objectsInRealm:realm]
        objectsWhere:@"category == %@", @"Dessert"];
```

For Vivino, the key point is not just the API shape, but how *Realm* is used. It functions as a persistent cache: data is overwritten on refresh, and *Realm* is not treated as the source of truth, so no conflict resolution or reconciliation logic is required. As with *Core Data*, this only works cleanly when teams enforce isolation.

Another *Realm* feature that stands out is its support for *live objects*. Query results and instances are automatically kept up to date as the underlying data changes. *Core Data* offers similar behavior, but it is scoped to a single managed object context, which is part of the reason *Realm* often feels simpler to use. Because *Realm* objects are so easy to work with, Vivino must be especially careful not to let them spread beyond the data layer.

Another developer who has experience with Realm is *Oliver Binns*, but he puts a different perspective:

> *In the past, Realm was a bit more approachable for junior developers - I think this has changed a bit since the release of SwiftData. Recently, I've been using it partly because one of the apps I've been helping with stores sensitive data, and we want to keep it encrypted while the app is closed… Realm supports this extra, more controllable encryption. The main downside is the build time is pretty slow, and with SPM it does a clean build regularly…*

What Oliver says is a good reminder that persistence choices are sometimes driven by security constraints and developer workflow costs, not just modeling style.

From a trade-off perspective, *Realm* is a third-party dependency. That can mean less alignment with Apple-first tooling and reliance on an external library's upgrade cadence. *Realm* trades Apple integration for simplicity - and works best when teams remember it's still a cache, not the truth.

With both *Core Data* and *Realm* in mind, we can now compare what actually differs in practice - and why neither is "better," only better suited to a team's constraints.

SwiftData: Delegated Persistence Through Simplicity

SwiftData is a relatively new, first-party framework that is focused on simplicity. Apple designed SwiftData to reduce setup and boilerplate, not to replace *Core Data* in all cases.

Just so we can be on the same page, this is how we define a model in SwiftData:

```
import SwiftData

@Model
final class Recipe {
    var title: String
    var category: String
}
```

Adding the `@Model` macro before the class definition is enough to add a new model to the scheme. SwiftData models are observable and integrate amazingly well with SwiftUI. Remember Realm's live objects? Apple took that approach and made it feel natural when combining SwiftData for SwiftUI.

That said, many interviewees actively avoid SwiftData. *Krzysztof* mentioned that its heavy use of property wrappers can make SwiftUI views slower, and *Stefan* described the framework as still immature. Looking across the interviews, a clear pattern emerges around where SwiftData fits well.

Danijela uses SwiftData as an indie developer to store user data and sync it via *CloudKit*, alongside static data shipped with the app. *Oliver* also uses SwiftData in personal projects. These examples suggest that SwiftData may not be the best choice for teams with complex data requirements or strict performance constraints. Still, it works very well for indie developers and personal projects. It requires minimal maintenance and comfortably covers a large portion of everyday use cases.

It's also worth remembering that *Danijela* uses SwiftData to support Optimistic UI, enabled by its integration with *CloudKit*. That brings us back to *Krzysztof*, who reaches for *GRDB* when he needs the same capabilities, but with complete control.

GRDB: When Teams Want Control Back

When we discussed Optimistic UI and offline-first design earlier in this chapter, one thing became very clear in *Krzysztof's* approach: visibility into what happens to data is non-negotiable. If we step back and look at the data frameworks we've covered so far, a pattern emerges. They all aim to simplify development by introducing abstractions, contexts, predicates, and relationships. Still, that simplicity comes at the cost of taking responsibility away from the developer and hiding what happens underneath.

That trade-off works well in many cases. But once teams introduce techniques such as complete data synchronization or Optimistic UI, the risk of hidden behavior increases. At that point, predictability matters more than convenience.

This is where *GRDB* enters the picture. Teams choose *GRDB* when they want a tool they direct, not a framework that dictates behavior. They want predictable queries, clear insight into reads and writes, and the flexibility to model sync state, versioning, and conflicts explicitly. Most importantly, they refuse to fight abstractions when correctness is non-negotiable.

GRDB wraps *SQLite* in a Swift-friendly layer while keeping every behavior explicit. Here's a short example of querying recipes with *GRDB*:

```swift
struct Recipe: FetchableRecord, Decodable {
    let id: Int
    let title: String
    let category: String
}

let recipes = try dbQueue.read { db in
    try Recipe.fetchAll(
        db,
        sql: """
        SELECT id, title, category
        FROM recipe
        WHERE category = ?
        ORDER BY title
        """,
        arguments: ["Dessert"]
    )
}
```

This example shows *GRDB's* defining characteristic: nothing is implicit. We can see precisely what is queried, how it is filtered, and how results are ordered. SQL is not a fallback here - it is a feature. Unlike Core Data's managed contexts or Realm's live objects, *GRDB* exposes raw SQL behavior directly. There is no magic - just **explicit behavior**.

That explicitness is precisely why *GRDB* fits complex synchronization scenarios so well. Pending operations, conflict resolution, and deterministic ordering are not edge cases; they are core concepts that we can model directly in the schema and queries.

On the truth-ownership spectrum, *GRDB* lives at the far end. It is the point at which teams accept full responsibility for local data and allow the app to own the offline truth, with the backend reconciling later.

That responsibility comes at a cost. With *GRDB*, we trade convenience and framework-driven behavior for clarity and precision. It's not better, or worse - it's heavier. But when teams need to stay extremely close to the truth, that weight is precisely what they seek.

Now that we've covered the spectrum and the tools developers and teams use, let's figure out which tool to pick.

Choosing the Right Tool

Let's start by aligning expectations: there is no "best" framework. Every choice comes with trade-offs in terms of responsibility, cost, truth, and ownership. Throughout this chapter, we've returned to the idea of truth ownership, so let's now place the different tools on that spectrum (Figure 8-5).

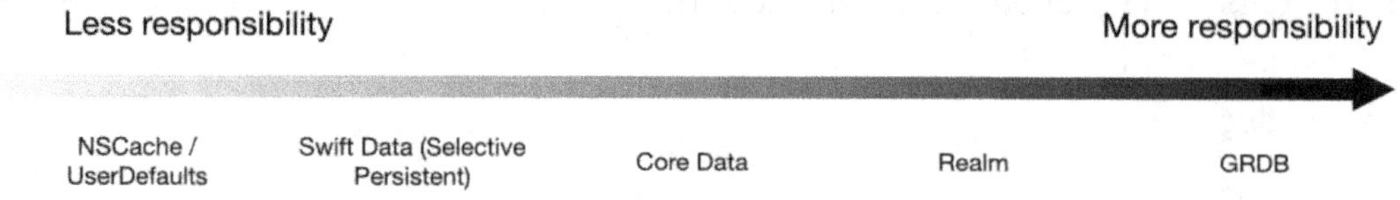

Figure 8-5. *The truth ownership spectrum, now with tools*

Looking at Figure 8-5, we can see how different tools reflect different levels of responsibility for data correctness. On the left side, tools like `NSCache` and `UserDefaults` help speed up the user experience, but nothing more than that. They are intentionally limited, making it hard to own the truth accidentally. On the other end of the spectrum, *GRDB* places almost all the responsibility on the app itself. It assumes that if something goes wrong, the app should know how to recover.

To decide where an app should sit on this spectrum, teams need to ask themselves a set of questions that clarify what they are willing to own and what they are not. For example:

- Should the app ever be correct **without the backend**?

- Is persistence mainly used to **improve user experience**, or for correctness?

- IIow much **hidden behavior** is the team comfortable carrying?

- Can the team design, implement, and maintain **sync logic**?

- Can **partially completed actions** live safely on the device?

- Are most data **small and stable**, or large and frequently changing?

- Do entities have **deep relationships**?

- What level of **responsiveness** do users expect?

- What is the long-term **maintenance cost** the team is comfortable with?

These questions help teams choose the *right goal*, not because a blog post claimed "9 reasons you should use `<framework>`," but because the tool matches what the product and team actually need.

When teams pick a framework as a goal, rather than as a consequence of these decisions, the same failures tend to repeat: using `UserDefaults` as a database, letting Core Data objects leak into UI code, treating Realm's live objects as a source of truth, or adopting GRDB only to use it as a cache.

Remember, frameworks don't define architecture. **Truth ownership does.**

Summary

We started this chapter with a simple question: *What is truth?*

We end it with a harder one: **how much of it are you willing to own?**

Throughout the chapter, we explored data management not as a question of frameworks, but as a question of truth ownership. Across teams and real-world systems, we saw a clear pattern: architectural decisions around data are really decisions about responsibility - who is allowed to be right, when, and at what cost. These are not technical details; there are product and team commitments.

We followed the journey of data to understand where truth lives, examined the tension between simplicity and responsibility, and explored how persistence and scale gradually pull teams toward greater ownership of correctness. We then looked at different tools and frameworks, not to rank them, but to understand how each reflects a distinct stopping point on the truth ownership spectrum. As Figure 8-5 shows, every step to the right increases responsibility for correctness, conflicts, and maintenance - and every tool choice is simply a consequence of where we decide to stop.

The key takeaway is sharper than "there is no best framework." There is only the **lightest tool that lets you own exactly the amount of truth your app and your team can afford**. Choosing how to manage data should never start with a framework. It must begin with the more profound questions of responsibility, cost, and user experience we explored throughout this chapter.

Own only the truth you can afford, and never let the tool choose how much that is.

The next chapter leaves *Xcode* behind and turns to something even more essential: our teammates, because no app is built alone.

Team Workflows

We do this for every feature, as we feel it pays off.

—Oliver Binns, Deloitte Digital

Introduction

We are in Chapter 9, and by now it should be clear that this book is not a typical technical manual. Most development books focus on Swift syntax, frameworks, and architectural patterns. Very few stop to examine what truly drives a team from idea to release: the workflow itself.

Team workflow is not a secondary concern. It is the engine behind how teams coordinate, align, and deliver. In many cases, it has a greater impact on outcomes than architecture decisions or the way we structured our design system.

In this chapter, we will

- Understand why finding a bug late in the process dramatically increases its cost

- Explore how teams control the distance a mistake is allowed to travel

- Break common myths around Git branching strategies

- Examine the structural levels of workflows

- Learn how to identify the level that best fits our team

This chapter is not about syntax. It is about coordination, risk, and structure. Let's begin by asking a simple question: how far are we willing to let a mistake travel before we catch it?

The Distance Matters More Than the Bug

When we talk about "Bugs," we usually refer to a mistake a developer made. For example, a button that doesn't do anything, a navigation problem, or just an index-out-of-bounds exception. It's easier for us, as developers and team managers, to look at bugs as isolated failures. When we isolate a failure, it's simpler to point to the root cause - "the developer didn't read the product requirements" or "the developer didn't check the array length before reading it." It is also simpler to define the solution – opening a bug in Jira or Linear and fixing it in an upcoming version or as part of a hotfix.

However, it is more complex to view bugs as workflow failures. Because the real cost of a bug is not the bug itself – it is the distance the bug travels before someone notices it. In other words, every workflow is an answer to one question:

How far are we willing to let a mistake travel before we catch it?

Let's dive into it for a second – imagine we have an end user, finding a bug. If we go back in the workflow, we can start with the QA tester who missed this issue. But – is it really the cause of the bug? We can ask ourselves many questions that can lead us not to a coding failure, but to a workflow failure:

- Is it an edge case or a common one?

- Did we have it in our test plan?

- If we had it in our test plan, did we also mention it in the requirements?

- If it were part of the requirements, did we discuss it during the kickoff meeting?

- Did we even have a kickoff meeting?

We can continue asking these sorts of questions. Still, the core idea is clear - when we work in a collaborative environment (indie developers - sorry for that), a failure is usually not isolated. And finding a mistake after release is not only a system failure; it also costs more.

The Price of Finding a Mistake

When we talk about the price of a mistake, it's tempting to focus just on hours: "three hours to fix a bug is three hours, right?" But just like we saw with architectural distance earlier, the deeper something goes into the system, the more expensive it is to pull back out. Fixing a mistake isn't just about how long it takes to change the code. It's about how far that mistake has spread.

If we find an issue during development, the cost is mostly in code edits. But if QA finds it? Now we need to log the bug, reproduce it, loop in QA and product, and verify the fix. That's more people, more tools, and more overhead. And if the bug reaches production? Add user reports, triage, emergency patches, and potential harm to business metrics or trust.

The stage matters - and the numbers back it up. According to a widely cited NIST (National Institute of Standards and Technology) study, a bug found in production can cost **up to 100× more** than one caught in the design phase. That estimate comes from their 2002 report on the economic impact of software errors, which is still referenced in many modern QA frameworks. And more recently, a 2021 IEEE study analyzing mobile apps found that user-reported bugs took **4–7× longer** to resolve than bugs caught internally. The deeper the bug, the wider the ripple.

That ripple includes triage, ticket grooming, regression testing, coordination delays, and the risk of introducing new bugs while patching the original one. Each downstream stage adds friction and cost - and teams know it. That's why they work so hard to build workflows that surface problems earlier.

Now, maybe you're thinking: *Okay, but this was true before AI. Does it still hold?* We've got code generators, test assistants, auto-refactor tools - surely that changes the equation?

Let's talk about that next.

AI Doesn't Break the Curve

Our next and final chapter looks at AI and how it's reshaping teams around the world. But let's be honest - this space moves so fast that anything I write today might feel outdated in a few months, maybe even weeks.

Still, one principle hasn't changed: AI can help us generate code faster. And tests. And sometimes even design ideas or product specs. But it doesn't flatten the team cost curve - it just shifts some of the prices. If the requirement is wrong, AI will simply build the wrong thing faster. And when users find the problem, it might help us fix it faster, too.

But the core truth stays the same: even with AI, the cheapest mistake is the one you catch during design - before it spreads, before it ripples, and before anyone writes a line of code.

But you know what? We always treat cost as development hours. But development hours are only a small portion of the cost.

The Cost Is More Than Just Time

To understand why bugs have such a high cost, even when they are easy to fix, we need to understand how our brains work. We often imagine the brain like a machine or a computer that we can stop and restart. That analogy is tempting, but it is misleading. While coding, we rely on a part of the brain called **working memory**. This is the part of the brain that holds the information we are actively using right now. In development, this includes the current feature, related files and abstractions, decisions we've already made, edge cases we still need to handle, and what we plan to do next.

Working memory is small and temporary. When we switch to another task, it fades quickly. The computer analogy still helps here, as long as we do not take it too far. Working memory behaves a bit like RAM. Switching tasks is less like putting the app in the background and more like restarting the system, as the state is gone.

So, when we return to a feature, we do not simply continue - we rebuild the mental context almost from scratch. Studies on task switching and productivity consistently show that this recovery can take up to 20 to 30 minutes, even when the interruption itself was short.

The damage depends not only on the feature's complexity but also on *when* we find the bug. During development testing, the context is still warm, and recovery may take only a minute or two. During the QA phase, the context is colder, and rebuilding it can take much longer. When a bug appears in production, the developer has already moved on. The code no longer lives in working memory, and reconstruction becomes slow, stressful, and expensive.

Early development estimates rarely account for this context-switching cost. Yet when bugs appear across multiple phases, the hidden cost adds up fast. Minutes turn into hours. Focus turns into fragmentation.

So, the real question is not whether mistakes will happen as they always do. The question is how to design workflows that catch them early, while the context is still alive, rather than letting them travel downstream. That's the point where connected workflows stop being a nice idea and start becoming a competitive advantage.

How Do Workflows Define Where Mistakes Are Allowed to Travel?

Now that we understand why bugs found later are more expensive, we can see the real purpose of workflows. A workflow is not just a process checklist. It defines how far a mistake is allowed to travel before someone stops it.

Each step exists for a reason. A kickoff meeting aligns the team on requirements. The QA phase exists to catch bugs before they reach production. When one of these steps fails, bugs do not disappear. They simply move further down the line.

Years ago, I worked on a large team with a high number of reported bugs. Management blamed the developers. But when we looked closely at the workflow, the real problems were elsewhere. Communication between the product manager and QA was weak. Communication between QA and developers was even weaker.

For example, when QA shares test plans early, developers can align their implementation with those scenarios. In practice, this often feels close to test-driven development, even without formal TDD. When that collaboration is missing, developers guess, QA compensates, and bugs slip through.

That experience taught me something important. Bug count and product quality are rarely purely technical problems. They are often the result of poor collaboration and inefficient workflows.

Teams invest heavily in tuning workflows based on their size and constraints, balancing speed against how late bugs are allowed to surface. A good workflow does not eliminate mistakes. It controls the distance they are allowed to travel.

How Teams Control Bug Distance

Remember the chapter on architecture and design patterns in Chapter 2? One key takeaway was that architecture is not the goal. It is a tool that helps a team, or an indie developer, build and maintain an app.

Dependency injection decouples code and adds flexibility. Modularization creates boundaries. Layers help teams reason about complexity. None of these exists for its own sake. They exist to help people work together and evolve the code safely.

The same idea applies to how teams manage their work. A workflow is not the goal. It is a tool. Code review is not about checking boxes. It is how developers collaborate, share context, and stay aligned around the codebase.

By defining workflows, teams control the balance between development speed and how far bugs are allowed to travel before they catch them. Faster workflows push issues downstream. Safer workflows stop them earlier. Every team chooses a point on that spectrum, whether intentionally or not.

One of the most important tools for shaping that workflow is how teams use Git.

The Myth of the Perfect Git Flow

Why are we talking about "Git" in a chapter about team workflows? When developers hear the word "Git," they often see it as a tool to "manage the history of our code." And while history is one of Git's best features, it is much more than that. To start, Git is a coordination system.

Teams use Git to

- **Isolate Unfinished Work:** A branch is not just a technical construct. It is a workflow decision. By creating a branch, a developer can start working on a task without interfering with anyone else. The code can be incomplete, wrong, or experimental - and remain safely contained.

- **Create Checkpoints for Review:** Pull requests are not just a feature of GitHub or GitLab. They are a collaboration mechanism. They define a moment where unfinished work becomes visible and open for discussion. This is where teams share context, challenge assumptions, and reduce uncertainty.

- **Control When Changes Become Visible:** Merging code is not a technical action. It is a team decision. Tapping "Merge" is easy; taking responsibility for what happens after is not. Every merge reflects a shared agreement on the change's maturity and the risk the team is willing to accept.

- **Define Responsibility and Ownership:** Every commit, review, and comment is tied to a person. This creates accountability not only for the code itself but also for the decisions made along the way. Git does not just track changes to files - it records how a team works together.

We can see that how we implement Git has a significant impact on our day-to-day workflows within the team.

So, one of the questions I asked our interviewees was "How do you use Git?" The answer indicated how the team works.

However, what struck me about the answers is that, even in Git, we can find a spectrum of implementations, including the classic "GitFlow" many developers are aware of. Even in a relatively short list of developers, the implementations ranged from a full GitFlow to a fast trunk-based workflow.

From GitFlow to Trunk-Based

Before we go any further, let's be precise about terminology.

When I say *"Git workflow,"* I really mean *"Git branching workflow."*

Branching is how we adapt Git to the way teams work. It reflects how we organize tasks, isolate risk, and collaborate. When we open a branch, we usually open a task – a feature, a bug fix, or an experiment. When we branch from another branch, it often signals something more specific: parallel work, dependencies, or scope uncertainty.

In that sense, Git branching is not just a technical detail. It mirrors how a team thinks and operates.

If branching reflects how teams work, we could expect to see dozens of different Git workflows. After all, every team works a little differently. But in practice, that's not what we see. Most teams today operate somewhere on a spectrum between two dominant approaches: GitFlow and trunk-based development. This spectrum raises an interesting question - does Git reflect how teams work? Or did teams adapt the way they work to fit a few well-known Git workflows?

To explore that, we'll start with GitFlow – the workflow that, for many years, became the default way teams structured their Git repositories.

GitFlow As a Standard

GitFlow is a branching strategy built around control and stability. Its popularity comes from a simple idea: separate ongoing development from released, production-ready code. By doing so, GitFlow helps teams work on multiple features, fixes, and versions while keeping releases predictable.

What I just described sounds complex, and it is. But for many teams, this complexity reflects reality.

When teams plan how to use Git, they usually end up asking the same questions:

- Where do we develop new features?

- Where do we stabilize?

- Where do we release from?

- Where do we fix bugs?

- Where do we apply urgent fixes?

These questions apply to every team. Without a clear strategy, even a team of three developers can quickly get into a mess.

To understand how GitFlow answers these questions, let's look at Figure 9-1.

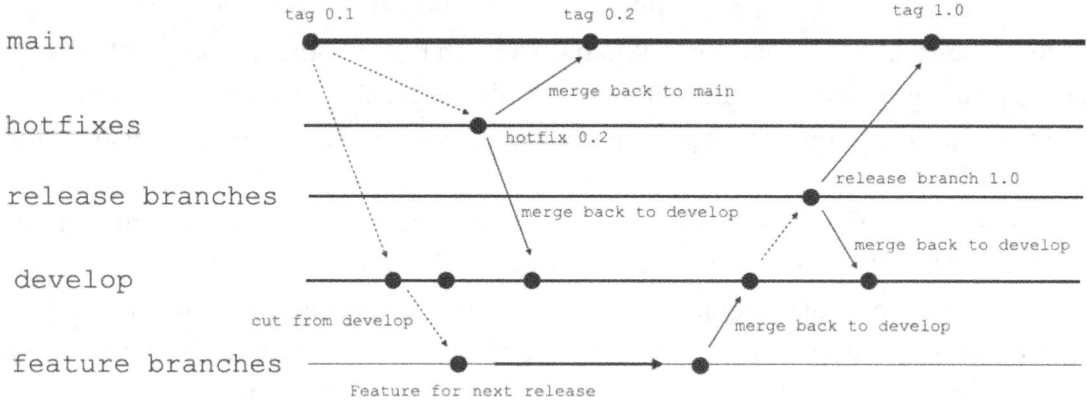

Figure 9-1. *GitFlow branching model*

At first glance, Figure 9-1 might look complex. But it shows how different branches fit into a typical team workflow. Each branch has a clear role.

- **main:** The `main` branch represents the production branch. Every released version is merged into `main` and usually tagged. That is why `main` reflects the code that is actually running on users' devices. Teams typically protect this branch and avoid committing directly to it.

- **develop:** The `develop` branch is the integration branch. Teams merge completed features and fixes into it to see how everything works together. QA often tests against this branch. Teams usually treat `develop` as releasable in principle, meaning they avoid merging unfinished or broken work.

- **Feature Branches:** Feature branches are created from `develop`. Each branch represents a single task: a feature, bug fix, refactor, or experiment. Once the work is done, the branch is merged back into `develop` and deleted. A common mistake is keeping feature branches alive for too long. That increases merge conflicts and disconnects the branch from ongoing changes.

- **Release Branches:** Teams cut a release branch from `develop` when they decide to stabilize a version. At this point, no new features are added. The focus shifts to bug fixes and release preparation. Once the version is stable, the branch is merged into `main`, tagged, and merged back into `develop`. This flow freezes the code for release while allowing other work to continue.

- **Hotfixes:** Hotfix branches are created directly from `main`, not from `develop`. They exist to handle urgent production issues that cannot wait for the next planned release. Once the fix is released, it is merged back into `develop` to ensure it becomes part of the next version.

Looking at these branches together, GitFlow clearly creates distance between code and production. Each branch adds a checkpoint. Features are isolated, integration is controlled, releases are stabilized, and production is protected. This model works well for teams that favor clear stages and parallel work, but it comes at the cost of speed and complexity. So, the question remains: which teams choose GitFlow, and why?

The next section may surprise you.

Do Indie Developers Use GitFlow?

GitFlow's complexity exists for a reason. It supports parallel work in larger teams, where developers can work on multiple features, fixes, and releases simultaneously. Because of that, before I started interviewing teams for this book, I assumed GitFlow was the default for most teams. I was wrong.

One of the biggest surprises came from an indie developer. Mikaela works alone, yet she uses GitFlow.

Mikaela was one of the first developers I interviewed, so her answer didn't raise any red flags at first. Only after talking to more teams did it start to feel unusual. An indie developer doesn't need to integrate work from other developers. There are no parallel features or competing release candidates to coordinate.

So, I asked Mikaela directly why she chose GitFlow. She said:

I chose it cause it's pretty simple and similar to what I've used at work.I use "main" as what's currently on the App Store, "dev" is the changes for the next version, and then feature branchesBut I may change it up and start just having main and feature branches only, and then just tag release commits when needed.

She didn't choose GitFlow because her solo project needed that structure. She chose it because it felt familiar and safe.

Mikaela's choice brings us back to a question I raised earlier in this chapter: does Git shape how teams work, or do teams shape Git to fit how they already work?

In Mikaela's case, the answer is clear. She took a workflow she already knew and applied it as-is. Developers rely on patterns. We do this constantly when we write networking code, design models, or build SwiftUI lists, and Git workflows are no different. GitFlow is simply a pattern many developers carry with them from team to team.

The second part of Mikaela's answer is just as important. She already sees GitFlow as overhead. Her instinct is to drop the dev branch and work only with `main` and feature branches, tagging releases when needed. For a solo developer, that's a natural move. The `develop` branch exists to integrate work from multiple developers. When you work alone, it solves a problem that doesn't exist.

At that point, she would no longer be using GitFlow. She would be using a trunk-based workflow.

Trunk-Based – The "New" GitFlow?

We often treat Git branching strategies as purely technical decisions. In practice, they behave more like trends. Just as design patterns do, they rise, dominate for a while, and then evolve as the industry matures. We saw the same pattern earlier with Coordinator, MVVM, and VIPER.

GitFlow became popular around 2014–2015, right as mobile apps started scaling seriously. Teams needed predictable release cycles, safe parallel work on complex features, and space for thorough manual QA. GitFlow gave them a clear structure - feature branches, release branches, hotfixes - and quickly became the default, even for smaller teams.

By 2019–2020, the balance began to shift. Release cycles accelerated. Automated testing became standard. Feature flags matured. Many teams still respected GitFlow but found the ceremony too heavy for their new pace. The sentence you started hearing more and more was

We still use GitFlow. But simpler...

This approach is exactly where Mikaela sits. When she described her workflow as "similar to what I've used at work," she was reflecting the industry state around 2020–2021, when a simplified GitFlow still felt like the safe, responsible choice. Since then, many teams (including some we interviewed) have continued simplifying further - moving toward faster integration, shorter branches, and greater trust in automation.

Let's look at Figure 9-2.

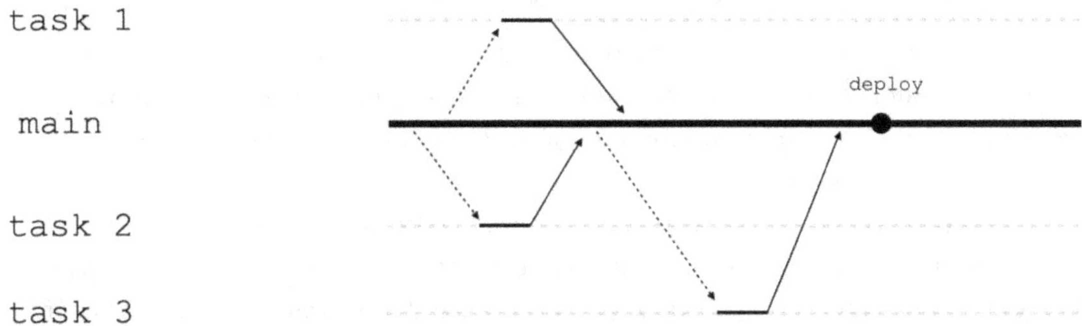

Figure 9-2. *A trunk-based strategy*

Figure 9-2 shows a different branching strategy called trunk-based development.

In a trunk-based workflow, developers work on a single persistent branch, main, and merge small, frequent changes into it.

The diagram illustrates this clearly. One thick main line runs straight across, while several very short branches (task 1, task 2, task 3) briefly diverge and merge back almost immediately. These are not long-running feature branches. They are short-lived task branches that exist only briefly and rarely overlap for more than a day.

Compared to GitFlow, trunk-based development is dramatically simpler, and that simplicity shows up in the team's day-to-day work. Developers never "go on a journey" for weeks on a private branch. They stay in sync with the rest of the codebase. Merges usually happen the same day or the next, which is why merge conflicts are relatively rare. When branches live for less than 24–36 hours, the chance of two people editing the same lines at the same time drops sharply.

Mikaela is far from alone in this shift. Noam Efergan and the Yazio team already run a full trunk-based workflow with multiple daily merges. Stefan uses a simplified version of GitFlow that leans heavily in the same direction. Krzysztof is actively moving away from GitFlow toward a lighter approach.

Even though this book isn't a scientific study, a clear pattern emerges from these conversations. Trunk-based development is increasingly taking the role GitFlow played a decade ago. The industry appears to be going through a similar shift to the one we saw around 2013–2015, this time toward simplicity.

To understand why this is happening, we first need to look at the real cost of trunk-based development and what it actually demands from a team.

How Does Everything Play Together

This isn't the first time I say that in the book, and probably won't be the last – but this book is not about coding; it's about culture. When we examine different teams, we care less about their coding solutions and more about how they deal with problems, culturally and process-wise.

That's why it will be a mistake to look at shifting to trunk-based development without the right context and isolated from other parallel trends and evolution. To get a broader context, we need to go back to Chapters 4 and 5, as well as look at the history of developers in that area. Looking at these chapters shows that testing and CI/CD go hand in hand and influence the team's rhythm. But one thing is missing there, and that's history.

Let's look at Figure 9-3.

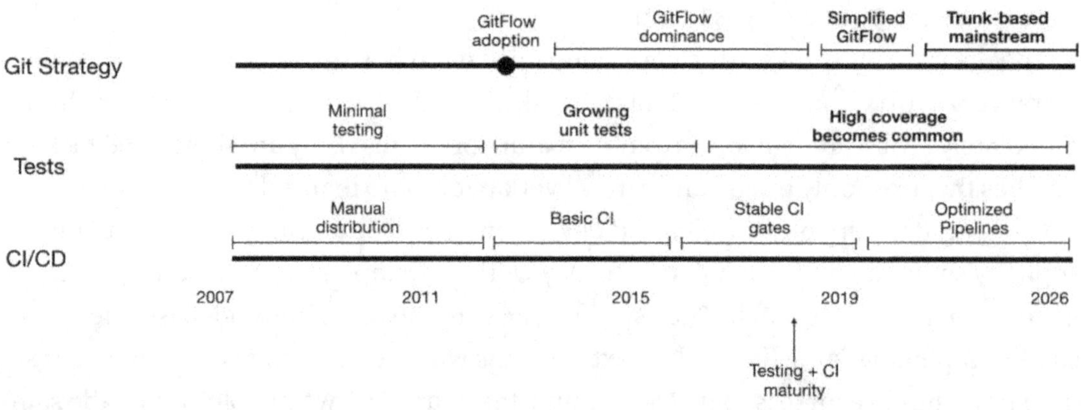

Figure 9-3. *How the maturity of the industry paved the way to trunk-based*

It's really challenging to understand how everything connects without placing the different tracks on a clear timeline. The story of our developers is simple – when we rely heavily on CI/CD and automated tests, it's easier to push changes more quickly and more frequently. Remember the team's rhythm we talked about? That's exactly it. The culture has changed, and Figure 9-3 shows that nicely.

Trunk-based development only works when feedback is fast.

Without automated testing and CI, constantly merging into main is reckless.

With fast feedback, it becomes the most honest workflow possible.

As teams grow, they trade speed for predictability.

Not because they love process, but because the cost of uncertainty increases.

The Different Levels of Workflows

When I was younger (and I was!), I was taught that to really understand something, we should ask "why?" three times to get to the bottom of the issue. Why did the kid get hurt? Because he climbed the tree. Why did he climb the tree? Because he wanted to grab the apple. Why did he want the apple? Because he was hungry. Boom. That's the real reason for the injury - not the climbing itself.

The same applies to branching strategies. It's tempting to say teams moved to trunk-based development because CI/CD improved. That's true - but it's only one layer of the story. CI maturity explains how teams can move faster. It doesn't explain why some teams still choose GitFlow.

So, let's dig deeper.

The Team's Workflows

When I asked developers how their workflows look, I received almost "boring" answers: kickoff meeting, discussion, implementation, pull request, code review, testing, and release. On the surface, every workflow sounded the same. But when I reviewed my notes, I noticed something interesting: the workflows were almost identical - except for small nuances.

And those nuances tell the real story.

Take kickoff meetings. Most teams hold them, but not in the same way. Vivino and Deloitte start every feature with a formal kickoff. Noam from Yazio told me they only hold kickoff meetings for large features. That sounds like a minor detail - but it isn't.

Or consider code reviews. All teams perform them. But Monika from Vivino described cross-squad reviews, in which developers from other iOS teams review pull requests. That's not just review - that's organizational alignment.

The same pattern appears with technical design documents. Vivino, Deloitte, and Danijela's previous workplace use formal tech design documents. Other teams don't.

And here's where it gets interesting: those same teams also use GitFlow.

Wait - what?

How do tech design documents, cross-squad reviews, and formal kickoff meetings have anything to do with a branching strategy?

The answer is that different teams have distinct structural patterns, typically organized into three levels.

The Three Levels of Workflow Patterns

To understand structural workflow patterns, we need to go back to a core idea from earlier chapters: the cost of distance. The real issue is not the bug itself, but how far it is allowed to travel before we catch it.

Every team makes a conscious or unconscious decision about that distance. Some teams can afford to discover issues in QA or even in production in exchange for speed. For others, that would be unacceptable. The workflow they design reflects that price.

Based on the interviews, we can roughly group teams into three levels. Let's start with the first one.

Level 1: Intuition-Driven (Indie Minimalism)

What workflow does an indie developer have? Do they even have one?

Indeed, indie developers don't use heavyweight processes like large corporations. But that doesn't mean they lack structure. A solo developer still thinks through a feature before building it, and that internal thinking is their kickoff meeting. They still review their own code. They still test before release. They still choose a branching strategy, even if it's lightweight. (And yes, Mikaela, I'm looking at you.)

In practice, indie developers follow the same classic flow as bigger teams (Figure 9-4).

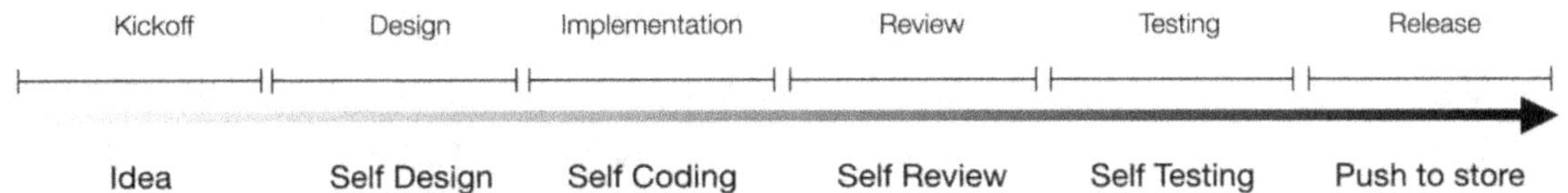

Figure 9-4. *Indie developer intuition workflow*

In Figure 9-4, we can see that the difference lies in scale and formality.

Documentation might exist only as code comments. QA is self-testing. Branching is simplified. Releases are fast and frequent.

This simplicity enables speed. But speed comes with a cost, when bugs are more likely to reach production. The key difference is that for indie developers, the price of that mistake is relatively small. The user base is smaller, and hotfixes can be shipped quickly. There are fewer dependencies and fewer stakeholders.

We already saw this pattern in the testing and CI/CD chapters. Now we can name it at the workflow level: a structure optimized for speed, driven more by intuition and momentum than by organizational constraints.

Interestingly, this pattern doesn't belong only to indie developers. Early-stage startups often operate the same way before their first launch. At that stage, speed matters more than long-term stability. The workflow reflects that priority.

Level 1 shows us what happens when one person handles the whole workflow. But what happens when the team grows? Can we still count on intuition, simplicity, and speed? In this case, the workflow expands, adding new checkpoints that help the team manage risks.

That's where Level 2 comes in.

Level 2: Team-Scale Process

The moment another developer joins the project, the dynamic changes. The "self-review" we saw in Figure 9-4 no longer suffices, because decisions now need to be explained and aligned. An idea that once lived only in one person's head must now be shared. Testing cannot rely solely on intuition, and assumptions must be made explicit. This shift does not come from distrust - it comes from scale. In Level 2, the price of mistakes increases, and so does the need for structure. The workflow itself does not change in shape, but it becomes heavier.

Level 2 typically represents small, growing teams. They still value speed and want to move forward quickly. Bugs found in QA - and even occasionally in production - are not catastrophic, as long as they are not high-severity. The team accepts a certain amount of risk in exchange for momentum. The key difference from Level 1 is that responsibility is no longer centralized in one person; it is distributed. Collaboration becomes part of the process, and that alone introduces friction.

We can see this pattern clearly in teams like Yazio, and Stream. Noam from Yazio shared that kickoff meetings usually happen only for large features. Stefan explained that at Stream, they keep things minimal: a short discussion, then straight to implementation. In all three cases, structure exists, but it is intentionally lightweight.

Selective or minimal kickoffs naturally introduce risk. Alignment may not be perfect, and different developers may interpret requirements slightly differently. Issues can surface during implementation and sometimes even after release. Yet these teams are comfortable operating this way. Their confidence does not come from extensive upfront planning, but from the systems that surround their development process.

With trunk-based development, strong CI/CD pipelines, and automated testing, they reduce the distance a mistake can travel. Critical bugs are unlikely to survive the pipeline, and when something does slip through, the team can respond quickly. Releases are frequent, fixes are fast, and the cost of change remains manageable. Level 2, therefore, is not about chaos or informality. It is about structured speed - a balance between collaboration and momentum, where infrastructure replaces ceremony as the primary safety net.

Figure 9-5 shows a classic team workflow in Level 2. If it looks similar to Figure 9-4, that's because the basic stages are still the same.

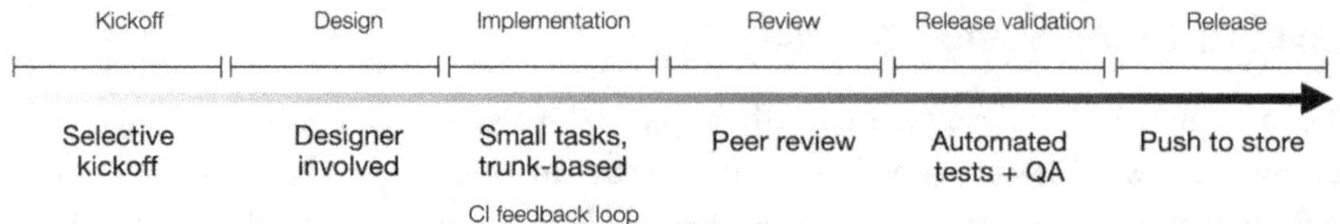

Figure 9-5. *Level 2 workflow*

In Figure 9-5, we can see selective kickoff meetings, small pull requests, and a strong reliance on automated testing. These teams understand that mistakes can reach the App Store, so they place a few lightweight checkpoints along the way - kickoff discussions, peer review, automated tests, and QA before release.

These checkpoints are intentionally not airtight. The goal is not to eliminate all risk, but to preserve flow. Critical issues are likely to be caught, while speed remains a priority.

If Level 2 focuses on protecting the team from critical bugs reaching production while preserving development speed, Level 3 shifts the focus. It not only protects against bugs - it protects against misalignment, coordination failures, and ripple effects across squads.

Level 3: Product-Scale Process

Teams operating at Level 3 are not simply adding more checkpoints. Their goal is different. The concern is no longer only preventing bugs from reaching production. It is preventing misalignment within and across teams. As the coordination scale increases, the potential business impact increases. The process becomes tighter not to slow development, but to protect the organization.

One clear change is the kickoff meeting. At Vivino, Deloitte, and Danijela's previous workplace, every feature begins with one. Oliver from Deloitte said, "We feel it pays off." Danijela described how, after the kickoff, the team sits together to create user stories and tasks. Monika explained that a design discussion and a short sync between developers follow the kickoff. These are not ceremonial steps. They are alignment mechanisms. In Level 2, some features skip kickoffs. Here, that is rarely the case.

Documentation also becomes more formal. Instead of relying only on Figma screens and Jira tickets, these teams write technical design documents. The goal is not bureaucracy. It is clarity. When multiple squads share components, documentation helps teams review decisions early and prepare better for implementation.

Code reviews change as well. In smaller teams, a peer review is often enough. At the product scale, review becomes a structural safeguard. Vivino conducts cross-squad code reviews. That creates shared ownership and reduces architectural silos. Monika also noted that the expectation is that code submitted for review is already perfect - accountability starts before the PR is opened. At Deloitte, Oliver requires reviewers to run the code locally. Danijela described a process that required two approvals. Different implementations, same intent: review is a serious checkpoint before release.

The branching strategy reflects this shift. While Level 2 teams often use trunk-based development, Level 3 teams typically use a GitFlow-style branching model. Features merge into the develop branch, where integration happens in a controlled environment before merging into main for release. Integration risk is absorbed in stages. The rhythm changes, and releases are coordinated and predictable. GitFlow is not the cause of this structure - it is the consequence of operating at product scale.

Let's have a look at Figure 9-6.

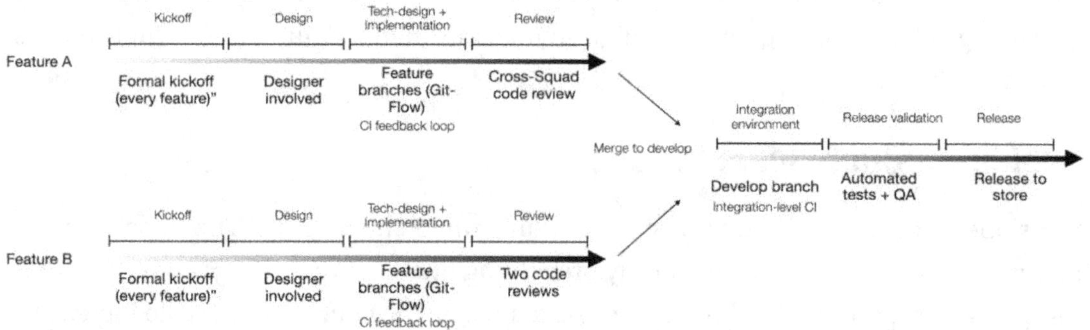

Figure 9-6. *Level 3 workflow*

Figure 9-6 shows the complexity of teams that prefer to catch the mistakes much earlier in the process. We can see two feature branches side by side, with formal kickoff meetings and extensive code reviews – sometimes by a developer from another team and, in other cases, by multiple developers.

Notice that these two branches get feedback from the CI during their implementation stage – do you remember our discussion in Chapter 5 about the outer and inner circles? So that's a good example of an inner circle. During the feature implementation stage, the developer receives immediate feedback from the CI about potential issues.

After the code reviews passed, the team merges the code into the integration environment – the develop branch, where it goes through the outer circle – a full CI process and a QA. From that point, the team creates a release branch and releases the app to the app store.

The integration branch also causes another interesting change in the process – periodicity releases.

Level 3's Coordinated Heartbeat

Another clear difference at Level 3 is release cadence. Unlike Levels 1 and 2, where teams often release whenever a feature is ready, product-scale teams usually release on fixed cycles - most commonly every two weeks. This pattern appeared repeatedly in the interviews. It is not accidental, nor is it simply a habit. It reflects how these organizations manage coordination at scale.

Technically, the develop branch in a GitFlow-style model allows a team to release at any time. Nothing prevents them from cutting a release earlier if everything looks stable. But in practice, these teams rarely operate that way. When we look back at Figure 9-6 and examine the workflow more closely, the reason becomes clear. Multiple squads work in parallel. Backend and mobile teams must stay aligned. QA needs to allocate time for regression testing. Sometimes marketing prepares campaigns or announcements around feature launches. In this environment, releases are no longer purely technical events. They are organizational events.

Without a shared rhythm, coordination quickly turns into chaos. One team may be ready while another is still stabilizing. QA may be overwhelmed by unpredictable release requests. Business stakeholders may not know when to prepare communication. The absence of cadence increases friction across the system. A fixed release cycle solves this by creating a predictable heartbeat for the entire organization.

At this scale, the team behaves like a coordinated system. The rhythm matters. You can accelerate it if needed, but it must remain synchronized across all participants. If releases happen randomly, misalignment appears in production - not necessarily as crashes, but as incomplete features, mismatched backend contracts, or partially integrated flows. The risk is no longer just a bug. It is systemic inconsistency.

An interesting question is how much time a fixed cycle takes. Danijela described two-week sprints and releases at her previous company, and Vivino releases a version every week. For many teams, two weeks is short enough to maintain a sense of progress and agility, but long enough to integrate parallel work, run integration-level CI, perform regression testing, and validate the release with QA. The fixed cycle also removes decision fatigue. There is no ongoing debate about whether to release today or wait until tomorrow. The schedule is clear. The train leaves on time.

At product scale, with shared libraries, multiple squads, and large user bases, predictability becomes more valuable than raw speed. The release cadence is not a limitation of GitFlow. It is a structural response to coordination pressure.

Now that we've gone through the different levels, let's try to summarize them so we can position ourselves correctly.

Picking Our Level

For some readers, the three-level framework will feel very familiar. For others, it may feel slightly detached from their day-to-day reality. That is expected. Many teams operate in hybrid modes. A startup with one iOS developer might adopt GitFlow yet still release every few days. A large organization might use trunk-based development but maintain a fixed two-week release cadence. The levels are not strict rules; they frame how teams coordinate their work from idea to release while balancing speed, safety, and alignment.

The model is descriptive, not prescriptive. It explains patterns that emerge as coordination pressure increases. Some teams move gradually from one level to another. Others intentionally mix practices. What matters is not compliance with a level, but awareness of the trade-offs involved.

To clarify the differences, Table 9-1 summarizes the three levels across several dimensions.

Table 9-1. *Workflow's three-level comparison*

Dimension	Level 1: Indie: Early stage	Level 2: Team Scale	Level 3: Product Scale
Team size	1–2 developers	Small team (3–8 devs)	Multiple squads
Coordination pressure	Minimal	Within-team alignment	Cross-squad alignment
Primary goal	Ship fast	Protect speed without breaking production	Protect organizational stability
Kickoff meetings	Rare or informal	Only for large features	Formal kickoff for every feature
Tech design documents	Usually none	Sometimes for complex work	Standard practice
Designer involvement	Informal/async	Often involved	Structured and synchronized
Branching strategy	Main + feature branches	Trunk-based	GitFlow
Pull requests + code reviews	Rare, informal	Small PRs, peer review	Structured reviews, sometimes cross-squad
QA process	Self-testing	Light QA before release	Dedicated QA + regression windows
Release cadence	When ready	Continuous /flexible	Fixed cycles (often two weeks)
Release trigger	Feature done	CI green	Release train schedule
Typical examples	Mikaela (indie), early startups	Yazio	Vivino, Deloitte

Table 9-1 highlights how teams at different scales approach similar challenges. Try to locate your own team in this table. Which column feels closest to your reality? Does it align with your current priorities - speed, simplicity, organizational stability?

There is no perfect workflow. There is only a workflow that fits our coordination scale and risk tolerance. The real question is not which level is "better," but whether our current process matches the pressure our team is operating under.

For example, does our team have a robust CI/CD infrastructure? Can we safely push changes to the main branch? How big is the team? What industry are we in, and how many users do we have? These questions' goal is to answer one simple question: how much risk are we willing to take? This can let us look at the table and pick what's relevant to us.

Summary

A team workflow is the invisible system that moves a product from idea to the App Store. Throughout this chapter, we explored why the real cost of a mistake is not the bug itself, but the distance it travels before we catch it. We saw how we shape the distance by branching strategies, CI/CD maturity, release cadence, and organizational alignment.

We examined Git not only as a version-control tool but also as a coordination mechanism. We compared GitFlow and trunk-based development and placed them on a broader historical timeline. Most importantly, we identified three structural workflow levels - intuition-driven, team-scale, and product-scale - and analyzed how coordination pressure transforms processes as teams grow.

There is no perfect workflow. There is only a workflow that matches a team's coordination scale, infrastructure maturity, and risk tolerance. When the structure is too light for the pressure a team operates under, instability follows. When it is too heavy, speed suffers. The goal is not to adopt trends, but to consciously design how far mistakes are allowed to travel.

In the next and final chapter, we turn to a force that is already reshaping these workflows: AI. Workflow design is about controlling distance and coordination, but AI may change our whole perspective. Great things to follow!

CHAPTER 10

Moving to the AI Era

Introduction

We're starting the last chapter of the book, and it's time to shift gears and open a topic that is probably the hottest subject today for developers - and much of the world: **the AI era**.

Unlike many of the topics we discussed earlier, AI is still very new. Tools, workflows, and patterns are not yet set in stone, and the landscape is evolving constantly. In this chapter, we'll explore how the developers I interviewed approach this change, each moving at their own pace.

In this chapter, we

- Discuss the **tension** between AI and developers

- Define the present: how developers are using AI in their **current workflows**

- Explore the idea of a **bottleneck shift** from execution to planning

- Take a **glimpse into the future** and see how developers might automate large parts of their workflows with AI

Let's jump into the first section and zoom out to understand where AI fits in.

The Assumption We Never Questioned

In the previous chapter, we explored real team workflows. We discussed trunk-based development as the evolving branching strategy. We examined CI discipline, PR culture, and one central idea: the distance a bug travels.

© Avi Tsadok 2026
A. Tsadok, *Real-World iOS Development*, https://doi.org/10.1007/979-8-8688-2815-7_10

When we zoom out, something becomes clear. That chapter was not about code. **It was about culture**. And if we zoom out even further, we see that most of this book is about culture. Architecture serves business goals. Testing reflects risk tolerance. Data management balances truth and experience. Navigation shapes how teams think about ownership. Every "technical" decision we discussed was, in reality, a human decision.

Developing a product, whether in a large team or as an indie, means planning, negotiating trade-offs, balancing constraints, and working within human limitations.

Let's recap a few of the core topics:

- **Architecture:** We said it must serve the company's business goals. Architecture helps developers support growth and scale the app responsibly.

- **Testing:** We know testing increases stability, but it comes at a cost. Every team must decide how much overhead they are willing to accept in exchange for safety.

- **Data:** Choosing a data strategy is not just technical. It shapes long-term scalability, UI performance, and how closely we stay connected to the source of truth.

At first glance, these topics look technical. In practice, they are deeply human, and because behind all of them lies one hidden assumption.

Humans write the code.

Everything in this book rests on this premise:

Humans design the architecture, choose the testing strategy, decide when to merge, and review pull requests, balancing speed and safety.

Developers make dozens of decisions every day, and those decisions shape the codebase and sometimes the business dramatically.

But our world is changing. And it is changing fast. During the time I spent writing this book, AI tools evolved so quickly that I had to revisit parts of what I had written. Capabilities improved. Boundaries shifted. What felt experimental became practical.

So here is the question that challenges the foundation of everything we discussed:

What happens when AI writes the code instead of humans?

Does architecture change? Do tests look different? What happens to CI when execution becomes cheap? Does branching strategy still matter? What happens to pull requests?

And more importantly, if writing code is no longer the bottleneck, **where do the real challenges move?**

These are not theoretical questions. They are already reshaping how teams work. However, the questions don't end. In fact, it's just the beginning of our story.

Dive into the Tensions Between Teams

Let's make this even more complex.

We already know there are powerful tools that exist that can dramatically speed up development. If AI is reshaping how we write code, we might expect teams to respond similarly. After all, this is one professional community. We face similar problems, use similar tools, attend the same conferences, and follow the same announcements from Apple, OpenAI, Anthropic, and others. It is almost impossible today to find a conference talk, blog post, or a book that does not position AI as a core development tool - including this one.

With that in mind, it's reasonable to expect some baseline adoption. A shared direction. A gradual but collective shift.

That is not what is happening.

When I spoke with developers for this book, I noticed something unexpected. There is no unified movement and no agreed-upon best practice. Instead, there is a wide spectrum of approaches.

Some teams are **moving fast**. They integrate tools like Copilot, Cursor, and Claude deeply into their workflows. They use AI to generate tests, create mocks, draft documentation, and even refactor complex code sections. For them, AI is not a side experiment; it has become part of the development infrastructure.

Other teams move much more cautiously. They experiment with AI for brainstorming, repetitive snippets, or documentation drafts, but they keep core logic, architectural decisions, and critical flows firmly in human hands. The boundary is clear: AI can assist, **but it does not lead.**

And then there are teams that barely use AI at all. In some cases, the reason is security constraints or regulatory requirements. In others, legacy architecture makes integration harder. But often, **the reason is cultural**. Some teams simply do not yet trust the tool enough to let it shape their workflow.

These differences are not minor. Different tools, different speeds, and different levels of trust directly influence how AI adoption unfolds inside each team. As execution becomes easier for some teams but not for others, velocity becomes uneven. The gap widens.

However, assuming this gap is only about how quickly developers produce code would miss the deeper shift. The real divergence does not lie in typing speed or automation. It lies in **how teams think**, review, and make decisions. What once felt like differences in architecture or testing strategy now reflects something deeper: different philosophies of adoption.

Before we dive in, let's try to frame our discussion – AI can serve us in so many ways, but as iOS developers, we mostly focus on vibe coding. So, let's briefly understand how vibe coding actually works.

How Vibe Coding Really Works

When we say "Vibe Coding," we mean coding by providing clear, simple, and free language instructions that generate code. In other words, vibe coding is what we all know as **prompts for an LLM**.

Chatting with an LLM feels, for most of us, still, like magic. As developers, we understand how it works, but when coding, this illusion of conversation hides structural risk.

Talking with a model feels like a real collaboration – we describe our intent, the model implements it, and the process continues until we refine it to our needs. We have an impression of something so creative and fluid, but underneath, vibe coding is just a statistical completion – it doesn't understand our product or architecture. What vibe coding really does is predict what is likely, not what is correct.

Context As the Hidden Constraint

The real constraint of vibe coding is the context – we can provide as much as we can, but ultimately the model sees **only what we give it** and operates within a limited context window. We, as developers, often have the full picture, but the model fills its unknown gaps with common patterns. This brings us back (again!) to Chapter 2 about architecture and design patterns – clear architecture and design patterns can improve the output quality. The larger and messier the codebase, the greater the risk to our project. Let's remember – vibe coding scales with architecture clarity, not with code size, and that's the key sentence here. Why? Because that defines the real skill developers need with vibe coding. Decomposition.

Decomposition Becomes the Real Skill

Vibe coding demos sometimes look like *"Build me a todo list app with lists and a persistent store."* This method works amazingly well for presentations, but can confuse developers. Is this how we should use vibe coding? *"Refactor this component"* or *"Build me a screen that fetches a list of users from the backend"*? Not exactly – remember what we said about providing context and clear instructions. High-quality vibe coding requires **breaking our work into small tasks**, defining constraints, rules, and examples. It also requires iterating over our process per component and reviewing the output. Senior engineers scale with AI, but for undisciplined engineers, AI is an extremely efficient engine to produce chaos faster.

Let's break this down for a second – we've talked about it in Chapter 2. Developers work in patterns – creating a request, defining a data structure, or creating a list in SwiftUI. These are all patterns we use over and over again, and for senior developers, many of the coding tasks feel repetitive. What vibe coding really does is save senior developers from these repetitive tasks. So, the danger shifts to other places – architecture, abstractions, incorrect logic, and product edge cases. These are the places the model can't handle without good context and instructions. And since AI-generated bad code can look convincing, vibe coding is where review discipline becomes critical. This also raises some serious questions: first, if we skip the struggle, where does deep understanding come from, and how will it affect our future development culture? And second, what is the new bottleneck within an iOS team? We'll get to that soon. If vibe coding reshapes how we execute, the next question becomes unavoidable:

What changes inside the team?

The Present: AI in the Real Workflow

Trying to discuss AI in a book poses two major challenges. First, things move quickly, and keeping up with all the changes is almost impossible. Second, unlike other topics, there is no reliable way to forecast where we are heading in this era.

Because of that, starting with the future does not seem like a good idea. Describing the interview findings and framing them to better understand today's reality is the best way to start.

And that is exactly what we are going to do now. AI adoption **also lies on a spectrum**, like other topics we explored in this book.

So, let's start at one end and move from there.

Minimal Implementation

Before we begin, one thing is important to note: the interviews were conducted at a specific point in time, at the end of 2025. There is a good chance that some things have changed since then. Still, it is interesting to see how different developers adopt AI tools at different paces.

For some developers, relying on AI for coding does not sound appealing. What is interesting is that each developer chose to avoid AI coding for a different reason.

Simplicity As a Strategy

Let's start with **Mikaela**. At the time of the interview, she chose to stay conservative and write her own Swift code. If we look at Mikaela's approach throughout the book, we can see that she consistently chooses simplicity as her strategy. She avoids complex design systems (Chapter 6), avoids local persistent stores and sync complexity (Chapter 8), and avoids complex navigation solutions such as coordinators (Chapter 7).

Mikaela follows a clear pattern: **if the problem does not exist yet, do not try to fix it**. For her, at least at the time of writing, AI coding tools introduce generated abstractions and the risk of architectural drift. More directly, Mikaela does not want code she has not fully reasoned about.

Remember, Mikaela is an indie developer who owns the backend, UI, architecture, and marketing. For her, AI adds unpredictability, which can be expensive when you are the only engineer, the only designer, the only marketing manager, and the only QA. We can see these patterns throughout the book.

Control and Clean Boundaries

Mikaela did not explicitly tell me why she avoided coding with AI. But by Chapter 10, I have gathered enough material to shape her developer profile.

With that in mind, let's move to **Danijela Vrzan** and examine a slightly different approach.

If we recap what we know about Danijela so far, one thing stands out: she likes to **stay in control**. In the testing chapter (Chapter 4), we saw that she worked at a company that maintained 90% test coverage and relied heavily on snapshot testing. This company also had strong design ownership (Chapter 6). Even in her indie projects, Danijela values structure. She defines clear model boundaries and carefully separates her SwiftData stores.

For a developer who comes from snapshot-testing-based CI, hundreds of tests, and well-defined design systems, AI can feel **risky**. AI tools often introduce hidden abstractions, blur architectural intent, and bypass deliberate decisions. It is easy to see why someone with Danijela's background would approach AI cautiously.

At first, her use of AI was limited. She used ChatGPT mainly for complex tasks involving obscure frameworks, especially when documentation was thin. She also relied on it to rewrite user-facing strings, shorten text to make it clearer, and generate inline code documentation.

Recently, however, her usage expanded. *"I only recently got into agentic coding,"* she told me. She experimented with Claude Code and Cursor and eventually decided to stick with Copilot for now. Danijela used it to implement a custom Quick Look Preview. Since it is an old and obscure framework with very little documentation available, AI helped her move much faster. As she described it, it *"created UI perfectly in a day."*

Still, her boundaries remain firm. *"I still review and read every single line of code and refactor everything. I don't want to lose my skills, and they definitely degrade if relying on AI to do everything."* She also admitted that she was hesitant at first: *"I was hesitant because I really enjoy writing code, but I'm trying not to let AI do everything and review every single line of code, so I know what's going on."*

Danijela's approach is not rejection - she uses AI to accelerate specific tasks, especially in areas where documentation is weak or the framework is unfamiliar. At the same time, she keeps architectural control, reviews every line, and protects her technical understanding. AI is **part of her workflow**, but it does not replace her judgment.

Now, as Monty Python used to say, "and now for something completely different." Using AI to build content.

Building Materials with AI

Up until now, we have looked at AI mainly as a tool for writing code or generating documentation. But AI's impact goes beyond the codebase. **Oliver Binns** shared a simple but powerful example: he uses AI to generate app icons for his personal projects. At first glance, generating an app icon does not seem like a big deal. But when Oliver puts on his indie developer hat, this small use case becomes much more meaningful.

Setting up an app requires **far more than writing code**. Building a real product demands design, copy, marketing materials, content, and yes, app icons. For indie developers, this is a heavy lift. In a world without AI, these requirements can become real obstacles, sometimes even blockers.

Oliver's example may look small, but it signals something much bigger. AI not only accelerates development for large teams with structured workflows. **It lowers the barrier to entry** for indie developers who want to build and ship complete products independently. What used to require a designer, a copywriter, or a marketing partner can now be prototyped, iterated on, and improved independently.

In that sense, AI is not just a coding assistant. It is a force multiplier for anyone trying to build a full-fledged product on their own.

Scoped Automation

What's interesting is that as teams grow larger, we often see a different pattern in how they use AI tools. Many larger teams have not yet fully embraced AI coding. Instead, they seem to be exploring where these tools fit into the development process.

Why do I call this section "Scoped Automation"?

In the previous section "How Vibe Coding Works," we discussed that AI coding performs best when dealing with common patterns. Now let's look at our daily tasks as iOS developers: creating reusable components, handling errors, tracking analytics events, building SwiftUI lists and forms, managing navigation, implementing View Models, and writing unit tests.

What all of these tasks have in common is that they rely on **repeated patterns.** We see them across many projects. As developers, we sometimes feel like we are inventing something new every time we write code, but much of our work follows established structures.

In fact, studies of large codebases suggest that **60–75% of development work consists of patterns that appear repeatedly across projects**. Architectural styles such as MVVM or VIPER reinforce this even further. Once we introduce a View Model, for example, its responsibilities and structure are usually predictable.

Let's look at Figure 10-1.

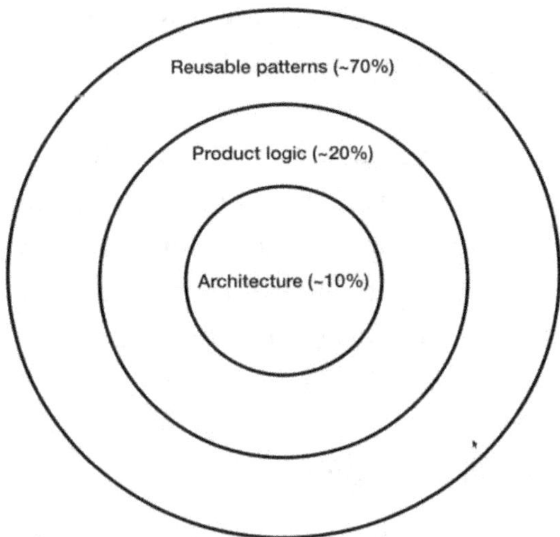

Figure 10-1. *Reusable patterns shared among development tasks*

Figure 10-1 divides development work into three layers:

- About **10% of our work consists of architectural decisions**: how we structure modules, design navigation flows, define data flow, and manage dependencies.

- Around **20% is product logic**: business rules, validation, edge cases, state management, and feature-specific behavior.

- But the largest portion of development work, roughly **70%**, consists of **reusable patterns**, such as the tasks we mentioned earlier.

When we look in the mirror, we often see ourselves as developers constantly making architectural and product decisions. In practice, however, much of our day-to-day work happens in this outer layer of repeated patterns.

So, if AI tools excel at generating these kinds of patterns, and most of our work revolves around them, a natural question emerges:

Why not let AI handle a portion of these routine tasks for us?

This is exactly what I call **scoped automation**.

Now, let's explore if that theory fits some of our interviewees. For example, generating unit tests.

Generating Unit Tests

One task our interviewees repeatedly mentioned is **generating unit tests**. Both **Stefan Blos** and **Monika Mateska** brought it up, and at first, that might sound like a strange task to delegate to AI. Why specifically unit tests?

However, at this point in the chapter, we should already have a sense of why developers choose this task as a natural candidate for AI assistance.

First, many developers see writing unit tests as **routine work**. We know they are important, but they do not directly add visible functionality to the product. From a product perspective, users never interact with them. Yet there are deeper technical reasons why unit tests are such a good fit for vibe coding.

Unit Tests Follow a Very Strict Pattern

Most unit tests follow a very predictable structure: **Arrange → Act → Assert**.

For example:

```
@Test("Calculate total with two items returns correct sum")
func calculateTotal() {
    // Arrange
    let calculator = CartCalculator()
    let items = [Item(price: 10), Item(price: 20)]

    // Act
    let total = calculator.calculateTotal(items)

    // Assert
    #expect(total == 30)
}
```

This is an extremely simple unit test, but its structure is the same as thousands of other tests across different projects. That predictability makes it a perfect target for language models, which excel at generating structured patterns.

Unit Tests Have a Small Context

Earlier, we discussed one of the main limitations of vibe coding: **context**. Human developers usually have the full picture of the system, while an AI model only sees the code we provide. However, this limitation almost disappears with unit tests.

Notice that we are talking about **unit tests**, not integration or UI tests. Unit tests usually operate on a **very small scope**: a single class, a single function, and simple inputs.

In the previous example, we only needed the `CartCalculator` class and the `calculateTotal` function. That's the entire context required to generate the test.

Compare that to implementing a full feature. Suddenly, we need to reason about networking, navigation, design systems, analytics, and application state. Writing production features requires system-level understanding - something LLMs still struggle with.

Unit Tests Are Derived Directly from the Code

Consider the following function:

```swift
func isValidEmail(_ email: String) -> Bool {
    let pattern = #"^[A-Z0-9._%+-]+@[A-Z0-9.-]+\.[A-Z]{2,}$"#
    return email.range(of: pattern, options: [.regularExpression,
    .caseInsensitive]) != nil
}
```

AI can easily generate test cases for this function, such as valid or invalid email addresses or empty strings. The function signature and return type already provide enough information to generate meaningful tests.

In many cases, the model doesn't need to fully understand the implementation. Instead, it **explores the function's input space**. What happens if the input is empty? What happens with edge values? What happens with invalid data?

Interestingly, this is very similar to how developers write their own tests. We explore variations of the input and verify that the output behaves as expected.

For a model trained on patterns, this task is a natural fit.

If generating unit tests works well because they rely on predictable patterns, we can ask a natural question: **what other parts of development share the same characteristics?**

Simple UI components are an obvious candidate.

Building UI Components

One thing **Zlatko** told me is that he finds vibe coding particularly useful for creating small UI components. **Vincent** mentioned something similar: he often uses AI tools for prototyping, which naturally involves generating UI as well.

That made me wonder: why are UI components such good candidates for vibe coding? After all, we've just discussed generating unit tests, but UI code seems more complex.

Let's look at the following code snippet:

```swift
struct PrimaryButton: View {
    let title: String
    let action: () -> Void

    var body: some View {
        Button(action: action) {
            Text(title)
                .font(.headline)
                .padding()
                .frame(maxWidth: .infinity)
                .background(Color.blue)
                .foregroundColor(.white)
                .cornerRadius(8)
        }
    }
}
```

The snippet above defines a reusable SwiftUI button called `PrimaryButton`. If we have built a few SwiftUI views before, it takes only a quick glance to understand what is happening. The structure is **immediately recognizable**: parameters at the top, followed by a `Button` that wraps a `Text` view and applies common modifiers like font, padding, and color.

We can read this code in seconds because we have **seen this structure hundreds of times before**. SwiftUI views rely heavily on predictable building blocks: containers such as `VStack` or `HStack`, visual elements like `Text` and `Image`, and chains of view modifiers that define styling and layout.

Just like unit tests, SwiftUI components follow highly repeatable patterns. These patterns appear across countless applications and codebases. Design systems make this repetition even stronger by defining standard components such as buttons, cards, and rows that are reused throughout the app.

Another reason UI components work well with vibe coding is their **limited scope**. A small component often lives in a single file and depends only on a few inputs, such as text, images, or actions. When the context is small, the model can generate useful code much more reliably. In practice, this also leads to a useful rule of thumb: when working with AI tools in SwiftUI, **keep the scope small and focused**.

However, UI generation also exposes an interesting limitation. SwiftUI has evolved rapidly over the years, and new APIs appear frequently. **Vincent** mentioned that AI tools are sometimes less productive when working with the newest SwiftUI APIs, simply because the models have not yet seen enough examples of them.

Language models rely heavily on repeated patterns. When the framework introduces new patterns, the model initially has less data to rely on, which can make the generated code less accurate.

Performing Small Refactors

Another interesting task AI can help with, according to **Zlatko**, is code refactoring. At first glance, refactoring seems like a task that requires deep reasoning and a strong understanding of the system. If that's the case, how can it be suitable for vibe coding?

The answer lies in distinguishing between **two types of refactoring**: those that operate in the **patterns layer** and those that operate in the **architecture layer**.

Let's look at the following example:

```swift
if user.age >= 18 {
    print("Adult")
} else {
    print("Minor")
}
```

The above example is a simple if-then-else statement. However, we can refactor it to a more convenient function:

```swift
func userCategory(for age: Int) -> String {
    age >= 18 ? "Adult" : "Minor"
}
```

This transformation does not require deep architectural reasoning. Similar to the previous examples of unit tests and SwiftUI components, this kind of refactor is a **predictable structural change**.

In fact, development tools have supported these transformations for years. IDEs can extract methods, rename variables, split large functions, and replace duplicated code with shared logic.

Another reason refactoring works well with AI tools is that it often begins with a **very clear instruction**. Developers might ask the model to *"extract this code into a function"* or *"split this SwiftUI view into smaller components."* As we discussed earlier in the chapter, clear prompts make it much easier for language models to produce useful results.

There is also a practical reason why developers enjoy using AI for refactoring: it reduces cognitive load. Refactoring frequently involves mechanical work such as moving code, renaming symbols, updating call sites, and fixing small compile errors. These steps are tedious but not conceptually difficult.

In this sense, refactoring becomes another example of **scoped automation** - a task where AI can handle repetitive transformations while the developer focuses on higher-level decisions.

All of these small tasks that accelerate our work as developers raise serious questions about the future of our workflows. Let's try to imagine what that future might look like.

The Bottleneck Shift – When Execution Gets Cheap

At this point in the chapter, we've seen how developers implement AI in their day-to-day work, each with its own pace. Now, it's time to turn our heads and try to imagine what the future holds for us. To do that, we first need to analyze the current situation and consider the influence of vibe coding not only on our code but also on our entire workflow and perhaps even on our organizational structure.

Let's talk about our current world of development, or the world as we knew it for years.

The Traditional (Old?) World

Unless you started developing after 2025, you probably recognize the traditional bottleneck in software development: **execution.**

Every feature begins with planning. Teams write PRDs (Product Requirements Documents), hold meetings, and discuss architecture before anyone writes a line of code. This is true not only in corporations and startups, but also among indie developers. Indie developers may skip long meetings and formal documents, but they still spend time thinking, designing, and planning before they start building.

All this ceremony has one clear purpose: **to protect the expensive part of development - execution.**

So, how expensive is execution? There is no definitive study that measures the exact ratio between planning and execution. However, a common estimate in software projects is that implementation and testing take **roughly three to four times longer than planning and design.** In other words, once development begins, most of the work still lies ahead.

And this estimate does not even include the cost of fixing bugs, which we explored in the previous chapter (Chapter 9).

Now look at Figure 10-2.

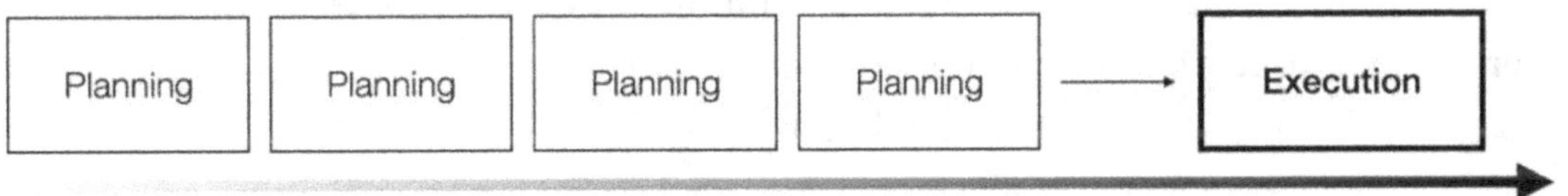

Figure 10-2. *Over-planning before execution*

Figure 10-2 illustrates a situation many developers recognize. A significant portion of time is spent on planning before the team finally reaches the execution phase.

But something interesting is happening now. We already saw how AI accelerates execution. Even developers who are cautious about AI adoption still use it for repetitive and patterned tasks. These tasks represent a large portion of day-to-day development work, and for iOS development, they can easily cover most **typical implementation tasks.**

This shift leads us in a clear direction: **execution becomes cheaper.** When that happens, the bottleneck does not disappear. It simply moves somewhere else. Welcome to the new world.

The World of AI-Driven Workflows

We don't have a time machine, and we can't tell the future, but we can certainly see the direction. We saw what some developers do with vibe coding, and I covered only the more conservative examples. If a large portion of our time is spent on repetitive, patterned tasks, we can imagine the impact this will have on execution in the coming years. **Writing code becomes faster and cheaper**.

But the change doesn't stop there. Refactoring, code modifications, and even bug fixing become cheaper as well. Earlier, we said that the bottleneck shifts. And it really will shift, straight to the top of the funnel.

Look again at Figure 10-2. What used to be the cheaper part of development – problem definition, high-quality PRDs, architectural design, reviews, and planning meetings – existed mainly to protect the execution phase from becoming **too expensive**. These steps helped teams reduce the risk of costly implementation mistakes.

But once execution becomes dramatically cheaper, the equation changes. The same activities that once protected development now become the most expensive part of the workflow.

Now that we understand where the bottleneck moves, we should ask ourselves what the response might be. One option is to speed up planning as well by using more AI tools that generate long, detailed PRDs and presentation decks. But maybe, just maybe, the better option is to rethink how teams work altogether.

Let's drill down a bit and see what that might mean.

The Changes That We'll Have to Make

We now have an amazing tool that can practically write code for us. The problem is that many teams still operate with a traditional workflow mindset, and our thinking remains single-dimensional. One obvious advantage of vibe coding is the ability to write code faster. But another advantage is just as important: **the ability to deliver faster**.

Think back to the trunk-based versus GitFlow discussion from the previous chapter. When we combine faster execution with workflows that support continuous delivery, we gain something even more valuable: **a more direct connection to reality**. Because AI makes execution fast and inexpensive, teams can test ideas quickly with real users instead of spending most of their time planning.

Here are several changes teams can make to adapt their workflow to this new environment:

- **Prioritize Prototyping Over Planning:** PRDs can be useful, but instead of investing large amounts of time in long and detailed documents, teams can often move faster by building a small working prototype. A prototype can sometimes define a feature more clearly than a document.

- **Demos Over Decks:** Many teams rely on long presentation decks during meetings. A working demo can often communicate the idea more effectively. Instead of hearing about the product, the team can interact with it and immediately see how it behaves.

- **Post-Launch Polish:** Combining trunk-based development with AI can enable a different approach to releases. A rough but functional version can replace the traditional demo phase. If the idea shows promise, the team can start rolling it out and continue refining it based on real user feedback. This is a significant shift from the traditional approach, but it may be more logical when execution is cheap and iteration is fast.

These are only some of the adjustments teams can make to remain effective in a world shaped by vibe coding. At first glance, vibe coding seems like a local improvement that simply speeds up development. In reality, accelerating execution can change much more than that. It can influence how teams plan, test ideas, and deliver products.

Interestingly, some of these principles also apply to the traditional world. Even if a team is not yet using vibe coding, many of these practices can still improve the flow of ideas from concept to product.

Some of the Things Are True Regardless of Vibe Coding

Years ago, when I worked as an iOS developer in a small startup, I noticed several recurring problems with my tasks. First, it was difficult to **estimate** when I would actually deliver a feature. Second, many **edge cases** were not clear at the beginning. And finally, the **user experience** often turned out different from what we initially imagined.

The last point was the most painful. I would build a feature around a certain architecture, only to discover later that the experience needed a significant change. At that point, making structural changes to the code was already expensive.

So, I tried a different approach. Instead of spending most of my time estimating, designing, and architecting the feature before writing code, I started doing something closer to what I described in the previous section.

I began the feature without committing to a strict estimate, or sometimes with only a very rough one. My goal was to **quickly build a rough end-to-end prototype** of the feature, including the main screens and API calls. The result was far from perfect. The UI was not polished, parts of the logic did not work, and the code was full of bugs. Sometimes I spent two days, sometimes a bit more, building that prototype. Remember, this was long before vibe coding was even imaginable. But building a prototype is mostly a function of time, not tools.

That prototype gave me several important advantages:

- **User Experience Understanding:** We did not have to wait two weeks to understand how the feature felt. Within a couple of days, I could show it to my manager or share it with QA and receive immediate feedback. Everyone could interact with the feature early. It did not need to be polished, and parts of the logic could still be incomplete. Even a rough version was enough to understand whether we were moving in the right direction.

- **Architectural Decisions:** When everything is still rough, it is also the best time to shape the architecture. Of course, I still did some technical thinking before starting. But during the prototyping phase, I discovered gaps that were impossible to anticipate earlier. Changing the architecture at that stage was relatively cheap. Deleting classes and rewriting parts of the code was not painful when the feature was only a few days old. If the demo revealed deeper issues, even radical changes were still manageable.

- **Clearer Estimations:** Estimation is a difficult skill because it is easier to estimate known work than unknown work. We can estimate how long it takes to build a list or a button, but it is much harder to estimate an unfamiliar integration, a complex animation, or a new navigation flow. One goal of the prototype was to touch every major part of the feature: integrations, APIs, animations, navigation, and more. The goal was not to produce perfect results. The goal was to encounter friction with the unknown and understand the real effort involved. No planning session can fully replace the insights that come from actually trying.

In many ways, the prototyping phase became **part of the planning phase**. Instead of spending most of the time writing documents or preparing presentation decks, I spent that time building something tangible. It took two or three days, but it was worth it.

Now imagine doing the same thing with vibe coding. If this approach was already valuable before AI, it becomes even more powerful when AI can accelerate the prototyping process.

With that in mind, let's take another step forward and see what a more advanced AI-driven workflow might look like.

A Glimpse of the Future

At this point, we have seen that developers have different ways of working with AI. However, in the previous section, we understood something deeper – the world as we know it is changing. As execution becomes cheaper, other parts of the workflow change, and these changes flip our workflows and turn them into something different.

Now, it's time to take an even bolder step into the future and imagine how this new workflow is **being automated end-to-end by AI**. One of the good things about this book is that it is built around real developers and use cases, which makes it easy to imagine things that are actually happening. Because this kind of future is already here. Let's turn to **Krzysztof** and see how he's using AI to be extremely productive.

The AI Development Pipeline

I use AI for everything.

—Krzysztof Zabłocki

Most developers approach AI mainly as a coding assistant. They ask it to generate a function, fix a bug, or explain a piece of code. **Krzysztof** takes a very different approach. Instead of using AI as a tool inside his workflow, he redesigns the entire workflow around AI. **Krzysztof** has always been focused on productivity. Like many developers, he invests heavily in tools that help him work faster. But with AI, he pushed that philosophy much further than most engineers.

For most developers, the spectrum of AI adoption is narrow. The main question is how much they rely on AI to generate code. Some use it occasionally for small tasks, while others rely on it more heavily during development. Krzysztof goes much further. Instead of asking how AI can help him write code faster, he asks a different question: **how can AI become the backbone of the entire development process?**

To understand this difference, we first need to look at the problem most developers have when working with AI.

The Problem Most Developers Have with AI

Many developers, not just iOS developers, remain somewhat skeptical about AI's ability to write code. They often admit that AI is useful for small repetitive tasks, but they struggle to believe it can do much more than that. In many cases, developers are disappointed with the code AI produces.

The reason is simple. Many developers still don't know how to work with these tools effectively. Let's look what a typical workflow for most developers would be:

- Open ChatGPT

- Write a prompt

- Copy-paste back the code

Their conclusion: "LLMs write bad code."

According to Krzysztof, however, the problem is not the model itself. In fact, he argues that modern LLMs have improved significantly in their recent versions. The real problem lies in the workflow.

Instead of adapting our workflow to the model, Krzysztof suggests doing the opposite. We should adapt the model to our team. In other words, we need to **teach the LLM our standards and our coding practices.**

Teaching the LLM Our Engineering Standards

To understand this idea, let's briefly recall how large language models work. At their core, LLMs predict the next word or token in a sequence based on patterns learned during training. Companies like OpenAI, Google, and Anthropic trained these models on massive collections of code and text. Through this training, the models learn patterns that allow them to generate code in many programming languages, including Swift.

However, Krzysztof points out an important limitation. Compared to languages such as JavaScript or Python, the amount of Swift code available for training is relatively small. In many cases, **the available code is also closer to demo-level examples than to real production code.**

As a result, when an LLM generates Swift code, it often reflects common patterns found in tutorials rather than the standards used in a specific team or project.

To solve this problem, Krzysztof applies a set of techniques that resemble the onboarding process we use for new developers joining a team. Instead of expecting the model to automatically understand our codebase, we gradually teach it how our team works.

Let's see some of these techniques:

- **Rules Files:** One of Krzysztof's core ideas is the use of rules files. These are Markdown files that describe his coding standards. They include architecture constraints, coding style, testing requirements, and general engineering guidelines. Before generating code, the LLM reads these files. In practice, this means Krzysztof teaches the model how his team writes code and what production-quality code should look like.

- **Examples Instead of Zero-Shot:** This is where the context we discussed earlier becomes important. Instead of relying on simple prompts, Krzysztof provides examples, anti-patterns, and good patterns. By showing the model what good and bad code look like, he significantly improves the quality of the generated output.

- **Decomposition:** This principle came up clearly in Krzysztof's interview, and I also discovered it myself when I started experimenting with LLMs. As Krzysztof told me, "You always want to create tasks. Don't do everything in one shot." At first, it feels tempting to throw an entire problem at the model and expect it to solve everything. In practice, however, LLMs perform much better when the problem is broken into smaller, well-defined tasks.

Looking at these three ideas, we can see what I meant earlier. Teaching an LLM is surprisingly similar to **onboarding a new developer**. We provide coding standards, examples, and guidelines so the new team member understands how we build software. The same approach works with AI.

But decomposition introduces another important idea. Breaking work into smaller tasks is not only helpful for AI. It also shapes the entire development workflow. And that leads to the next question in Krzysztof's approach:

What is the **role of the human** in this pipeline? Or – how does the developer pipeline look now when we combine AI and human touch? Let's detail what an AI development looks like.

The AI Development Pipeline

Krzysztof's development workflow looks something like this:

- Pull tasks from Linear

- Generate a PRD

- Break the work into subtasks

- Generate code

- Code review

- Fix compile errors

- Open GitHub Pull Request

What makes this pipeline unusual is that **every stage is handled by AI**. After Krzysztof brought LLM-generated code close to production quality, he began automating more of the development process. Using orchestration tools such as **LangGraph**, models such as **Claude**, and routing layers such as **OpenRouter**, he built a system that enables AI to run the entire pipeline automatically. As Krzysztof puts it, "*I can do in two hours what used to take two days.*"

At this point, a natural question appears: where is the developer in this pipeline? Since AI handles most of the coding work, the human role shifts. Instead of writing every line of code, the developer **acts as a checkpoint** across the pipeline, reviewing decisions, validating results, and ensuring the system still makes sense. In other words, AI dramatically reduces the cost of execution, but understanding the system's architecture, constraints, and long-term direction still requires human judgment.

Now that we understand what the pipeline looks like, let's drill down to some of the tools I have mentioned. After all, without the right tooling, all of these ideas stay theoretical.

Tools and Infrastructure

We are in an era when a new tool pops up every day, and perhaps this section will feel outdated by the time this book goes to print. But, in most cases, the principles stay the same, and we can translate these tools to other tools in the future.

Let's start with **OpenRouter**.

Control AI Traffic with OpenRouter

One of the things that characterizes both Krzysztof's workflow and the broader world of AI is the growing number of available models, each with different strengths. Some models are better at reasoning, others at coding, and new versions appear constantly. If we want to optimize our pipeline in such a rapidly evolving environment, we need **a flexible way to switch between models**. OpenRouter is an example of such a tool.

OpenRouter provides a single API that gives developers access to multiple LLM providers. Instead of integrating separately with services such as OpenAI, Anthropic, or Google, developers can call one endpoint and select the model they want to use. This means one SDK, one API, and one billing system.

Based on Krzysztof's interview, his pipeline is built from multiple AI agents. Since different models perform better at different tasks, OpenRouter allows him to experiment easily and choose the right model for each stage of the pipeline.

As Krzysztof told me, "*You need to learn the different models.*" Learning them is not just about reading documentation - it **requires experimentation**. Developers often need to run the same workflow with different models to assess performance. OpenRouter makes this process straightforward.

Another benefit is availability. If a specific model becomes slow or temporarily unavailable, OpenRouter can **route requests to alternative providers**, helping ensure the pipeline continues to run.

In many ways, OpenRouter acts as an **abstraction layer on top of LLM** providers. Just as developers decouple their applications from specific infrastructure components, tools like OpenRouter allow AI systems to remain flexible as models and providers continue to evolve.

Let's move to another interesting tool that can help us build **the pipeline itself**.

Building Workflows with LangGraph

We've discussed pipelines and how tools like OpenRouter make it easier to switch between different models, but we still need a way to orchestrate the entire workflow. One of the primary tools Krzysztof uses for this purpose is **LangGraph**, a framework designed to orchestrate multi-step AI workflows.

LangGraph allows developers to structure complex pipelines involving multiple AI agents – planning, coding, reviewing - while controlling how these agents interact with one another.

With LangGraph, we define a **graph of steps** in the workflow. In Krzysztof's case, those steps might include generating a PRD, breaking the work into subtasks, generating code, reviewing it, and fixing errors. LangGraph is designed to support collaboration among multiple AI agents. For example, a planning agent could use a Google model, such as Gemini, while a coding agent could use an Anthropic model, such as Claude.

Another key concept in LangGraph is **shared state**. When we imagine a pipeline of agents, we often think about agents passing text messages to one another. Instead, LangGraph passes a structured state object through the workflow. In practice, this state is often defined in a file such as `workflow_state.json` (or as a typed object in code), and it evolves as the pipeline runs. For example:

```
{
  "task": "Add password reset feature",
  "prd": "User can request password reset via email...",
  "subtasks": [],
  "code": null,
  "review_feedback": null
}
```

Each field represents a stage in the workflow:

- `task`: The high-level goal the system is trying to achieve

- `prd`: A product requirements description generated by a planning agent

- `subtasks`: A list of smaller tasks derived from the PRD, used to break down the work

- code: The generated implementation (initially `null` until the coding step runs)

- `review_feedback`: Comments or issues raised by a reviewing agent after inspecting the code

This JSON represents the current state of the workflow. You can think of it as the pipeline's shared memory. Each step in the graph reads the state, performs its task, and updates the state before passing it to the next step.

LangGraph also supports **iterations and loops**. In the interview, Krzysztof described a scenario where the system fixes compile errors and retries the process. LangGraph allows workflows to repeat steps until specific conditions are met, making automated pipelines significantly more robust.

Finally, remember how Krzysztof described the developer's role as a **checkpoint rather than an executor**? LangGraph supports **human-in-the-loop workflows**, allowing a developer to inspect the system state, interrupt execution, approve a step, or modify the workflow before it continues.

LangGraph can therefore serve as an important building block when constructing AI-driven development pipelines. While other orchestration tools exist, frameworks designed specifically for coordinating AI agents are becoming increasingly important for teams looking to automate larger parts of their workflows.

Next – not a tool, but a nice tip I received during the interview.

Not a Tool, But a Small Tip

We already know that a core idea when working with LLMs is providing detailed context. What most developers do is try to write the most detailed prompt they can. The problem is that typing on a keyboard is **not the same as speaking**. Because typing takes effort, we naturally skip details to save time. Sometimes, however, those missing details are exactly what makes the difference between average and great results.

One of Krzysztof's tips for working with LLMs is surprisingly simple: **speak to the computer instead of typing**. By removing the friction of typing, we tend to describe the problem more fully and naturally.

For developers, speaking to a computer to generate code may sound strange. But in many ways, this is the essence of vibe coding: describing what we want in natural language rather than implementing every step ourselves.

How to Continue from Here?

This chapter is unique - and it's also the last chapter of a unique book. Unlike other topics we discussed, it is still difficult to say what the "right" approach to AI development is. The field is evolving extremely quickly, and we are clearly at the beginning of a major shift whose final direction nobody fully understands.

But even from what we know today and from the developers I interviewed, we can already see several clear signals.

- **Use AI for Repetitive Tasks:** We don't have to go all the way to enjoy the benefits of vibe coding. As we saw, many developers already use AI to create UI components, define data structures, or generate unit tests. Krzysztof told me that 99% of his coding is done with AI, but even automating the small tasks we repeat every day can create a meaningful productivity boost.

- **Stay Constantly Updated:** This was one of the chapters in which new tools appeared even as I was writing it. That alone says a lot. Nobody knows exactly what the future of AI-assisted development will look like, but one thing is certain: developers who stop learning will eventually fall behind. Staying up to date has always been important in software development, but with AI, the pace of change is dramatically faster.

- **A Huge Opportunity for Indie Developers:** We saw how Krzysztof built workflows that, before the AI era, would likely have required an entire team. We also saw developers like Danijela using AI for documentation and other supporting tasks. For independent developers, AI removes many of the barriers that once made building a full product difficult. Design, content, documentation, and even parts of development are becoming dramatically easier to handle on your own.

AI introduces something fundamentally new into the world of software development. For the first time, developers are not just writing software - they are increasingly **orchestrating systems that generate software.**

And if the stories in this book show anything, it's that the teams who learn how to work with these systems, rather than compete with them, will shape what the next era of development looks like.

Chapter and Book Summary

There's a reason I chose AI as the topic for the last chapter of the book. All the previous chapters describe how developers and teams work today. This chapter's radical turn is not meant to contradict anything we've discussed, but to invite us to think about how everything we've seen might evolve as AI becomes part of our workflows.

In this chapter, we

- Learned how **vibe coding** really works, including its constraints and the importance of decomposition

- Explored how developers **are already integrating** AI into their daily work

- Saw how AI **shifts the economics of development**, where execution becomes the cheaper part of the process

- Got a **glimpse of the future** through the workflows Krzysztof is building

There is no doubt that writing about AI will always feel incomplete. No matter how hard we try to document it, the landscape changes faster than any book can keep up. In the end, how we adopt and implement AI is up to us.

And perhaps that's the most symbolic part of this chapter. The entire idea behind this book was to capture something that LLMs cannot easily produce: **authentic voices from developers working in the field**. Conversations, experiences, and perspectives from people building real products. And yet, the final chapter inevitably brings us to AI.

It may feel as if our job as iOS developers is becoming easier. In some ways, it is. But the reality is more complex. We still need to understand frameworks, capabilities, architecture, and design patterns. Now we must also learn to work with AI systems that are increasingly participating in the development process.

How these skills come together is the **real challenge ahead.**

Index

K

L

M

N

T